Just Briefs

ASPEN PUBLISHERS

Just Briefs

Second Edition

Laurel Currie Oates
Director, Legal Writing Program
Seattle University School of Law

Anne Enquist
Associate Director, Legal Writing Program
Seattle University School of Law

Connie Krontz
Legal Writing Professor
Seattle University School of Law

 Wolters Kluwer
Law & Business

AUSTIN   BOSTON   CHICAGO   NEW YORK   THE NETHERLANDS

To contact Customer Care, e-mail customer.care@aspenpublishers.com,
call 1-800-234-1660, fax 1-800-901-9075, or mail correspondence to:

> Aspen Publishers
> Attn: Order Department
> PO Box 990
> Frederick, MD 21705

Printed in the United States of America.

1 2 3 4 5 6 7 8 9 0

ISBN 978-0-7355-6231-8

Library of Congress Cataloging-in-Publication Data

Oates, Laurel Currie, 1951-
  Just briefs / Laurel Currie Oates, Anne Enquist, Connie Krontz. — 2nd ed.
    p. cm.
  Includes bibliographical references and index.
  ISBN 978-0-7355-6231-8 (pbk. : alk. paper) 1. Briefs—United States. I. Enquist,
Anne, 1950- II. Krontz, Connie, 1953- III. Title.

  KF251.O18 2008
  808'.06634—dc22

2007049897

About Wolters Kluwer Law & Business

Wolters Kluwer Law & Business is a leading provider of research information and workflow solutions in key specialty areas. The strengths of the individual brands of Aspen Publishers, CCH, Kluwer Law International and Loislaw are aligned within Wolters Kluwer Law & Business to provide comprehensive, in-depth solutions and expert-authored content for the legal, professional and education markets.

CCH was founded in 1913 and has served more than four generations of business professionals and their clients. The CCH products in the Wolters Kluwer Law & Business group are highly regarded electronic and print resources for legal, securities, antitrust and trade regulation, government contracting, banking, pension, payroll, employment and labor, and healthcare reimbursement and compliance professionals.

Aspen Publishers is a leading information provider for attorneys, business professionals and law students. Written by preeminent authorities, Aspen products offer analytical and practical information in a range of specialty practice areas from securities law and intellectual property to mergers and acquisitions and pension/benefits. Aspen's trusted legal education resources provide professors and students with high-quality, up-to-date and effective resources for successful instruction and study in all areas of the law.

Kluwer Law International supplies the global business community with comprehensive English-language international legal information. Legal practitioners, corporate counsel and business executives around the world rely on the Kluwer Law International journals, loose-leafs, books and electronic products for authoritative information in many areas of international legal practice.

Loislaw is a premier provider of digitized legal content to small law firm practitioners of various specializations. Loislaw provides attorneys with the ability to quickly and efficiently find the necessary legal information they need, when and where they need it, by facilitating access to primary law as well as state-specific law, records, forms and treatises.

Wolters Kluwer Law & Business, a unit of Wolters Kluwer, is headquartered in New York and Riverwoods, Illinois. Wolters Kluwer is a leading multinational publisher and information services company.

To my parents, Bill and Lucille Currie,
my husband, Terry, and my children, Julia and Michael.
Thank you.

To my family, Steve, Matt, Mary, and Jeff Enquist,
for their love, support, and patience.

To my husband, Ray, and my daughter, Emma,
for their love and support.

Summary of Contents

Contents

Preface

The title of this book and its double meaning might be a bit of a misnomer. The book is about "just" briefs in the sense that we intend it to remind you that your briefs to the court should work toward a just result; however, it is not a book just about briefs because it includes more than brief writing. *Just Briefs* is really a book about the larger topic of effective advocacy as it plays out in trial and appellate briefs, oral argument, and the thinking process that informs both.

"Effective advocacy" might not make a jazzy title, but we find the topic of effective advocacy tremendously engaging. Admittedly, the process of researching, analyzing, and writing a brief that is effective advocacy can be arduous and time consuming. But it is also deeply rewarding. When lawyers write a persuasive brief or make a compelling argument, they make a difference. They protect the rights of their clients, they help enforce or change the law, and they make sure that the legal system works as it was intended to work.

Thus, as you work through the chapters in this book, keep your eye on the larger goal of becoming an effective advocate. Instead of focusing primarily on getting an A on your brief or oral argument, focus on learning to be the best advocate that you can be. Learn how to develop a theory of the case that will appeal to both the judge's head and heart, learn how to tell your client's story, and learn how to construct persuasive arguments. In addition, work on developing your writing skills. Learn how to make your points clearly, precisely, concisely, even eloquently. Finally, think about the role you need and want to play as an advocate. As you think through how zealous you want to be when representing your client, remember that your own reputation as an attorney affects your ability to persuade. Your reputation and your credibility might ultimately be your most effective tools as an advocate.

Acknowledgments

One of the pleasures of writing a derivative work is that it allows the authors to think about all of the people who have helped them along the way. In our case, the preparation of this work has reminded us of all of the people who helped us as we wrote the first, second, third, and fourth editions of *The Legal Writing Handbook* and the first and second editions of *Just Writing*.

We would like to begin by thanking our students and colleagues who, in the eighties, provided the inspiration and insights that led to the writing of *The Legal Writing Handbook*. We would, however, also like to thank our most recent students and colleagues whose suggestions and corrections made each edition better than the earlier one. In particular, we would like to thank the following individuals: Susan McClellan, Lori Bannai, Mimi Samuel, Janet Dickson, Mary Bowman, Lucas Cupps, Janet Chung, Nancy Wanderer, and Jessie Grearson. In addition, we would like to thank our law librarian, Stephanie Wilson, who helped us with the research on the new legal issues in this edition, and our former students, Jean Jorgenson and Amanda Froh, who allowed us to use their briefs as starting points for the sample briefs in Chapter 2.

Finally, we would like to thank the editors at Aspen for their support and advice and our administrative assistant, Lori Lamb, for her assistance in preparing the manuscript.

Laurel Oates
Anne Enquist
Connie Krontz

January 2008

Just Briefs

Writing a Trial Brief

§ 1.1 Motion Briefs

Much of litigation is a motions practice. For example, as a trial attorney, you will file motions for temporary relief, to compel discovery, to suppress evidence, to dismiss, or for summary judgment. Although not all of these motions will be supported by briefs, many will.

§ 1.1.1 Audience

In writing a brief in support of or in opposition to a motion, your primary audience is the trial judge.

Sometimes you will know which judge will read your brief. Either the brief will have been requested by a specific judge, or you will know which judge will hear the motion. At other times, though, you will not know which judge will read your brief. The motion will be read by whichever judge is hearing motions on the day that your motion is argued.

If you know which judge will read your brief, write your brief for that judge. Learn as much as you can about that judge, and then craft a brief that he or she will find persuasive. If you do not know which judge will read your brief, write a brief that will work for any of the judges who might hear your motion. Although a particular approach might work well with one judge, do not risk using that approach if it might offend other judges.

In whichever situation you find yourself, keep the judge's schedule in mind. It is not uncommon for a judge hearing civil motions to hear twenty motions in a single day. If in each of these cases each party has filed a twenty-page brief, the judge would have 800 pages to read. Given this workload, it is not surprising that for most judges the best brief is the short brief. Know what you need and want to argue, make your argument, and then stop.

Also keep in mind the constraints placed on trial judges. Because trial judges must apply mandatory authority, they need to know what the law is, not what you think it should be. Whenever possible, make the easy argument: set out and apply existing law.

§ 1.1.2 Purpose

In writing to a trial judge, you have two goals: to educate and to persuade. You are the teacher who teaches the judge both the applicable law and the facts of the case. You are not, however, just a teacher. You are also an advocate. As you teach, you will be trying to persuade the court to take a particular action.

§ 1.1.3 Conventions

The format of a particular brief will vary from jurisdiction to jurisdiction and, even within a jurisdiction, from court to court. Consequently, you need to check the local rules. Is there a local rule that prescribes the types of information that should be included in the brief, the order in which that information should be presented, and the particular format? If there is no local rule, check with other attorneys or with the court clerk to see if there is a format that is typically used.

§ 1.2 *State v. Patterson*

In this chapter, our example case is *State v. Patterson*, a criminal case in which the defendant has filed a motion to suppress the identifications obtained at a show-up shortly after an assault and at a line-up held four days later. See the documents on pages 4-9.

§ 1.3 Developing a Theory of the Case

Good advocates do not just set out the facts and the law. Instead, they use the facts and the law to construct a compelling story.

A good story, or theory of the case, appeals both to the head and to the heart. The theory of the case puts together the law and the facts in a way that is legally sound and that produces a result that the court sees as just.

There are at least two ways of coming up with a good theory of the case. The first is to look at the case through your client's eyes. According to your client, what happened? Why did the other people involved do what they did? Why did your client act as he or she did? Why does your client think that what he or she did was legally right? Justified? Is there law that supports your client's view of what happened?

The second way is to look at the cases involving the same issue in which the court reached the result that you want the court to reach in your case. In those cases, what was the winning party's theory of the case? What legal arguments did that party make? How did it characterize what happened? What was the court's reaction? Did the trial court "buy" the winning party's theory of the case or come up with its own theory of the case?

In our case, Patterson says that he did not commit the crime. He was simply at the wrong place at the wrong time. At the time that crime was committed, Patterson was doing laundry, moving his car, and getting ready to meet his wife for dinner. Although Martinez has identified him as her assailant, she did so only because police pointed him out to her and suggested to her that he was the man who had assaulted her. In addition, Patterson does not match Martinez's and Clipse's description of the assailant. Although both Martinez and Clipse told the police that the assailant was in his late thirties or early forties, Patterson is only twenty-two. In contrast, the State says that Patterson is the person who assaulted Martinez. Martinez has identified Patterson as her assailant, his car matches the one that Martinez and Clipse have described, and a gun was found in his apartment.

§ 1.4 The Caption

In some jurisdictions, motion briefs are printed on pleading, or numbered, paper, but in other jurisdictions they are printed on regular paper. In addition, in many jurisdictions, the caption is set out on the first page beginning on about line 5. The parties' names are set out on the left-hand side, and the case number and the title of the document are set out on the right-hand side. See pages 49 and 59.

PRACTICE POINTER

Many jurisdictions now allow, or even require, the parties to file their pleadings and briefs electronically. Thus, before filing your brief, check your local rules.

Form 9.28	**SEATTLE POLICE DEPARTMENT**	Case Number
CSS 21.122		06-49721

DATE 08-12-06   **TIME** 6:05 P.M.   **PLACE** Police Headquarters

STATEMENT OF: Beatrice Marie Martinez

    My name is Beatrice Marie Martinez, and I live at 801 East Harrison #202, and my phone number is 329-9679. I am 17 years old. Today, at 4:30 p.m. I left my apartment, beginning my walk to work; Angelo's Restaurant at 5th & Pike. I walked southbound on Harvard to Denny Way, then westbound on Denny Way to Boylston. I again walked southbound on Boylston, until I came to East Howell Street. As I was walking westbound on East Howell Street, a red, old station wagon was going eastbound, and it attracted my attention because it slowed down and the driver was looking at me. I didn't think much of it, and turned the corner, now walking southbound in the 1700 block of Belmont. As I turned the corner, I again saw the old red station wagon, coming northbound on Belmont. As I came to an apartment building, the station wagon pulled in front of me, blocking the sidewalk, and the driver kept looking at me. The driver jumped out of the car, and shouted "Hey." I looked at him, and he had what looked to me to be a .38 pointed at my stomach. I stepped back, and heard someone else yell "Hey," and I ran across the street and hid behind a wall. I also pushed buttons, trying to get someone to let me inside the apartment house. The man who appeared to be in his early 40s, white, 165-170 lbs., 5'7-8 blondish brown hair, wearing dark jacket, and glasses, jumped back into the station wagon, and took off down the street. A man ran up, and took me to his apartment to call police. The police came, and took a report and were taking me home, when I saw the man, walking in front of us. Although at first I was not sure that the man was the man who had attacked me but police arrested him, and I again went back to the apartment, at the request of the police. I was brought downtown by the man who had the apartment, to give this statement. This is a true and correct statement, to the best of my knowledge.

STATEMENT
TAKEN BY: *Det. Al Yuen*   SIGNED: *Beatrice Martinez*

WITNESS: WITNESS:

Form 9.28   **SEATTLE POLICE DEPARTMENT**   Case Number

CSS 21.122   06-49721

DATE 08-14-06   **TIME** 6:47 P.M.   **PLACE** Police Headquarters

---

STATEMENT OF: Chester Joseph Clipse

My name is Chester Joseph Clipse, I'm a 19 year old white male. I live at 600 E. Olive St., Apt. 110. Today at about 4:50 p.m., I was walking home, and as I approached my apartment building, at Corner of E. Olive St. and Belmont, I saw a man in a red dodge wagon driving up the street slowly. He pulled into my parking stall, so I approached, to see what he was doing. He approached a girl, who was on the sidewalk, and she screamed. At this time, I saw the man had a gun, and I yelled "Hey." He turned, and ran to his car, putting the gun under his coat. The girl ran across the street, and the guy backed out, and took off down the street, northbound. At that moment, a meter maid came down street, and I flagged him down, telling him what happened. The meter maid took off after the man, and I took the girl to my apartment house to get her off the street. I went with officers and positively identified the car, which was parked in the 600 Block of E. Howell. The driver was a white man about late 30's or early 40's. He was about 5'9 or 5'10, and about 180-185 lbs. He had brown wavy hair, and was wearing a green outfit. After the officers had left, I saw him walking up the street, and I saw officers confront him. The officers sent me back inside with the girl.

This is a true and correct statement to the best of my knowledge.

STATEMENT TAKEN BY: Det. Al Yuen   **SIGNED:** Chester Clipse

WITNESS: **WITNESS:**

Form 9.28	**SEATTLE POLICE DEPARTMENT**	Case Number
CSS 21.122		06-49721

DATE 08-15-06   **TIME** 3:22 P.M.   **PLACE** Police Headquarters

STATEMENT OF: Dean Patterson

On August 13-14, I worked my usual 11-7 shift as a security guard. When I got home, I went to bed and slept until about 1:00 p.m. At 2:30, my wife, a nurse at a nearby hospital, received a call asking her to come to work at 3:00 p.m. She told them that she could come in and, at about 3:00, I drove her to work. When I got back, I couldn't find a parking spot in front of our building and was forced to park almost a block away. Between 3:00 and 4:30 I did two loads of laundry, watched an old movie on T.V., and talked on the phone with both a friend, Karen Callendar, and my wife. I made my last trip to the laundry room at about 4:30 p.m.. On my way back, I decided to check my car to see how much gas I had. After I checked the gas, I moved the car to a parking spot right in front of our building. At about 5:00, I left the apartment and began walking toward the hospital, where I planned to join my wife at 5:15 for her dinner break. When I was about two blocks from our apartment, I was stopped and arrested. The gun that was found in my apartment is the gun that I was issued by the security company that I work for.

STATEMENT TAKEN BY: Det. Al Yuen   **SIGNED:** Dean Patterson

WITNESS: **WITNESS:**

**IN THE SUPERIOR COURT OF THE STATE OF WASHINGTON
FOR KING COUNTY**

STATE OF WASHINGTON,	)	
	)	
Plaintiff,	)	NO. 06-49721
	)	
vs.	)	INFORMATION
	)	
DEAN EUGENE PATTERSON,	)	
	)	
Defendant.	)	
	)	

I, Norm Mason, Prosecuting Attorney for King County, in
the name and by the authority of the State of Washington,
by this Information do accuse Dean Eugene Patterson of the
crime of assault in the second degree, committed as follows:

That the defendant Dean Eugene Patterson, in King
County, Washington, on or about August 14, 2006, did know-
ingly assault Beatrice Martinez, a human being, with a
weapon and other instrument or thing likely to produce
bodily harm, to-wit: a revolver;

Contrary to RCW 9A.36.021 (1)(C), and against peace and
dignity of the State of Washington.

Norm Mason

NORM MASON
Prosecuting Attorney

Michael T. Frankel

By Michael T. Frankel
MICHAEL T. FRANKEL
Assistant Chief Criminal Deputy
Prosecuting Attorney

Witnesses for state:

Chester Joseph Clipse
Beatrice Marie Martinez
Richard Edward Martin
Terry William Hindman
William P. Cox
Al Yuen
Roy Moran

Information

Line-Up Document

Form 9.3   SHOW-UP IDENTIFICATION
CSS 21.53   Seattle Police Department
Rev. 9-72   Criminal Investigation Division

Case Number: _06-49721_   Date: _8-16-06_
                                            Time: _1400_

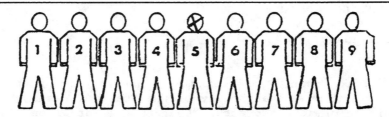

I have just witnessed a show-up consisting of _5_ person(s).

I identify the above number(s) _5_

the person(s) who _assaulted me_
                    (robbed me, assaulted me, etc.)
on _August 14_   _4:40_   at _1700 Belmont_
     (date)   (time)   (address)

The person(s) I have indicated above have been identified
to me as: _____
_____Dean Patterson_____
_____

Witness
  or
(Victim) _Beatrice Martinez_ _801 E. Harrison # 202_
        (Signature)   (address)
                                          _329-9679_
                                              (phone)
Statement taken by: _Det. Al Yuen_ Witness: _____
Show-up prepared by: _"   "_   Location: _____
Photographs taken by: _Det. R. Reed_____
                        (name)
                                          (division)
Attorney present: _Jerry Kellogg_____
                   (name)

Waiver signed: Yes _____   No _X_

Line-Up Document

Form 9.3
CSS 21.53
Rev. 9-72

SHOW-UP IDENTIFICATION
Seattle Police Department
Criminal Investigation Division

Case Number: _06 - 49721_   Date: _8-16-06_
                                             Time: _1400_

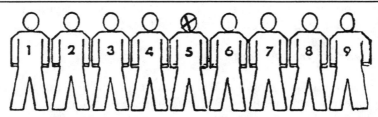

I have just witnessed a show-up consisting of ~~five~~ person(s).
I identify the above number(s) _No Id_
the person(s) who _____
                        (robbed me, assaulted me, etc.)
on _8-14-06_   _16:45_   at _600 East Olive Street_
    (date)   (time)   (address)

The person(s) I have indicated above have been identified
to me as: _____
_____
_____

(Witness)
or
Victim: _Chester Clipse, 600 East Olive Street_
         (Signature)   (address)   (phone)

Statement taken by: _Det. Al Yuen_ Witness: _____

Show-up prepared by: _"   "_ Location: _____

Photographs taken by: _Det. R. Reed_ _____
                        (name)   (division)

Attorney present: _Terry Kellogg_ _____
                    (name)

Waiver signed: Yes _____   No _X_

§ 1.5 The Statement of Facts

Never underestimate the importance of the facts. Particularly at the trial court level, it is the facts, not the law, that usually determine the outcome.

§ 1.5.1 Select the Facts

Like the statement of facts in an objective memo, the statement of facts in a motion brief contains three types of facts: background facts, legally significant facts, and emotionally significant facts.

a. Background Facts

Background facts play a different role in persuasive writing than they do in objective writing. In an objective statement of facts, the writer includes only those background facts that are needed for the story to make sense. In contrast, in drafting a persuasive statement of facts, you can also use background facts to create a favorable context. See section 1.5.3(a).

b. Legally Significant Facts

Because most courts require that the statement of facts be "fair," in writing the statement of facts you must include all of the legally significant facts, both favorable and unfavorable. Thus, in our example case, both the State and the defendant must include all of the facts that will be relevant in determining whether the identifications obtained at the show-up and at the line-up should be suppressed and whether Martinez and Clipse should be allowed to make in-court identifications.

c. Emotionally Significant Facts

Although you must include all of the legally significant facts, you do not need to include all of the facts that are emotionally significant. Although as a defensive move you may sometimes include an emotionally significant fact that is unfavorable, recharacterizing it or minimizing its significance, most of the time you will not. It is more common to include only those emotionally significant facts that favor your client.

The harder question is how to handle emotionally significant facts that are unfavorable to the other side. Should you sling mud, or should you take a higher road and omit any reference to those facts? The answer is that it depends: it depends on the fact, on the case, and on the attorney. If the fact's connection to the case is tenuous, most attorneys would not include it. If, however, the case is weak and the fact's connection is closer, many attorneys would include it, some using it as a sword, others using it much more subtly.

§ 1.5.2 Select an Organizational Scheme

In selecting an organizational scheme, consider two factors. First, decide which organizational scheme makes the most sense. Does it make more sense to use a chronological organizational scheme, a topical organizational scheme, or a topical organizational scheme with the facts within each topic set out in chronological order? Second, decide which organizational scheme will allow you to set out the facts in such a way that you are able to present your story and your theory of the case most effectively.

In our example case, it makes sense to set out the facts in chronological order. In deciding whether to suppress the evidence, the trial judge will want to know what happened first, second, and third. A chronological organizational scheme will also allow each side to tell its story. The only difference will be that Patterson will start his story with his activities on the day in question, and the State will start its story where it started for the victim: with the assault.

§ 1.5.3 Present the Facts

In writing the statement of facts for an objective memo, you set out the facts accurately and objectively. You did not present the facts in the light most favorable to your client.

In writing the statement of facts for a motion brief, you still need to set out the facts accurately. One of the fastest ways to lose a case is to leave out legally significant facts or to misrepresent either the legally significant or emotionally significant facts. Being accurate does not mean, however, that you need to set out the facts objectively. You are permitted and, in fact, expected to present the facts in such a way that they support your theory of the case.

In presenting the facts, attorneys use a number of different techniques. They create a favorable context, they tell the story from their client's point of view, they emphasize the facts that support their theory of the case and de-emphasize those that do not, and they select their words correctly.

a. Create a Favorable Context

A court will view a fact differently depending on the context in which it is presented. Consider, for example, the following sentence.

EXAMPLE 1

He pulled out his gun and, at point-blank range, shot the woman in the head.

After reading this sentence, what is your reaction? Who is the "bad guy"? Who is the victim? For most, it is the gunman who is the bad guy. Having shot a woman at point-blank range, he is a cold-blooded killer who should be found guilty of murder. Now read the following sentence.

EXAMPLE 2

Pushing his young son out of harm's way, he pulled out his gun and, at point-blank range, shot the woman in the head.

Although the gunman has shot a woman, he is no longer a cold-blooded killer. He is a father shooting to save his son. The context has changed, and the gunman is no longer the bad guy. He and his son are the victims. Consider one final sentence.

EXAMPLE 3

Having stalked his victim for days, the gunman pushed his young son behind him, pulled out his gun and, at point-blank range, shot the woman in the head.

Do we still have a father shooting to save his son? The answer is no. Now we have a gunman who is worse than the cold-blooded killer in the first example: we have a stalker who shoots a woman in front of his own son. Another context, a different verdict.

As the preceding examples illustrate, one way to create a favorable context is to start the story where it favors your client. In the following example, Patterson uses this technique. Instead of starting his statement of facts with the assault or his arrest, he starts it by describing what he was doing on the day of the assault. By starting with these facts, he is able to start the story with facts that support his theory of the case: he is an innocent pedestrian who happened to be in the wrong place at the wrong time. Note how the writer works in the fact that Patterson is married, that he has a job, and that he does nice things; for instance, he takes his wife to work, does the laundry, and arranges to meet his wife during her dinner break.

EXAMPLE 4 **THE FIRST THREE PARAGRAPHS OF THE DEFENDANT'S STATEMENT OF FACTS**

At 7:30 on Monday morning, August 14, 2006, twenty-two-year-old Dean Patterson finished his shift as a security guard and walked to his apartment. After having breakfast with his wife, Patterson went to bed and slept until about 1:00 p.m. At about 2:30 p.m., Patterson's wife received a phone call asking her to work at the local hospital, where she is employed as a nurse. She got ready, and Patterson dropped her off at the hospital at about 3:10. When he returned, Patterson could not find a parking place close to his apartment and had to park several blocks away.

At about 3:30 p.m., Patterson called his wife to find out how long she would have to work. They had plans to go to a movie that evening, and he wanted to know whether he should change those plans. At about 3:50 p.m., Patterson took a load of laundry to the apartment complex's laundry room. When he returned to his apartment, Patterson watched part of an old movie. At about 4:20, Patterson went back to the laundry room to put the clothes in the dryer. On his way back, he walked to where his car, an older model red station wagon, was parked to see if he needed to get gas. As he did so, Patterson noticed a parking spot much closer to his apartment and, after checking his gas gauge, moved his car to that spot. After parking his car, Patterson got out of the car and, because the driver's side door does not lock from the outside, walked to the passenger side to lock the doors. As he did so, he nodded to a parking enforcement officer who was driving by.

By this time, it was 4:30, and Patterson decided to phone his wife again. He arranged to meet her at 5:15 for her dinner break. Patterson picked up the laundry and then left the apartment a little before 5:00 to meet his wife.

The State also creates a favorable context. However, instead of starting its statement of facts by describing Patterson's actions, it begins the story where it started for the victim. In the first paragraph of its statement of facts, the State describes the assault and then the show-up and line-up.

EXAMPLE 5 THE FIRST PARAGRAPH OF THE STATE'S STATEMENT OF FACTS

On Monday, August 14, 2006, Beatrice Martinez was assaulted with a deadly weapon. At a show-up held thirty to forty minutes after the attack, Martinez positively identified the defendant, Dean E. Patterson, as her assailant. Four days after the assault, Martinez picked Patterson out of a line-up, once again positively identifying him as her assailant.

b. Tell the Story from the Client's Point of View

One of the most powerful persuasive devices is point of view. In most cases, you will want to tell the story as your client would tell it.

One way of telling the story from your client's point of view is to make your client the "actor" in most of your sentences. Note how in the defendant's statement of facts, the writer has made Patterson or his wife the subject in most of the main clauses; in the State's statement of facts, the writer has made Martinez the subject in most of the main clauses.

In the following examples, the subject of each sentence is in bold.

EXAMPLE 1 EXCERPT FROM DEFENDANT'S STATEMENT OF FACTS

At 7:30 on Monday morning, August 14, 2006, twenty-two-year-old **Dean Patterson** finished his shift as a security guard and walked to his apartment. After having breakfast with his wife, **Patterson** went to bed and slept until about 1:00 p.m. At about 2:30 p.m., **Patterson's wife** received a phone call asking her to work at the local hospital where she is employed as a nurse. **She** got ready, and **Patterson** dropped her off at the hospital at about 3:10. When he returned, at about 3:30 p.m., **Patterson** called his wife to find out how long she would have to work. **They** had plans to go to a movie that evening, and **he** wanted to know whether he should change those plans. At about 3:50 p.m., **Patterson** took a load of laundry to the apartment complex's laundry room. When he returned to his apartment, **Patterson** watched part of an old movie. At about 4:20, **Patterson** went back to the laundry room to put the clothes in the dryer. On his way back, **he** walked to where his car, an older model red station wagon, was parked to see if he needed to get gas. As he did so, **Patterson** noticed a parking spot much closer to his apartment and, after checking his gas gauge, moved his car to that spot. After parking his car, **Patterson** got out of the car and, because the driver's side door does not lock from the outside, walked to the passenger side to lock the doors. As he did so, **he** nodded to a parking enforcement officer who was driving by.

By this time, **it** was 4:30, and **Patterson** decided to phone his wife again. **He** arranged to meet her at 5:15 for her dinner break. **Patterson** picked up the laundry and then left the apartment a little before 5:00 to meet his wife.

EXAMPLE 2   EXCERPT FROM THE STATE'S STATEMENT OF FACTS

On Monday, August 14, 2006, **Beatrice Martinez** was assaulted with a deadly weapon. At a show-up held thirty to forty minutes after the attack, **Martinez** positively identified the defendant, Dean E. Patterson, as her assailant. Four days after the assault, **Martinez** picked Patterson out of a line-up, once again positively identifying him as her assailant.

---

c. Emphasize the Facts that Support Your Theory of the Case, and De-emphasize Those that Do Not

In addition to presenting the facts from the client's point of view, good advocates emphasize those facts that support their theory of the case and de-emphasize those that do not. They do this by using one or more of the following techniques.

1. Airtime

Just as listeners remember best the songs that get the most airtime, readers remember best the facts that get the most words. Consequently, favorable facts should be given considerable "airtime," and unfavorable ones should be given little or no "play." In our example case, if Patterson is going to persuade the court that the identifications are unreliable, he needs to de-emphasize the fact that Martinez saw the car twice. Although he cannot omit the fact that the car drove by twice, he does not need to give this fact very much airtime. In contrast, if the State is going to persuade the court that Martinez's identifications are reliable, it needs to emphasize the fact that she saw the car twice. Thus, the State wants to give this fact as much airtime as possible. In the following examples, the relevant facts are in bold.

| EXAMPLE 1 | **EXCERPT FROM THE DEFENDANT'S STATEMENT OF FACTS** |

At about 4:30 p.m. on the same day, seventeen-year-old Beatrice Martinez left her apartment to walk to work. As she was walking southbound on Belmont, **a car that had driven by earlier pulled in front of her.** The man got out of his car, took one or two steps toward Martinez, and then pulled a gun from his pocket. As soon as she spotted the gun, Martinez screamed, looked away, and then, crying, ran across the street. The entire encounter was over in three or four seconds.

| EXAMPLE 2 | **EXCERPT FROM THE STATE'S STATEMENT OF FACTS** |

As she was walking north on Belmont, Martinez observed an older model red station wagon with a chrome luggage rack as it passed slowly by her. Moments later, the same car came down the street again. This time, the driver pulled his car in front of Martinez, stopping his car so that it blocked her path. As Martinez watched, the driver got out of his car and walked toward her. The man then took a gun from his coat pocket and pointed it at Martinez. Martinez looked at the gun, looked back up at her assailant, and then, crying, ran back across the street to safety.

2. Detail

Just as readers tend to remember best those facts that get the most airtime, they also tend to remember best those facts that are described in detail. The more detail, the more vivid the picture; the more vivid the picture, the more likely it is that the reader will remember the particular facts. Thus, airtime and detail work hand in hand. In contrast, to de-emphasize unfavorable facts, good advocates describe them in general terms.

Look once again at the following examples, this time comparing the way in which the defendant and the State describe the assailant's car. By leaving out the description of the car, is the defendant setting out all of the legally significant facts? What inference does the State want the judge to draw?

| EXAMPLE 1 | **EXCERPT FROM THE DEFENDANT'S STATEMENT OF FACTS** |

At about 4:30 p.m. on the same day, seventeen-year-old Beatrice Martinez left her apartment to walk to work. As she was walking southbound on Belmont, **a car that had driven by earlier pulled in front of her**. The man got out of his car, took one or two steps toward Martinez, and then pulled a gun from his pocket. As soon as she spotted the gun, Martinez screamed, looked away, and then, crying, ran across the street. The entire encounter was over in three or four seconds.

EXAMPLE 2   **EXCERPT FROM THE STATE'S STATEMENT OF FACTS**

As she was walking north on Belmont, Martinez observed **an older model red station wagon with a chrome luggage rack** as it passed slowly by her. Moments later, the same car came down the street again. This time, the driver pulled his car in front of Martinez, stopping his car so that it blocked her path. As Martinez watched, the driver got out of his car and walked toward her. The man then took a gun from his coat pocket and pointed it at Martinez. Martinez looked at the gun, looked back up at her assailant, and then, crying, ran back across the street to safety.

---

3. Positions of Emphasis

Because readers tend to remember best information that is placed in a position of emphasis (the beginning and end of a section, the beginning and end of a paragraph, and the beginning and end of a sentence), whenever possible, place the facts that you want to emphasize in one of these positions. Conversely, if you want to de-emphasize a fact, bury it in the middle. Place it in the middle of a sentence, in the middle of a paragraph, or in the middle of a section.

In the following examples, the defendant wants to emphasize that Martinez told the police that her assailant was in his early forties. As a consequence, he places that fact near the end of the paragraph. In contrast, because the State wants to de-emphasize that fact, it places it in the middle of a sentence in the middle of a paragraph.

EXAMPLE 1   **EXCERPT FROM THE DEFENDANT'S STATEMENT OF FACTS**

Because she was still upset, Martinez was able to give Officer Yuen only a general description of her assailant. She described him as being a short, white male with blondish-brown hair who was wearing glasses and a dark jacket. In addition, **she told the police that her assailant was in his early forties.** Patterson is twenty-two.

EXAMPLE 2   **EXCERPT FROM THE STATE'S STATEMENT OF FACTS**

Martinez told the police that her assailant was a white male who was about 5'7" tall and who weighed about 165-170 pounds, that her assailant had wavy blondish-brown hair, **that her assailant appeared to be in his early forties,** and that at the time of the assault, her assailant was wearing a dark jacket and glasses.

In the next set of examples, the defendant wants to de-emphasize that he owns an older model red station wagon but the State wants to emphasize that fact.

| EXAMPLE 3 | **EXCERPT FROM THE DEFENDANT'S STATEMENT OF FACTS** |

At about 3:50 p.m., Patterson took a load of laundry to the apartment complex's laundry room. When he returned to his apartment, Patterson watched part of an old movie. At about 4:20, Patterson went back to the laundry room to put the clothes in the dryer. On his way back, he walked to where his car, **an older model red station wagon,** was parked to see if he needed to get gas. As he did so, Patterson noticed a parking spot much closer to his apartment and, after checking his gas gauge, he moved his car to that spot. After parking his car, Patterson got out of the car and, because the driver's side door does not lock from the outside, he walked to the passenger side to lock the doors. As he did so, he nodded to a parking enforcement officer who was driving by.

| EXAMPLE 4 | **EXCERPT FROM THE STATE'S STATEMENT OF FACTS** |

Later that day, the police searched **Patterson's car, an older model red station wagon with a chrome luggage rack,** and his apartment. In the apartment, they found a gun.

4. Sentence Length

Just as airtime and detail work together, so do positions of emphasis and sentence length. Because readers tend to remember information placed in shorter sentences better than information placed in longer sentences, good advocates place favorable facts in short sentences in a position of emphasis. For instance, in Example 1, not only did defense counsel place the favorable fact in a position of emphasis, but he also put that fact in a relatively short sentence. In Example 2, the State not only buried the unfavorable fact in the middle of the paragraph, it also placed that fact in the middle of a long sentence.

| EXAMPLE 1 | **EXCERPT FROM THE DEFENDANT'S STATEMENT OF FACTS** |

Because she was still upset, Martinez was able to give Officer Yuen only a general description of her assailant. She described him as being a short, white male with blondish-brown hair who was wearing glasses and a dark jacket. In addition, she told police that her assailant was in his early forties. **Patterson is twenty-two.**

| EXAMPLE 2 | **EXCERPT FROM THE STATE'S STATEMENT OF FACTS** |

Martinez told the police that her assailant was a white male who was about 5'7" tall and who weighed about 165-170 pounds, that her assailant had wavy blondish-brown hair, **that her assailant appeared to be in his early forties,** and that at the time of the assault, her assailant was wearing a dark jacket and glasses.

PRACTICE

Another way to emphasize a favorable fact is by highlighting discrepancies. For example, in the preceding Example 1, Ms. Elder places the fact that the defendant is twenty-two next to fact that Ms. Martinez told police that her assailant appeared to be in his early forties. By juxtaposing these two facts, Ms. Elder is able to highlight the discrepancies. In contrast, the prosecutor puts the fact that the Mr. Patterson is twenty-two in one paragraph and the fact that Ms. Martinez told police that her assailant was in his early forties in a different paragraph.

5. Active and Passive Voice

Good advocates use the active voice when they want to emphasize what the actor did and the passive voice when they want to draw the reader's attention away from the actor's actions. Consider the following examples.

EXAMPLE 1   **ACTIVE VOICE**

Patterson assaulted Martinez.

EXAMPLE 2   **PASSIVE VOICE**

Martinez was assaulted.

Because the State wants to emphasize that it was Patterson who assaulted Martinez, the prosecutor would use the language in Example 1. In contrast, because the defendant states that he is not the person who assaulted Martinez, he would use the language set out in Example 2. For more on the active and passive voice, see Section 5.1 in *Just Writing, Second Edition.*

6. Dependent and Main Clauses

Another technique is to put favorable facts in the main clause and unfavorable facts in a dependent clause. Compare the following examples. The defendant wants to emphasize the fact that Clipse was unable to make an identification and de-emphasize the fact that Martinez was able to make an identification, but the State wants to do the opposite.

EXAMPLE 1   **EXCERPT FROM THE DEFENDANT'S BRIEF**

Later that day, the police searched Patterson's car and apartment. In the apartment, the police found the gun issued to Patterson by his employer. Four days later, the police held a line-up at the police station. **Although Martinez identified Patterson as the man who had approached her, Clipse did not identify Patterson.**

EXAMPLE 2   EXCERPT FROM THE STATE'S BRIEF

A line-up was held four days later. **Although Clipse was unable to identify the man who had assaulted Martinez, Martinez identified Patterson as her assailant.**

---

d. Choose Your Words Carefully

Words are powerful. Not only do they convey information, but they also create images. Consider, for example, the labels that might be used to describe Mr. Patterson:

> Mr. Dean Patterson
> Dean Patterson
> Patterson
> Dean
> the suspect
> the accused
> the defendant

Defense counsel would probably want to use "Mr. Patterson," "Dean Patterson," or "Patterson" in referring to her client, but the prosecutor might use "the defendant." By using his name, defense counsel reminds the judge that her client is a real person. The title "Mr. Patterson" makes Patterson seem less like a person charged with a felony and more like an average respectable citizen. In contrast, by using the label "defendant" the State suggests that Patterson is guilty.

PRACTICE

Because legal proceedings are formal proceedings, as a general rule, do not refer to parties or to witnesses by just their first names. The only time that you might want to break this "rule" is when referring to a child.

Other word choices can also subtly persuade the court. For instance, in the following paragraph the defendant wants to set up his argument that Officer Yuen's actions tainted the identifications. Thus, he uses "agreed" to suggest that Martinez's identification was prompted by Officer Yuen's questions, "questioned" to suggest that the officers' actions would have indicated to Martinez and Clipse that Patterson was guilty, and "watched" to remind the court that Martinez and Clipse may have been influenced by the officers' actions.

| EXAMPLE 1 | **EXCERPT FROM THE STATE'S STATEMENT OF FACTS** |

Even though Martinez was unable to see the man's face, she **agreed** with the officer that the man looked like her assailant. At this point, Officer Yuen stopped the car, got out, and approached Patterson. As he was **questioning** Patterson, Officer Cox drove up with Clipse. While Martinez and Clipse **watched,** Officers Cox and Yuen **continued questioning** Patterson. Officer Cox then returned to Martinez and Clipse and walked them back to Clipse's apartment. While Officer Cox did so, Officer Yuen placed Patterson under arrest.

§ 1.5.4 Checklist for Critiquing the Statement of Facts

I. Organization

- The facts have been presented in a logical order (chronologically or topically).
- When possible, the facts have been presented in an order that favors the client.

II. Content

- The writer has included both the relevant procedural facts (procedural history) and the facts on which the case is based (statement of facts).
- All of the legally significant facts have been included.
- The emotionally significant facts that favor the client have been included.
- An appropriate number of background facts have been included.

III. Persuasiveness

- The writer has presented the facts so that they support the writer's theory of the case.
- The writer has presented the facts in a favorable context.
- The writer has presented the facts from the point of view that favors the client. (In telling the client's story, the writer has used the client as the subject of most sentences.)
- The writer has emphasized favorable facts and de-emphasized unfavorable ones.
  - Favorable facts have been given more airtime than unfavorable facts.

- Favorable facts have been described in detail; unfavorable facts have been described more generally.
- The positions of emphasis have been used effectively. When possible, favorable facts have been placed at the beginning and end of the statement of facts, at the beginning and end of a paragraph, and at the beginning and end of a sentence.
- Short sentences and short paragraphs have been used to emphasize favorable facts; unfavorable facts have been placed in longer sentences in longer paragraphs.
- Active and passive voices have been used effectively.
- Favorable information has been emphasized by placing it in the main, or independent, clause; unfavorable facts have been placed in dependent, or subordinate, clauses.
- Words have been selected not only for their denotation but also for their connotation.

§ 1.6 Drafting the Issue Statement

§ 1.6.1 Select the Lens

The issue statement is the lens through which the judge views the case. Select the correct lens, and you improve your chances that the court will see the case as you see it and decide the motion in your client's favor. The difficulty, of course, is in selecting the lens. How do you select just the right one? Unfortunately, there is no easy answer. Because selecting the lens is, at least in part, a creative act, there is no foolproof formula.

There are, however, some strategies that you can try. First, think about your theory of the case. Given your theory, how should you frame the issue? Second, look at how the court framed the issues in cases that are similar to yours. In the cases in which the courts suppressed the evidence, how did the court frame the issue? Did the court focus on the defendant's rights? On the police's abuse of its power? On discrepancies in the testimony? Then look at the cases in which the courts did not suppress the evidence.

Finally, brainstorm. From what other angles can you view the case? What other labels can you attach? Think outside the box.

§ 1.6.2 Select a Format

Most courts do not prescribe a format for an issue statement. Although you should have the same number of issue statements as you have main argumentative headings, you can state the issue using the under-does-when format, the whether format, or the multisentence format.

EXAMPLE 1   "UNDER-DOES-WHEN" FORMAT

Under the Fourteenth Amendment, should the Court grant the defendant's motion to suppress Martinez's show-up identification (1) when a police officer pointed out Patterson to Martinez, repeatedly asking the shaken Martinez whether Patterson looked like her assailant; (2) when, during the second or two that Martinez had to view her assailant, her attention was focused on his gun and not his face; and (3) when Martinez told the police that her assailant was in his early forties and Patterson is only twenty-two years old?

EXAMPLE 2   "WHETHER" FORMAT

Whether the Court should grant the defendant's motion to suppress Martinez's show-up identification (1) when a police officer pointed out Patterson to Martinez, repeatedly asking the shaken Martinez whether Patterson looked like her assailant; (2) when, during the second or two that Martinez had to view her assailant, her attention was focused on his gun and not his face; and (3) when Martinez told the police that her assailant was in his early forties and Patterson is only twenty-two years old.

EXAMPLE 3   MULTISENTENCE FORMAT

On August 14, 2006, a man jumped out of his car, approached Martinez, and pointed a gun at her. As soon as she saw the gun, Martinez screamed and, crying, ran across the street. Shortly after the assault, a police officer twice asked Martinez whether a pedestrian looked like her assailant. Although Martinez could not see the pedestrian's face, she agreed. The police then questioned the pedestrian, Dean Patterson, while Martinez and another witness watched. Both Martinez and the witness told the police that Martinez's assailant was in his late thirties or early forties. Patterson is twenty-two. Under these circumstances, should the Court suppress Martinez's show-up and line-up identifications and prevent Martinez and Clipse from making in-court identifications?

PRACTICE POINTER   Once you select a format, use that format for each of your issue statements. Do not write one issue statement using the under-does-when format, a second issue statement using the whether format, and a third using the multisentence format. Also remember that you are not bound by opposing counsel's choices. You do not need to use the same format that he or she used, and you do not need to have the same number of issue statements. Do not let your opponent dictate your strategy.

§ 1.6.3 Make Your Issue Statement Subtly Persuasive

Your issue statement should be subtly persuasive. After reading it, the judge should be inclined to rule in your client's favor.

There are two techniques that you can use to make your issue statements persuasive. First, state the legal question so that it suggests the conclusion you want the court to reach. For example, if you want the court to grant the motion, ask whether the court should grant the motion. In contrast, if you want the court to deny the motion, ask whether the court should deny the motion. Second, include the facts that support your position, and present those facts in the light most favorable to your client.

For instance, in our example case, the defendant wants to state the legal question so that it suggests that the court should grant his motion to suppress. In contrast, the State wants to frame the question so that it suggests that the court should deny the defendant's motion.

EXAMPLE 1   **THE DEFENDANT'S STATEMENT OF THE LEGAL QUESTION**

"Whether the Court should grant the motion to suppress when . . . ."

EXAMPLE 2   **THE STATE'S STATEMENT OF THE LEGAL QUESTION**

"Whether the Court should deny the motion to suppress when . . . ."

The defendant also wants to set out the facts so that they suggest that the police procedures were unnecessarily suggestive and that Martinez's identifications are unreliable. Accordingly, the defendant wants to set out the facts that establish that the procedure was suggestive. (Instead of allowing Martinez to identify Patterson independently, a police officer pointed out Patterson and repeatedly asked the shaken Martinez whether he looked like her assailant.) In addition, the defendant wants to set out facts that establish that Martinez had a limited opportunity to view her assailant and that her description was inaccurate. Note that in both instances the writers set out the facts related to the first part of the test first and then the facts related to the second part of the test.

EXAMPLE 3   **THE DEFENDANT'S ISSUE STATEMENT**

Under the Fourteenth Amendment, should the Court grant Mr. Patterson's motion to suppress Martinez's show-up, line-up, and in-court identifications and Clipse's in-court identification when (1) a police officer pointed out Patterson to Martinez, repeatedly asking the shaken Martinez whether Patterson looked like her assailant; (2) the police questioned Patterson in front of Martinez and Clipse; (3) during the second or two that Martinez had to view her assailant, her attention was focused on his gun and not his face; and (4) both Martinez's and Clipse's descriptions were inaccurate?

The defendant wants to set out the facts that indicate that the police procedures were unnecessarily suggestive and that Martinez's identifications are unreliable, but the State wants to downplay the police officer's questions and emphasize instead that Martinez had a good opportunity to view her assailant.

EXAMPLE 4 · THE STATE'S ISSUE STATEMENT

Should the Court deny the defendant's motion to suppress when the police merely asked the victim whether a pedestrian was her assailant and when the victim observed her assailant on two occasions for several seconds in broad daylight?

Thus, writing a persuasive issue statement is a three-step process. You must select the appropriate lens, choose a format, and then craft your issue statement so that it is subtly persuasive.

§ 1.6.4 Checklist for Critiquing the Issue Statement

I. Format

- There is the same number of issue statements as there are main argumentative headings.
- The writer has used one of the conventional formats: under-does-when, whether, or multisentence.
- The same format has been used for each question presented.

II. Content

- The issue statement states the legal question and includes references to the legally significant facts. In addition, when appropriate, it also includes a reference to the rule of law.
- The legal questions have been framed so that they support the writer's theory of the case.

III. Persuasiveness

- The legal question has been framed so that it suggests an answer favorable to the client.

- Favorable facts have been emphasized, and unfavorable ones de-emphasized.
- Words have been selected for both their denotation and their connotation.

IV. Writing

- The judge can understand the issue statement after reading it through once.
- Punctuation has been used to divide the issue statement into manageable units of meaning.
- When appropriate, parallel constructions have been used.
- In both the main and subordinate clauses, the subjects and verbs are close together.
- The issue statement is grammatically correct, correctly punctuated, and proofread.

§ 1.7 Ordering the Issues and Arguments

§ 1.7.1 Present the Issues and Arguments in a Logical Order

In many cases, logic dictates the order of both the issues and, under each issue, the arguments. Threshold questions (for example, issues relating to whether the court has jurisdiction or to the statute of limitations) must be discussed before questions relating to the merits of the case. Similarly, the parts of a test must be discussed in order and, when one argument builds on another, the foundation argument must be presented first.

Although in our example case there is only one issue—whether the court should grant the defendant's motion to suppress—under that issue are several subissues. The court must decide (1) whether to suppress Martinez's show-up identification, (2) whether to suppress Martinez's line-up identification, and (3) whether to suppress any in-court identifications that Martinez or Clipse might make.

Logic dictates, at least in part, the order in which these three subissues should be discussed. Because an impermissibly suggestive show-up would taint the line-up and in-court identifications, you should discuss the show-up before the line-up and both the show-up and the line-up before the in-court identifications.

Logic also dictates the order of the arguments. Before it will suppress an identification, the court must find (1) that the police procedures were impermissibly suggestive and (2) that, under the totality of the circumstances, the resulting identifications are unreliable. Consequently, the defendant must discuss suggestiveness first.

In deciding whether an identification is reliable, the court considers five factors: (1) the witness's opportunity to see her assailant; (2) the witness's degree of attention; (3) the accuracy of the witness's description; (4) the witness's level of certainty; and (5) the length of time between the crime and the confrontation. Does logic dictate that these factors be discussed in any particular order?

§ 1.7.2 Decide Which Issues and Arguments Should Be Presented First

First impressions count. As a consequence, when logic does not dictate the order of your issues or arguments, put your strongest issues and your strongest arguments first. In addition, some attorneys like to end their brief with a strong argument. Although this strategy allows you to take advantage of the positions of emphasis, it also creates a risk. If the judge does not finish your brief, he or she might not see one of your strong arguments.

§ 1.8 Drafting the Argumentative Headings

§ 1.8.1 Use Your Argumentative Headings to Define the Structure of the Arguments

Just as posts and beams define the form of a building, argumentative headings define the form of the argument. When drafted properly, they provide the judge with an outline of the argument.

EXAMPLE 1   **DEFENDANT'S ARGUMENTATIVE HEADINGS**

I.   THE COURT SHOULD GRANT MR. PATTERSON'S MOTION TO SUPPRESS MARTINEZ'S SHOW-UP, LINE-UP, AND IN-COURT IDENTIFICATIONS AND CLIPSE'S IN-COURT IDENTIFICATION.

[Text]

A.   Martinez's show-up identification should be suppressed because the police procedures were impermissibly suggestive and because Martinez's identification is unreliable.

[Text]

1.   The police procedures were impermissibly suggestive because the police officer repeatedly asked Martinez whether Patterson looked like her assailant and because the officers questioned Patterson in Martinez's presence.

[Text]

2. Martinez's identification is unreliable because Martinez was able to view her assailant for only a few seconds, her attention was focused on the gun and not his face, and her description of her assailant does not match the description of Patterson.

[Text]

B. <u>Martinez's line-up identification should be suppressed because it was tainted by the show-up.</u>

[Text]

C. <u>Martinez should not be permitted to make an in-court identification because such an identification would be tainted by the impermissibly suggestive show-up and the line-up.</u>

In addition to defining the structure of the argument, argumentative headings also act as locators. By using the headings and subheadings, a judge can locate a particular argument. Argumentative headings also help the writer. As a practicing attorney, you will seldom have large blocks of time available for writing. Instead, you will have to squeeze in an hour here and two hours there. If you prepare your argumentative headings first, you can use what time you have effectively and write the sections one at a time.

§ 1.8.2 Use Your Argumentative Headings to Persuade

In addition to using argumentative headings to define the structure of your argument, use the headings to persuade.

Begin your heading by setting out a positive assertion. If you want the court to grant your motion to suppress, make that assertion: "The Court should grant the motion to suppress . . . ." In contrast, if you want the court to deny the motion to suppress, make that assertion: "The Court should deny the motion to suppress . . . ."

EXAMPLE 1   **NOT EFFECTIVE: NOT A POSITIVE ASSERTION**

The Court should not grant the motion to suppress . . . .
The Court should not suppress Martinez's show-up identification . . . .

EXAMPLE 2   **EFFECTIVE: POSITIVE ASSERTION**

The Court should deny the motion to suppress . . . .
The Court should admit Martinez's show-up identification . . . .

After setting out your assertion, you will usually want to set out the facts or reasons that support your assertion. The most common format is as follows:

Assertion	because	facts or reasons that support your assertion
Martinez's line-up identification should be suppressed	because	it was tainted by the impermissibly suggestive show-up.

In those instances in which you do not set out the reasons in your heading, use subheadings or sub-subheadings to set out the reasons. Look again at the headings and subheadings in the defendant's argumentative headings. Although the writer has not included a "because" clause in the main heading, she has included them in the subheadings and sub-subheadings.

EXAMPLE 3 **DEFENDANT'S ARGUMENTATIVE HEADINGS**

I. THE COURT SHOULD GRANT MR. PATTERSON'S MOTION TO SUPPRESS MARTINEZ'S SHOW-UP, LINE-UP, AND IN-COURT IDENTIFICATIONS AND CLIPSE'S IN-COURT IDENTIFICATION.

[Text]

A. Martinez's show-up identification should be suppressed because the police procedures were impermissibly suggestive and because Martinez's identification is unreliable.

[Text]

1. The police procedures were impermissibly suggestive because the police officer repeatedly asked Martinez whether Patterson looked like her assailant and because the officers questioned Patterson in Martinez's presence.

[Text]

2. Martinez's identification is unreliable because Martinez was able to view her assailant for only a few seconds, her attention was focused on the gun and not his face, and her description of her assailant does not match the description of Patterson.

[Text]

B. Martinez's line-up identification should be suppressed because it was tainted by the show-up.

[Text]

C. <u>Martinez should not be permitted to make an in-court identification because such an identification would be tainted by the impermissibly suggestive show-up and the line-up.</u>

§ 1.8.3 Make Your Headings Readable

If the judge does not read your headings, they do not serve either of their functions: they do not provide the judge with an outline of your argument, and they do not persuade. To make sure that your headings are read by the judge, keep them short and make them easy to read. As a general rule, your headings should be no more than three typed lines.

In the following example, the writer has tried to put too much information in her heading. As a result, the heading is too long, and the sentence is difficult to understand.

EXAMPLE 1 | **HEADING IS TOO LONG AND DIFFICULT TO UNDERSTAND**

1. The police procedures were impermissibly suggestive because the witness viewed only one person, the police repeatedly asked the witness whether that person looked like her assailant, and the police questioned the person in front of the witness, and because the person was simply walking down the street and not trying to escape and the witness was not likely to die or disappear, there was no reason to conduct a one-person show-up.

The following heading is much better. Instead of trying to put her entire argument into her heading, the writer has included only her most important points.

EXAMPLE 2 | **HEADING IS SHORTER AND EASIER TO UNDERSTAND**

1. The police procedures were impermissibly suggestive because the police officer repeatedly asked Martinez whether Patterson looked like her assailant and because the officers questioned Patterson in Martinez's and Clipse's presence.

§ 1.8.4 Follow the Conventions: Number, Placement, and Typefaces

By convention, you should have one, and only one, main argumentative heading for each issue statement. You set out the question in your issue statement and answer it in your main heading. Although subheadings and sub-subheadings are optional, if you include one, you should have at least two. You might or might not elect to include text between the main heading and the first subheading or between a subheading and the first sub-subheading.

PRACTICE

Historically, only three typefaces were used. When briefs were prepared using typewriters, the main headings were set out using all capital letters, the subheadings were underlined, and the sub-subheadings were set out using regular typeface. Although many attorneys still use this system, others have adopted different systems, for example, setting out the main headings in bold rather than all capitals. Check with your local court and firm to see what is commonly done in your jurisdiction.

EXAMPLE 1 **TYPEFACES FOR MAIN HEADING, SUBHEADINGS, AND SUB-SUBHEADINGS**

I. FIRST MAIN HEADING [Answers question set out in first issue statement.]

[If appropriate, set general rules here.]

A. <u>First subheading</u>

[If appropriate, set out specific rules here.]

1. First sub-subheading

[Set out argument here.]

2. Second sub-subheading

[Set out argument here.]

B. Second subheading

[Set out argument here.]

II. SECOND MAIN HEADING [If you had two issue statements, answers question set out in the second issue statement.]

[If appropriate, set out general rules here.]

A. <u>First subheading</u>

[Set out argument here.]

B. <u>Second subheading</u>

[Set out argument here.]

C. <u>Third subheading</u>

[Set out argument here.]

§ 1.8.5 Checklist for Critiquing the Argumentative Headings

I. Content

- When read together, the headings provide the judge with an outline of the argument.

II. Persuasiveness

- Each heading is in the form of a positive assertion.
- Each assertion is supported, either in the main heading or through the use of subheadings.
- The headings are case-specific; that is, they include references to the parties and the facts of the case.
- Favorable facts are emphasized and unfavorable facts are de-emphasized or omitted if not legally significant.
- Favorable facts have been placed in the positions of emphasis.
- Favorable facts have been described vividly and in detail.
- Words have been selected both for their denotation and their connotation.

III. Conventions

- The writer has used the conventional typefaces for main headings, subheadings, and sub-subheadings.
- There is never just one subheading or just one sub-subheading in a section.

IV. Writing

- The judge can understand the heading after reading it through once. (Headings are not more than two or three lines long.)
- Punctuation has been used to divide the heading into manageable units of meaning.
- When appropriate, parallel constructions have been used.
- In both the main and subordinate clauses, the subject and verb are close together.
- The headings are grammatically correct, correctly punctuated, and proofread.

§ 1.9 Drafting the Arguments

Most of us have had arguments. As children, we fought with our parents over cleaning our rooms or over how late we could stay out. As adults, we have fought with friends, roommates, spouses, and partners over household chores, budgets, and world events.

Although most of us have had arguments, very few of us have been taught how to make arguments. We know how to express our anger and frustration; we do not know how to set out an assertion and then systematically walk our listener through our "proof." Even fewer of us have been taught how to set out our proofs persuasively.

It is, however, exactly these skills—the ability to set out an assertion, to walk your reader through your proof, and to present that proof persuasively—that you will need to develop if you are going to write an effective brief. Good advocates have the mental discipline of a mathematician. They think linearly, identifying each of the steps in the analysis, and then walk the judge through those steps in a logical order. They also have the creativity and insight of an advertising executive. They know their "market," and they know both the image they want to create and how to use language to create it. In short, they have mastered both the science and the art of advocacy.

§ 1.9.1 Identify Your Assertions and Your Support for Those Assertions

An argument has two parts: an assertion and the support for that assertion.

a. Setting Out Your Assertion

An assertion can take one of two forms. It can be procedural, setting out the procedural act you want the court to take, or it can be substantive, setting out the legal conclusion you want the court to reach.

EXAMPLE 1   **TYPES OF ASSERTIONS**

Procedural

The court should grant the motion to suppress.

The court should deny the motion to suppress.

Substantive

The police procedures were impermissibly suggestive.

The witness's identification is reliable.

---

b. Supporting Your Assertion

Although your assertion is an essential part of your argument, it is not, by itself, an argument. How many judges would be persuaded by the following exchange?

Defense counsel:	Your Honor, the Court should grant the Defendant's motion to suppress.
Prosecutor:	Your Honor, we respectfully disagree. The Court should deny the motion.
Defense counsel:	No, Your Honor, the Court should grant the motion.
Prosecutor:	No. The Court should deny the motion.

An exchange in which the defendant asserts that the police procedures were impermissibly suggestive and the prosecutor asserts that they were not is equally unpersuasive. Standing alone, assertions do not persuade. They must be supported.

In law, that support can take one of several forms. You can support an assertion by applying a statute or common law rule to the facts of your case, by comparing or contrasting the facts in your case to the facts in analogous cases, or by explaining why, as a matter of public policy, the court should rule in your client's favor.

In the first example set out here, the defendant supports his assertion by applying the rule to the facts of his case. In the second example, the defendant supports his assertion by comparing the facts in his case to the facts in the analogous cases, and, in the third example, he supports his assertion using public policy.

EXAMPLE 2 **DEFENDANT SUPPORTS HIS ASSERTION BY APPLYING THE RULES TO THE FACTS OF HIS CASE**

Assertion: The police procedures were impermissibly suggestive.

Support: Rule: One-person show-ups are inherently suggestive. *See Neil v. Biggers*, 409 U.S. 188, 199, 93 S. Ct. 375, 34 L. Ed. 2d 401 (1972).[1] When the police present the witness with a single suspect, the witness usually infers that the police believe that the person being presented committed the crime. *Id.*

Application: In this case, the police presented Martinez with a single suspect: Dean Patterson. In doing so, the police suggested to Martinez that Patterson was the man who had assaulted her.

EXAMPLE 3 **DEFENDANT SUPPORTS HIS ASSERTION BY COMPARING THE FACTS IN HIS CASE WITH THE FACTS IN AN ANALOGOUS CASE**

Assertion: The police procedures were impermissibly suggestive.

Support: Analogous case: In *State v. Booth*, 36 Wn. App. 66, 67-68, 671 P.2d 1218 (1983), the police brought the witness to the scene

---

[1] Because this brief is a brief to a Washington court, the writer has used the Washington citation rules.

of the arrest and showed him a single suspect, who was sitting with his back to the witness in the back seat of the police car. The court held that the police procedures were impermissibly suggestive. *Id.* at 70.

Application: As in *Booth*, in our case the police showed the witness a single suspect and asked her to identify him before she had an opportunity to see his face. The only difference between the two cases is the identity of the person in the police car. While in *Booth* it was the suspect who was in the car, in our case it was the witness.

EXAMPLE 4   **THE DEFENDANT SUPPORTS HIS ASSERTION BY USING PUBLIC POLICY**

Assertion: The police procedures were impermissibly suggestive.

Support: Policy: To protect the rights of defendants, the courts should suppress unreliable identifications.

Application: Because Martinez's identifications are unreliable, Patterson will be denied his right to a fair trial if Martinez's show-up and line-up identifications are admitted.

If there is only one argument that supports your assertion, make that argument. If, however, you can make several different arguments, think about whether you want to include all of those arguments. Will your brief be more persuasive if you set out only one strong argument, or will it be more persuasive if you set out three, four, or five arguments? Identifying the arguments is the science; deciding which arguments to include is the art.

§ 1.9.2 Select an Organizational Scheme

In making their arguments, most advocates use one of two types of reasoning: deductive or inductive. When you use deductive reasoning, you set out your assertion and then the support for that assertion. In contrast, when you use inductive reasoning, you set out your support first, and then walk the judge through your support to your conclusion.

Deductive Reasoning

Assertion: The identification is not reliable.

Support: The identification is not reliable because Martinez viewed her assailant for only two or three seconds.

               The identification is not reliable because Martinez's attention was focused on the gun and not on her assailant's face.

               The identification is not reliable because Martinez's description of her assailant was inaccurate.

The identification is not reliable because, at least initially, Martinez was not certain that Patterson was her assailant.

Inductive Reasoning

Support: Martinez viewed her assailant for only two or three seconds.

Martinez's attention was focused on the gun and not on her assailant's face.

Martinez's description of her assailant was inaccurate.

At least initially, Martinez was not certain that Patterson was her assailant.

Conclusion: Because Martinez viewed her assailant for only two or three seconds, because her attention was focused on the gun and not on her assailant's face, because her description of her assailant was inaccurate, and because, at least initially, she was not certain that Patterson was her assailant, Martinez's identification is not reliable.

If you use deductive reasoning, you will usually use a version of the following blueprint. Note the similarities between this blueprint and the blueprints that you use to organize the discussion section in an objective memo. Also note that the example shows two different ways of setting out the arguments. Under the first subheading, the assertion is set out first. Under the second subheading, the assertion is set out after the rules and the descriptions of the cases. You should use whichever format is, in your case, most likely to be effective.

EXAMPLE 1 BLUEPRINT FOR AN ARGUMENT USING DEDUCTIVE REASONING

1. MAIN HEADING

   [Text set out in the light most favorable to your client.]

   A. <u>First subheading</u>

      1. Assertion

      2. Rules set out in the light most favorable to your client

      3. Descriptions of the analogous cases

      4. Your arguments

      5. Your response to your opponent's arguments

   B. <u>Second subheading</u>

      1. Rules set out in the light most favorable to your client

      2. Descriptions of the analogous cases

   3. Assertion

   4. Your arguments

   5. Your response to your opponent's arguments

When you use inductive reasoning, you will usually integrate the rules, the descriptions of the cases, and your response to the other side's arguments into each of your arguments.

EXAMPLE 2 **BLUEPRINT FOR AN ARGUMENT USING INDUCTIVE REASONING**

   I. MAIN HEADING

      A. First subheading

         1. First argument

         2. Second argument

         3. Third argument

         4. Fourth argument

         5. Conclusion

      B. Second subheading

         1. First argument

         2. Second argument

         3. Third argument

         4. Conclusion

There are also several other organizational schemes that you may use. For example, if, in your case, the facts are your best argument, start by setting out the facts. Then show how those facts are similar to the facts in cases in which the court reached the conclusion you want the court to reach.

EXAMPLE 3 **FACTS SET OUT FIRST**

   I. MAIN HEADING

      [Text set out in the light most favorable to your client.]

      A. First subheading

         1. Facts of your case

         2. Comparison of the facts in your case to the facts in analogous cases

         3. Courts' holdings in analogous cases

4. Response to other side's arguments

5. Conclusion

In the following example, defense counsel used this strategy in arguing that the show-up was impermissibly suggestive. Because none of the cases supported her position, defense counsel began her argument by setting out her assertion and the facts that support that assertion.

EXAMPLE 4 **EXCERPT FROM THE DEFENDANT'S BRIEF**

A. The police procedures were impermissibly suggestive because the police officer repeatedly asked Martinez whether Patterson looked like her assailant and because the officer questioned Patterson in Martinez's presence.

In this case, Officer Yuen's actions suggested to Martinez that he believed Patterson was her assailant.

While driving Martinez home, Officer Yuen pulled up behind Patterson and asked Martinez whether Patterson looked like her assailant. When Martinez did not respond, Officer Yuen repeated his question, asking "Is that the man who assaulted you?"

Although Martinez could not see Patterson's face, after hesitating, she agreed with Officer Yuen that Patterson looked like her assailant. At that point, Officer Yuen pulled up behind Patterson, got out of the police car, and began questioning him. A few minutes later, Officer Cox and Clipse arrived, and both Officer Yuen and Officer Cox questioned Patterson while Martinez and Clipse watched.

In contrast, if your best argument is an argument based on an analogous case, start by describing that case.

EXAMPLE 5 **EXCERPT FROM THE STATE'S BRIEF**

A. Merely asking the victim whether a pedestrian was her assailant does not make a permissible show-up impermissibly suggestive.

There are no published Washington cases in which the courts have held that a show-up was impermissibly suggestive. Instead, in a Division I case, the court held that the show-up was not impermissibly suggestive when the police picked up the witness at a tavern and told him that they wanted to take him to his apartment to see if he could identify his assailant. *State v. Rogers*, 44 Wn. App. 510, 515-16, 722 P.2d 1249 (1986). When the witness, an elderly individual who was not wearing his glasses, arrived at his apartment, he identified the defendant when the defendant came out of the building. *Id.* There was a uniformed police officer in front of the defendant and another uniformed police officer following behind him. *Id.*

Similarly, in *State v. Booth*, 36 Wn. App. 66, 70-71, 671 P.2d 1218 (1983), the court held that the show-up was not impermissibly suggestive when the police asked the witness to accompany them to the place where the defendant had been arrested and the witness identified the defendant after seeing him in the back of a police car. *Id.* at 67-68; *accord State v. Guzman-Cuellar*, 47 Wn.2d 326, 734 P.2d 966 (1987) (show-up not impermissibly suggestive when eyewitnesses were shown the defendant, who was in handcuffs standing next to a police car.)

Although you want to set out the pieces of your argument in the order that the judge expects to see them, you also want to emphasize your best arguments. Therefore, instead of using a format mechanically, use it creatively to accomplish your purpose.

§ 1.9.3 Present the Rules in the Light Most Favorable to Your Client

Although the structure of the argument section is similar to the structure of the discussion section, the way in which you present the rules is very different. In an objective memo you set out the rules objectively, but in a brief you set them out in the light most favorable to your client. Without misrepresenting the rules, you want to "package" them so that they support your assertion.

To set out the rules in the light most favorable to your client, use one or more of the following techniques.

A. Create a favorable context.
B. State favorable rules as broadly as possible and unfavorable rules as narrowly as possible.
C. Emphasize favorable rules and de-emphasize unfavorable rules.
  1. Emphasize the burden of proof if the other side has the burden; de-emphasize the burden of proof if you have the burden.
  2. Give favorable rules more airtime and unfavorable rules less airtime.
  3. Place favorable rules in a position of emphasis and bury unfavorable ones.
  4. Place favorable rules in short sentences or in the main clause, and place unfavorable rules in longer sentences or in dependent clauses.
D. Select your words carefully.

Compare the following examples, identifying the techniques that the writers used.

EXAMPLE 1 · OBJECTIVE STATEMENT OF THE RULE

In deciding whether identification testimony is admissible, the courts apply a two-part test. Under the first part of the test, the defendant must prove that the police procedures were impermissibly suggestive. If the court finds that the procedure was impermissibly suggestive, the State then has the burden of showing that, under the totality of the circumstances, the reliability of the identification outweighs the suggestive police procedure. *Manson v. Braithwaite*, 432 U.S. 98, 108, 97 S. Ct. 2243, 53 L. Ed. 2d 140 (1977).

EXAMPLE 2 · RULES STATED IN THE LIGHT MOST FAVORABLE TO THE DEFENDANT

The United States Supreme Court has developed a two-part test to ensure a criminal defendant the procedural due process guaranteed to every individual by the Fourteenth Amendment. *Manson v. Braithwaite*, 432 U.S. 98, 108, 97 S. Ct. 2243, 53 L. Ed. 2d 108 (1977).

Under the first part of the test, the defendant need show only that the identification that he seeks to suppress was obtained through the use of impermissibly suggestive police procedures. *Id.* Once this has been established, the onus shifts to the State to prove that, under the totality of the circumstances, the witness's identification is so reliable that it should be admitted even though it was obtained through impermissibly suggestive means. *Id.*

EXAMPLE 3 · RULES STATED IN THE LIGHT MOST FAVORABLE TO THE STATE

Identifications should not be kept from the jury unless the procedures used in obtaining the identifications were so suggestive and unreliable that a substantial likelihood of irreparable misidentification exists. *Simmons v. United States*, 390 U.S. 377, 384, 88 S. Ct. 967, 19 L. Ed. 2d 1247 (1968).

In deciding whether identification evidence is admissible, the courts employ a two-part test. Under the first part of the test, the defendant has the burden of proving that the identification evidence that he seeks to suppress was obtained through impermissibly suggestive procedures. *Manson v. Braithwaite*, 432 U.S. 98, 108, 97 S. Ct. 2243, 53 L. Ed. 2d 140 (1977). Only if the defendant satisfies this substantial burden is the second part of the test applied.

Even if the court determines that the police procedures were impermissibly suggestive, the evidence is admissible if, under the totality of the circumstances, the identifications are reliable. Due process does not compel the exclusion of an identification if it is reliable. *Id.*

Let's begin by comparing the opening sentences of all three examples. In Example 1, the writer simply states that the court applies a two-part test. There is no attempt to create a favorable context.

EXAMPLE 4   OBJECTIVE STATEMENT OF THE RULE

In deciding whether identification testimony is admissible, the courts apply a two-part test.

In contrast, in Examples 2 and 3, the writers "package" the rule, using policy to create a context that favors their respective clients. The key language is shown in boldface type.

EXAMPLE 5   RULES STATED IN THE LIGHT MOST FAVORABLE TO THE DEFENDANT

The United States Supreme Court has developed a two-part test to ensure a criminal **defendant the procedural due process guaranteed to every individual by the Fourteenth Amendment.**

EXAMPLE 6   RULES STATED IN THE LIGHT MOST FAVORABLE TO THE STATE

Identifications should not be kept from the jury unless the procedures used in obtaining the identifications were so suggestive and unreliable that a substantial likelihood of irreparable misidentification exists.

In addition to creating a favorable context, the parties have emphasized or de-emphasized the burden of proof, depending on whether they have the burden or the other side has the burden. Compare the highlighted passages.

EXAMPLE 7   OBJECTIVE STATEMENT OF THE RULE

Under the first part of the test, **the defendant must prove** that the police procedures were impermissibly suggestive.

EXAMPLE 8   RULES STATED IN THE LIGHT MOST FAVORABLE TO THE DEFENDANT

Under the first part of the test, **the defendant need show** only that the identification that he seeks to suppress was obtained through the use of impermissibly suggestive police procedures.

EXAMPLE 9   RULES STATED IN THE LIGHT MOST FAVORABLE TO THE STATE

Under the first part of the test, **the defendant has the burden of proving** that the identification evidence he seeks to suppress was obtained through impermissibly suggestive procedures.

Similarly, both sides try to lead the court to the desired conclusions. Defense counsel presumes that the defendant will meet his burden; the State presents the second part of the test as an alternative. Even if the State loses on the first part of the test, it wins on the second. Once again, in excerpts from earlier Examples 2 and 3 the key language is shown in boldface type.

EXAMPLE 10 **RULES STATED IN THE LIGHT MOST FAVORABLE TO THE DEFENDANT**

Once this has been established, the onus shifts to the State to prove that, under the totality of the circumstances, the witness's identification is so reliable that it should be admitted even though it was obtained through unnecessarily suggestive means.

EXAMPLE 11 **RULES STATED IN THE LIGHT MOST FAVORABLE TO THE STATE**

In deciding whether identification evidence is admissible, the courts employ a two-part test. Under the first part of the test, the defendant has the burden of proving that the identification evidence he seeks to suppress was obtained through impermissibly suggestive procedures. *Manson v. Braithwaite*, 432 U.S. 98, 113, 97 S. Ct. 2243, 53 L. Ed. 2d 140 (1977). **Only if the defendant satisfies this substantial burden is the second part of the test applied.**

Even if the court determines that the police procedures were impermissibly suggestive, the evidence is admissible if, under the totality of the circumstances, the identifications are reliable. Due process does not compel the exclusion of an identification if it is reliable. *Id.*

Finally, look at the words that each side uses:

Defendant	State
ensure	so suggestive
guaranteed	burden
onus shifts	substantial burden
so reliable	compel

Instead of using the language they saw in the cases or the first word that came to mind, each side selected its words carefully, with the goal of subtly influencing the decision-making process.

§ 1.9.4 Present the Cases in the Light Most Favorable to Your Client

When you use analogous cases to support your argument, present those cases in the light most favorable to your client. If a case supports your position, emphasize the similarities between the facts in the analogous case and the facts in your case. On the other hand, if a case does not support your position, emphasize the differences.

In our example case, both sides use *State v. Booth*, 36 Wn. App. 66, 671 P.2d 1218 (1983), a case in which the court held that the identification was reliable. The relevant portion of the court's opinion is set out in Example 1.

EXAMPLE 1   EXCERPT FROM *STATE v. BOOTH*

"The facts provide several indicia of reliability. Ms. Thomas was driving slowly, it was a clear day, and she observed Booth for approximately forty-five seconds. Her attention was greater than average because he had money in his hands and was running. In addition, her attention was particularly drawn to the car with Missouri plates because she had lived in Missouri. Finally, the identification took place thirty to forty minutes later and was unequivocal. On the basis of these facts we find that reliability outweighed the harm of suggestiveness and the identification was properly admitted."

Because the court found that the identification was reliable, the defendant wants to distinguish *Booth*. As a consequence, in discussing opportunity to view, the defendant wants to emphasize that in *Booth* the witness viewed the defendant for almost a minute, while in our case the witness viewed her assailant for only a few seconds.

EXAMPLE 2   HOW THE DEFENDANT MIGHT DESCRIBE *STATE v. BOOTH*

An identification will not be found to be reliable unless the witness had an adequate opportunity to view the defendant. This was the situation in *Booth*. In that case, a bystander was able to view the defendant for almost a minute. *Id.* at 70. Because she was able to view the defendant for an extended period of time under good conditions, the court concluded that her identification was reliable. *Id.* In contrast, in our case Martinez viewed her assailant for only two or three seconds.

Conversely, the State wants to emphasize the similarities between the facts in its case and the facts in *Booth*. Thus, it tries to minimize the amount of time that the witness had to view the defendant.

EXAMPLE 3   HOW THE STATE MIGHT DESCRIBE *STATE v. BOOTH*

The courts do not require that the witness have viewed the defendant for an extended period of time. For example, in *Booth*, the court found the witness's identification was reliable even though the witness had viewed the defendant for less than a minute. *Id.* at 70.

---

§ 1.9.5 Present the Arguments in the Light Most Favorable to Your Client

In addition to presenting the rules and analogous cases in the light most favorable to your client, you also want to set out the arguments in the light most favorable to your client. As a general rule, set out your own arguments first, give your own arguments the most airtime, and use language that strengthens your arguments and undermines the other side's arguments.

a. Present Your Own Arguments First

You will almost always set out your own arguments first. By doing so, you can take advantage of the position of emphasis, emphasizing your argument and de-emphasizing the other side's arguments.

The following example shows what you do not want to do. By setting out the defendant's assertions, the State gives the defendant's arguments extra airtime. The court gets to read the defendant's argument in the defendant's brief and then again in the State's brief.

EXAMPLE 1   INEFFECTIVE ARGUMENT

The defendant argues that the police procedures were impermissibly suggestive because the police showed Martinez a single suspect, Patterson, and because they asked Martinez whether Patterson looked like her assailant.

It is our contention that the police procedures were not impermissibly suggestive. One-person show-ups are not per se impermissibly suggestive; if the show-up occurs shortly after the commission of the crime during a search for the suspect, it is permissible. *See State v. Booth*, 36 Wn. App. 66, 70-71, 671 P.2d 1218 (1983).

The following example is substantially better. Instead of starting its arguments by setting out the defendant's assertions, the State starts by setting out a favorable statement of the rule. It then sets out its own argument, integrating its responses to the defendant's arguments into its own arguments.

EXAMPLE 2   MORE EFFECTIVE ARGUMENT

One-person show-ups are not per se impermissibly suggestive: a show-up is permissible if it occurs shortly after the commission of a crime during a search for the suspect. *See State v. Booth*, 36 Wn. App. 66, 70-71, 671 P.2d 1218 (1983).

In this case, the show-up occurred within forty-five minutes of the assault. It also occurred before the police officers had completed their investigation: Officer Yuen saw Patterson as he was leaving the crime scene to take Martinez home.

Under these circumstances, Officer Yuen would not have been doing his job if, upon seeing a man who matched the assailant's description, he had not asked Martinez whether the man looked like her assailant. The officer's question, "Is that the man?" was not enough to turn a permissible show-up into one that was impermissibly suggestive.

b. Give the Most Airtime to Your Own Arguments

Most of the time, you will want to give more airtime to your own arguments than you do to the other side's arguments. Your goal is to respond to or counter the other side's arguments without giving them too much airtime. Compare the following examples. In the first example, the State gives too much airtime to the defendant's age. In the second, the State counters the defendant's arguments without overemphasizing them.

EXAMPLE 1   INEFFECTIVE ARGUMENT

On the whole, Martinez's description was accurate. When she was interviewed, Martinez told the police that her assailant was a white male, that he was approximately 5'7" tall, that he weighed between 165 and 170 pounds, that he had blondish-brown hair, that he was wearing a dark jacket, and **that he appeared to be in his early forties. In fact, the defendant is twenty-two.**

This discrepancy in age is insignificant. It is often difficult to guess a person's age: some people appear older than they are, and others appear younger. Thus, the court should give little weight to the fact that Martinez misjudged the defendant's age. On the basis of the other information Martinez gave to the police, the police were able to identify the defendant as the assailant.

EXAMPLE 2   MORE EFFECTIVE ARGUMENT

In this case, Martinez was able to give the police a detailed description of her assailant. When she was interviewed, she told the police that her assailant was a white male with blondish-brown hair, that he was approximately 5'7" tall and weighed between 165 and 170 pounds, **that he appeared to be in his early forties,** and that he was wearing a dark green jacket. This description is accurate in all but one respect. **Although Martinez misjudged the defendant's age,** she accurately described his hair, his height and weight, and his clothing.

c. Use Language that Strengthens Your Arguments and Undermines the Other Side's Arguments

In setting out your own arguments, do not use phrases such as "We contend that . . . ," "It is our argument that . . . ," "We believe that . . . ," or "We feel . . . ." Just set out your assertions.

EXAMPLE 1	**DEFENDANT'S BRIEF**

Ineffective

It is our contention that the police procedures were impermissibly suggestive.

More Effective

The police procedures were impermissibly suggestive.

On the other hand, when it is necessary to set out the other side's argument, use an introductory phrase that reminds the court that the statement is just the other side's assertion or argument.

EXAMPLE 2	**DEFENDANT'S BRIEF**

Although the State contends that Martinez's identification is reliable, Martinez had only a second or two to view her assailant.

d. Use the Same Persuasive Techniques You Used in Setting Out the Facts, Issues, Rules, and Analogous Cases

Finally, when appropriate, use the same persuasive techniques that you used in writing the other parts of your brief. For instance, use the positions of emphasis to your best advantage. Place your best points at the beginning or end of a section or paragraph. In addition, whenever possible, put your strong points in short sentences or, in a longer sentence, in the main clause. Finally, select your words carefully. Choose words that convey not only the right denotation but also the right connotation.

Also remember that persuasive arguments are not written; they are crafted. In first drafts, concentrate on content and organization; in subsequent drafts, work on writing persuasively.

§ 1.9.6 Checklist for Critiquing the Argument

I. Content

- Has the writer set out his or her assertions?
- Has the writer supported his or her assertions?
  - If appropriate, has the writer applied the applicable statute or common law rule to the facts of his or her case?

- If appropriate, has the writer compared and contrasted the facts in the analogous cases to the facts in his or her case?
- If appropriate, has the writer explained why, as a matter of public policy, the court should rule in his or her client's favor?
- Has the writer cited to the key relevant authorities?
- Are the writer's statements of the rules and descriptions of the cases accurate?

II. Organization

- Has the writer used one of the conventional organizational schemes—for example, deductive or inductive reasoning?
- Has the writer used an organizational scheme that allows him or her to emphasize the strongest parts of his or her arguments?

III. Persuasiveness

Rules

- Has the writer presented the rules in the light most favorable to his or her client?
  - Did the writer create a favorable context?
  - Did the writer state favorable rules as broadly as possible and unfavorable rules as narrowly as possible?
  - Did the writer emphasize favorable rules and de-emphasize unfavorable ones?
  - Did the writer select words both for their denotation and for their connotation?

Analogous Cases

- Has the writer presented the cases in the light most favorable to his or her client?
  - Did the writer create a favorable context?
  - Did the writer state favorable holdings as broadly as possible and unfavorable holdings as narrowly as possible?
  - Did the writer emphasize favorable facts and de-emphasize unfavorable ones?
  - Did the writer select words both for their denotation and for their connotation?

Arguments

- Did the writer present his or her own arguments first?
- Did the writer give his or her own arguments the most airtime?
- Did the writer use language that strengthens his or her arguments and weakens his or her opponent's arguments?

§ 1.10 The Prayer for Relief

The final section of the brief is the prayer for relief or the conclusion. In some jurisdictions, the prayer for relief is very short. The attorney simply sets out the relief that he or she wants.

EXAMPLE 1   **EXCERPT FROM THE DEFENDANT'S BRIEF**

Prayer for Relief

For the reasons set out above, Mr. Patterson respectfully requests that the Court suppress Martinez's show-up and line-up identifications and that the Court not permit Martinez or Clipse to make an in-court identification.

In other jurisdictions, the attorney sets out the relief that he or she is requesting and summarizes the arguments.

EXAMPLE 2   **EXCERPT FROM THE DEFENDANT'S BRIEF**

Conclusion

The Court should suppress Martinez's show-up identification because the police officer's questions were impermissibly suggestive and because, given Martinez's limited opportunity to view her assailant and the inaccuracies in her description, her identification is unreliable.

The Court should also suppress Martinez's line-up identification and any in-court identifications that Martinez or Clipse might make: both the line-up and the in-court identifications have been tainted by the impermissibly suggestive show-up.

---

§ 1.11 Signing the Brief

Before the brief is submitted to the court, it must be signed by an attorney licensed to practice law in the jurisdiction. The following format is used in many jurisdictions.

Submitted this _____ day of _____, 200 ____.

_____

Attorney for the Defendant

Because the following briefs were filed in a case being heard by a Washington trial court, the attorneys used one of the formats typically used in Washington for motions to suppress. In addition, the attorneys used the Washington citation rules and not *The Bluebook* or *ALWD Citation Manual* rules. Because the briefs were written before the hearing on the motion to suppress, the attorneys could not include citations to a record. Instead, in setting out the facts they set out the facts that they believed they could establish during the hearing.

Before drafting a brief for another court, check the local rules for the required format, for the format used for citations to legal authorities, and for the rules governing citations to the record.

EXAMPLE 1	**DEFENDANT'S BRIEF**

1

2

3

4

5   THE SUPERIOR COURT OF KING COUNTY, WASHINGTON

6 STATE OF WASHINGTON,   )   Case No.: No. 06-01-2226
)

7   Plaintiff,   )   DEFENDANT'S BRIEF IN SUPPORT
)   OF MOTION TO SUPPRESS

8   v.   )

9 DEAN E. PATTERSON,   )

10   Defendant.   )

11

12   **Statement of Facts**

13   At 7:30 a.m. on Monday, August 14, 2006, twenty-two-year-old Dean

14 Patterson finished his shift as a security guard and walked to his apartment.

15 After having breakfast with his wife, he went to bed and slept until about 1:00

16 p.m. At about 2:30 p.m., Patterson's wife received a phone call asking her to

17 work at the local hospital where she is employed as a nurse. Patterson's wife

18 got ready, and Patterson dropped her off at the hospital at about 3:10 p.m.

19   At about 3:30 p.m., Patterson called his wife to find out how long she

20 would have to work: they had plans to go to a movie that evening, and he

21 wanted to know whether he should change those plans. At about 3:50 p.m.,

22 Patterson took a load of laundry to the apartment complex's laundry room.

23 When he returned to his apartment, Patterson watched part of an old movie.

24 At about 4:20 p.m., Patterson went back to the laundry room to put the

25 clothes in the dryer. On his way back, he walked to where his car, an older

Defendant's Brief in Support   Alicia Hamsa
of Motion to Suppress   1   Office of the Public Defender
                                 Seattle, Washington

1   model red station wagon, was parked to see if he needed to get gas. As he

2   did so, Patterson noticed a parking spot much closer to his apartment and,

3   after checking his gas, moved his car to that spot. After parking his car, Pat-

4   terson got out of the car and, because the driver's side door does not lock

5   from the outside, walked to the passenger side to lock the doors. As he did

6   so, he nodded to a parking enforcement officer who was driving by.

7   By this time, it was 4:30 p.m., and Patterson decided to phone his wife

8   again. He arranged to meet her at 5:15 p.m. for her dinner break. Patterson

9   retrieved the laundry and then left the apartment a little before 5:00 p.m.

10 to meet his wife.

11   At about 4:30 p.m. on the same day, seventeen-year-old Beatrice Marti-

12 nez left her apartment to walk to work. As she was walking southbound on

13 Belmont, a car that had driven by earlier pulled in front of her. The man got

14 out of his car, took one or two steps toward Martinez, and then pulled a gun

15 from his pocket. As soon as she spotted the gun, Martinez screamed, looked

16 away, and then, crying, ran across the street. The entire encounter was over

17 in three or four seconds.

18   At about 4:50 p.m. Chester Clipse was walking home when he saw a

19 man in a red station wagon driving slowly down the street. When the man

20 started to pull into Clipse's parking stall, Clipse began walking toward him

21 to tell him that he could not park there. As he did so, Clipse saw the man

22 get out of his car and walk toward a girl who was on the sidewalk. He then

23 heard the girl scream, and as she screamed, Clipse saw that the man had a

24 gun. Clipse yelled "Hey," and the man turned and ran to his car, putting the

25 gun under his coat. As the girl ran across the street, the man got back into

26 his car, backed out, and drove away, traveling northbound on Belmont.

Defendant's Brief in Support   Alicia Hamsa
of Motion to Suppress   2   Office of the Public Defender
                                                Seattle, Washington

1　　　At the same time, a parking enforcement officer drove down the street.

2　　Clipse flagged him down, told him what had happened, and described the car

3　　and the man. The parking enforcement officer called 911 and then left to try to

4　　locate the car. Because the girl was still crying, Clipse took her to his landlady's

5　　apartment. He then went back outside and waited for the police.

6　　　　When the police arrived, Clipse told Officers Yuen and Cox what had

7　　happened. Clipse told the police that the man was white, about 5'10" tall,

8　　and about 180 to 185 pounds. He also told the officers that the man was

9　　wearing a green outfit and that he was in his late thirties or early forties.

10　　Patterson is twenty-two.

11　　　　While Clipse was talking to the police, Officer Cox received a radio mes-

12　　sage indicating that the parking enforcement officer had located a car that

13　　matched the one that Clipse had described. While Officer Cox took Clipse in

14　　his patrol car to see if Clipse could identify the car the parking enforcement

15　　had located, Officer Yuen went inside to interview Martinez.

16　　　　Because she was still upset, Martinez was able to give Officer Yuen only

17　　a general description of her assailant. She described him as being a short,

18　　white male with blondish-brown hair who was wearing glasses and a dark

19　　jacket. In addition, she told police that her assailant was in his early forties.

20　　　　After interviewing Martinez, Officer Yuen took the still shaken Martinez

21　　to his car to take her home. When they had traveled less than a block, Officer

22　　Yuen noticed a white male wearing dark-colored clothing. As he drove up

23　　behind him, Yuen asked Martinez, "Is that the man?" When Martinez did

24　　not immediately answer, Yuen asked the question again: "Is that the man

25　　who assaulted you?"

26

1   Even though Martinez was unable to see the man's face, she agreed with

2   the officer that the man looked like her assailant. At this point, Officer Yuen

3   stopped the car, got out, and approached Patterson. As he was question-

4   ing Patterson, Officer Cox drove up with Clipse. While Martinez and Clipse

5   watched, Officers Cox and Yuen continued questioning Patterson. Officer

6   Cox then returned to Martinez and Clipse and walked them back to Clipse's

7   apartment. While he did so, Yuen placed Patterson under arrest.

8   Later that day, the police searched Patterson's car and apartment. In the

9   apartment, the police found the gun issued to Patterson by his employer. Four

10   days later, the police held a line-up. Although Martinez identified Patterson as

11   the man who had approached her, Clipse did not identify Patterson.

12   **Issue**

13   Under the Fourteenth Amendment, should the Court grant Mr. Patterson's

14   motion to suppress Martinez's show-up, line-up, and in-court identifications

15   and Clipse's in-court identification when (1) a police officer pointed out Pat-

16   terson to Martinez, repeatedly asking the shaken Martinez whether Patter-

17   son looked like her assailant, (2) the police questioned Patterson in front of

18   Martinez and Clipse, (3) during the second or two that Martinez had to view

19   her assailant, her attention was focused on his gun and not his face, and (4)

20   both Martinez's and Clipse's descriptions were inaccurate?

21   **Argument**

22   I.   THE COURT SHOULD GRANT MR. PATTERSON'S MOTION TO SUP-
          PRESS MARTINEZ'S SHOW-UP, LINE-UP, AND IN-COURT IDENTIFICA-
23   TIONS AND CLIPSE'S IN-COURT IDENTIFICATION.

24

25   The United States Supreme Court has developed a two-part test to ensure

26   a criminal defendant the procedural due process guaranteed to every indi-

Defendant's Brief in Support
of Motion to Suppress   4   Alicia Hamsa
                                                Office of the Public Defender
                                                     Seattle, Washington

1   vidual by the Fourteenth Amendment. *Manson v. Braithwaite*, 432 U.S. 98,

2   113, 97 S. Ct. 2243, 53 L. Ed. 2d 140 (1977).

3   Under the first part of the test, the defendant need show only that the

4   identification that he seeks to suppress was obtained through the use of

5   unnecessarily suggestive police procedures. *Id.* Once the defendant has

6   established that the procedure was suggestive, the onus shifts to the State to

7   prove that, under the totality of the circumstances, the witness's identification

8   is so reliable that it should be admitted even though it was obtained through

9   suggestive means. *Id.*

10   A.   Martinez's show-up identification should be suppressed because
              the police procedures were impermissibly suggestive and because
11   Martinez's identification is unreliable.

12

13   The courts have repeatedly condemned the practice of showing a witness

14   a single suspect. *See, e.g., Stovall v. Denno*, 388 U.S. 293, 302, 87 S. Ct. 1967,

15   18 L. Ed. 2d 1199 (1967); *State v. Rogers*, 44 Wn. App. 510, 515, 722 P.2d

16   1349 (1986); *State v. Kraus*, 21 Wn. App. 388, 391-92, 584 P.2d 946 (1978).

17   Although such show-ups are not per se impermissibly suggestive, they should

18   be admitted only if the show-up occurred during the prompt search for the

19   suspect and if the State proves that the witness's identification is reliable.

20   *State v. Rogers*, 44 Wn. App. at 515.

21   1.   The police procedures were impermissibly suggestive because the
              police officer repeatedly asked Martinez whether Patterson looked
22   like her assailant and because the officer questioned Patterson in
23   Martinez's presence.

24   In this case, Officer Yuen's actions suggested to Martinez that he believed

25   that Patterson was her assailant.

26

Defendant's Brief in Support   Alicia Hamsa
of Motion to Suppress   5   Office of the Public Defender
                                                       Seattle, Washington

1   While driving Martinez home, Officer Yuen pulled up behind Patterson

2   and asked Martinez whether Patterson looked like her assailant. When Mar-

3   tinez did not respond, Officer Yuen repeated his question, asking "Is that the

4   man who assaulted you?"

5   Although Martinez could not see Patterson's face, after hesitating, she

6   agreed with Officer Yuen that Patterson looked like her assailant. At that

7   point, Officer Yuen pulled up behind Patterson, got out of the police car, and

8   began questioning him. A few minutes later, Officer Cox and Clipse arrived,

9   and both Officer Yuen and Officer Cox questioned Patterson while Martinez

10   and Clipse watched.

11   Unlike *State v. Kraus*, 21 Wn. App. at 392, in which the show-up iden-

12   tification occurred during a prompt search for the robber, in this case the

13   show-up did not occur while the police were searching for Martinez's assailant.

14   Instead, it occurred while the officer was driving Martinez home. In addi-

15   tion, unlike *Stovall*, 388 U.S. at 302, in which the police held the show-up

16   because they were concerned that the suspect might die, in this case, there

17   were no exigent circumstances. In fact, because the police had located a car

18   that matched the description of the one driven by the assailant, they could

19   have identified the owner of the car and any individuals who had driven it

20   and placed them in a line-up.

21   2.   Martinez's identification is unreliable because Martinez was able to
22   view her assailant for only a few seconds, her attention was focused
             on the gun and not his face, and her description of her assailant does
23   not match the description of Patterson.

24   The key inquiry in determining the admissibility of a witness's identifica-

25   tion is its reliability. *Manson v. Braithwaite*, 432 U.S. 98, 114, 97 S. Ct. 2243, 53

26   L. Ed. 2d 140 (1977). In determining whether an identification is reliable, the

1   courts consider the witness's opportunity to view the person who committed

2   the crime, the witness's degree of attention, the time between the crime and

3   the confrontation, the witness's level of certainty, and the accuracy of the

4   witness's prior description. *Neil v. Biggers*, 409 U.S. 188, 199-200, 93 S. Ct.

5   375, 34 L. Ed. 2d 401 (1972); *State v. Rogers*, 44 Wn. App. 510, 516, 722 P.2d

6   1349 (1986); *State v. Booth*, 36 Wn. App. 66, 71, 671 P.2d 1218 (1983).

7   For example, in *State v. Rogers*, the court held that the witness's identi-

8   fication was reliable when the witness had a good opportunity to view the

9   defendant because he spent almost 20 minutes with the defendant before the

10 defendant assaulted him and knocked off his glasses. *Id.* at 512. During that

11 20 minutes, the witness's attention was focused on the defendant because

12 the defendant had come to his apartment asking for beer and cigarettes. *Id.*

13 at 512-13. Finally, the witness was certain that it was the defendant who had

14 assaulted him, and his description of the defendant was essentially accurate.

15 *Id.* at 516.

16   Similarly, in *State v. Booth*, the court held that the witness's identifica-

17 tion was reliable when the witness viewed the defendant for approximately

18 45 seconds and her attention was focused on the defendant because the

19 defendant had money in his hands and was running, and the car that the

20 defendant entered had Missouri plates and the witness had lived in Missouri.

21 *Id.* at 71. In addition, the witness's identification was reliable because it was

22 unequivocal. *Id.*

23   In contrast, in this case Ms. Martinez's identification is not reliable. First,

24 in this case, Martinez did not have a good opportunity to view her assailant.

25 Unlike the witness in *Rogers*, who was with his assailant for almost twenty

26 minutes, and the witness in *Booth*, who observed the robber for at least forty-

Defendant's Brief in Support   Alicia Hamsa
of Motion to Suppress   7   Office of the Public Defender
                                                        Seattle, Washington

1   five seconds, Martinez was able to view her assailant for only a few seconds.

2   During the pretrial hearing, Martinez testified that she had seen her assailant

3   for two or three seconds before she turned and ran. Although Martinez testified

4   that she had noticed the car on a prior occasion, she did not testify that she

5   had noticed the driver. In a similar case, the court held that the witness had

6   not had a good opportunity to view the robber when the witness was with

7   the robber for five to six minutes and viewed him for two or three minutes.

8   *State v. McDonald*, 40 Wn. App. 743, 747, 700 P.2d 327 (1985).

9   Second, Martinez's attention was not focused on her assailant. Unlike

10   the witness in *Booth*, whose attention was focused on the robber because he

11   was running and carrying money and got into a car with license plates from

12   the witness's home state, Martinez's attention was focused on the car and

13   then on the gun that her assailant was holding. As Martinez has testified, she

14   looked at the gun, then glanced at the man holding it, and then ran.

15   Third, although the show-up occurred within about forty-five minutes

16   of the assault, Martinez's level of certainty was low. The first time that Offi-

17   cer Yuen asked Martinez whether Patterson looked like the man who had

18   assaulted her, she did not respond. In addition, the second time that Officer

19   Yuen asked her the same question, she said only that Patterson looked like

20   him. She did not say, "Yes, that is him."

21   Finally, Martinez's description was inaccurate. Although Martinez told

22   the police that her assailant was in his early forties, Patterson is twenty-two.

23   While sometimes an individual will believe that an individual is two, three,

24   or even five years older than the individual actually is, it is extremely uncom-

25   mon for someone to be off by twenty years.

26

1   In this case, Martinez identified Patterson as her assailant only because

2   Officer Yuen suggested to her that Patterson was the man who had assaulted

3   her. In addition, the State cannot prove that Martinez's identification is reliable.

4   Martinez did not have a good opportunity to view her assailant, her attention

5   was not focused on her assailant, her identification was uncertain, and her

6   description was inaccurate. As a consequence, Patterson's due process rights

7   would be violated if Martinez's identification is admitted.

8   B.   <u>Martinez's line-up identification should be suppressed because it was</u>
             <u>tainted by the show-up.</u>
9

10   When the initial identification is obtained through impermissibly sug-

11   gestive procedures, subsequent identifications must also be suppressed

12   unless the State can prove that the subsequent identifications are reliable.

13   *State v. McDonald*, 40 Wn. App. at 746. In *McDonald*, the court reversed the

14   defendant's conviction, concluding that the procedures used at the line-up

15   were impermissibly suggestive and that the State had not proved that the

16   witness's subsequent in-court identification was reliable. *Id.*

17   Similarly, in this case the procedures were impermissibly suggestive, and

18   the State cannot prove that Martinez's subsequent identifications are reliable.

19   See section 1A (2), *supra*. Martinez picked Patterson out of the line-up, not

20   because she remembered him as her assailant, but because the police had

21   suggested to her that he was her assailant.

22   C.   <u>Martinez and Clipse should not be permitted to make an in-court</u>
             <u>identification because such an identification would be tainted by the</u>
23   <u>impermissibly suggestive show-up and the line-up.</u>

24

25   Just as Martinez's line-up identification was tainted by the impermissibly

26   suggestive show-up, Martinez's and Clipse's in-court identifications have also

Defendant's Brief in Support   Alicia Hamsa
of Motion to Suppress   9   Office of the Public Defender
                                                                Seattle, Washington

1   been tainted. Although the police did not ask Clipse whether Patterson looked

2   liked the man who had assaulted Martinez, Clipse watched as the police ques-

3   tioned Patterson. In addition, Patterson was with Martinez, who may have

4   told him that Officer Yuen believed that Patterson was her assailant.

5   **Prayer for Relief**

6   For the reasons set out above, Mr. Patterson respectfully requests that the

7   Court suppress Martinez's show-up and line-up identifications and that the

8   Court not permit Martinez or Clipse to make an in-court identification.

9   Dated this 23rd day of September, 2006.

10

11   _____
                                      Attorney for Defendant
                                      Washington Bar No. 00000

12

13

14

15

16

17

18

19

20

21

22

23

24

25

26

Alicia Hamsa
Office of the Public Defender
Seattle, Washington

EXAMPLE 2 **STATE'S BRIEF**

1

2

3

4

5   THE SUPERIOR COURT OF KING COUNTY, WASHINGTON

6   STATE OF WASHINGTON,   )   Case No.: No. 06-01-2226
)
7   Plaintiff,   )   STATE'S BRIEF IN OPPOSITION TO
)   DEFENDANT'S MOTION TO SUPPRESS
8   v.   )
)
9   DEAN E. PATTERSON,   )
)
10   Defendant.   )
     _____   )
11

12   **Statement of Facts**

13   On Monday, August, 14, 2006, Beatrice Martinez was assaulted with a

14 deadly weapon. At a show-up held thirty to forty minutes after the attack,

15 Martinez identified the defendant, Dean E. Patterson, as her assailant. Four

16 days after the assault, Martinez picked Patterson out of a line-up, once again

17 identifying him as her assailant.

18   Ms. Martinez left her apartment at about 4:30 p.m. to walk to work

19 at Angelo's, a restaurant. As she was walking north on Belmont, Martinez

20 observed an older model red station wagon with a chrome luggage rack as

21 it passed slowly by her. Moments later, the same car came down the street

22 again. This time, the driver pulled his car in front of Martinez, stopping his

23 car so that it blocked her path. As Martinez watched, the driver got out of his

24 car and walked toward her. The man then took a gun from his coat pocket

State's Brief in Opposition to   Mary Kingsburgh
Defendant's Motion to Suppress   1   Asst. Prosecuting Attorney
                                                          King County
                                                    Seattle, Washington 98122

1   and pointed it at Martinez. Martinez looked at the gun, looked back up at her

2   assailant, and then, crying, ran back across the street to safety.

3   At about the same time, Chester Clipse was walking south on Belmont. As

4   he approached his apartment, Clipse saw a man in a red station wagon pull

5   into his parking spot. Clipse immediately started walking toward the man to tell

6   him that he could not park there. A moment later, Clipse saw the man get out

7   of his car and approach a young woman who had suddenly stopped. As Clipse

8   watched, the man pulled out a gun and pointed it at the young woman.

9   Both Martinez and Clipse screamed, and the man turned and ran to

10   his car, putting the gun under his coat. As the young woman ran across the

11   street, the man got back into his car, backed out, and drove away, traveling

12   northbound on Belmont.

13   Clipse ran to the young woman, Ms. Martinez, to make sure that she

14   had not been hurt. As he was comforting her, a parking enforcement officer

15   drove up the street. Clipse stopped him, told him what had happened, and

16   gave him a description of the station wagon. The parking enforcement officer

17   called 911 and then left to search for the station wagon.

18   Clipse took Martinez into his landlady's apartment and then went back

19   outside to wait for the police. When the police arrived, Clipse told Officers

20   Yuen and Cox what had happened. Clipse described the car and told the

21   police that the man was white, that he was about 5'10'' tall and about 180

22   to 185 pounds, that he was in his late thirties or early forties, and that he

23   was wearing a green outfit.

24   While Clipse was talking to the police, Officer Cox received a radio mes-

25   sage indicating that the parking enforcement officer had located a red station

26

State's Brief in Opposition to
Defendant's Motion to Suppress   2

Mary Kingsburgh
Asst. Prosecuting Attorney
King County
Seattle, Washington 98122

1   wagon. While Officer Cox took Clipse in his car to see if Clipse could identify

2   the car, Officer Yuen went inside to interview Martinez.

3   Martinez told the police that her assailant was a white male who was

4   about 5'7'' tall and who weighed about 165 to 170 pounds, that her assailant

5   had wavy blondish-brown hair, that her assailant appeared to be in his early

6   forties, and that at the time of the assault, her assailant was wearing a dark

7   jacket and glasses.

8   After interviewing Martinez, Officer Yuen offered to drive Martinez home,

9   and Martinez accepted the offer. When they were less than a block from the

10   scene of the assault, Officer Yuen saw a man matching the description given

11   to him by Martinez. Officer Yuen asked Martinez whether the man was her

12   assailant. After getting a good look at the man, Martinez answered "Yes."

13   Officer Yuen stopped the car and, after telling Martinez to stay in the car,

14   approached the man. As he was doing so, Officer Cox drove by and stopped.

15   While Officer Cox escorted Martinez and Clipse back to Clipse's apartment

16   building, Officer Yuen arrested the man, Dean Patterson.

17   Later that day, the police searched Patterson's car, an older model red

18   station wagon with a chrome luggage rack, and his apartment. In the apart-

19   ment, they found a gun.

20   A line-up was held four days later. Although Clipse was unable to identify

21   the man who had assaulted Martinez, Martinez identified Patterson as her

22   assailant.

23   **Issue**

24   Should the Court deny the defendant's motion to suppress when the

25   police merely asked the victim whether a pedestrian was her assailant and

26

State's Brief in Opposition to
Defendant's Motion to Suppress   3

Mary Kingsburgh
Asst. Prosecuting Attorney
King County
Seattle, Washington 98122

1   when the victim observed her assailant on two occasions for several seconds

2   in broad daylight?

3   **Argument**

4   I.   THE COURT SHOULD DENY THE DEFENDANT'S MOTION TO SUP-
          PRESS BECAUSE THE POLICE PROCEDURES WERE NOT IMPER-
5   MISSIBLY SUGGESTIVE AND THE VICTIM'S IDENTIFICATION IS
6   RELIABLE.

7   Identifications should not be kept from the jury unless the procedures

8   used in obtaining the identifications were so suggestive and unreliable that

9   a substantial likelihood of irreparable misidentification exists. *See Simon v.*

10   *United States*, 390 U.S. 377, 384, 89 S. Ct. 1127, 22 L. Ed. 2d 402 (1969).

11   In deciding whether identification evidence is admissible, the courts

12   employ a two-part test. Under the first part of the test, the defendant has

13   the burden of proving that the identification evidence that he or she seeks

14   to suppress was obtained through impermissibly suggestive procedures.

15   *Manson v. Braithwaite*, 432 U.S. 98, 113, 97 S. Ct. 2243, 5 L. Ed. 2d 140.

16   Only if the defendant satisfies this substantial burden is the second part of

17   the test applied. *Id.*

18   Even if the court determines that the police procedures were imper-

19   missibly suggestive, the evidence is admissible if, under the totality of the

20   circumstances, the identifications are reliable. *Simmons v. United States*, 390

21   U.S. at 384. Due process does not compel the exclusion of an identification

22   if it is reliable. *Id.*

23   A.   <u>Merely asking the victim whether a pedestrian was her assailant does
24   not make a permissible show-up impermissibly suggestive.</u>

25   There are no published Washington cases in which the courts have held

26   that a show-up was impermissibly suggestive. Instead, in a Division I case,

State's Brief in Opposition to   Mary Kingsburgh
Defendant's Motion to Suppress   4   Asst. Prosecuting Attorney
                                                                    King County
                                                          Seattle, Washington 98122

1 the court held that the show-up was not impermissibly suggestive when the

2 police picked up the witness at a tavern and told him that they wanted to

3 take him to his apartment to see if he could identify his assailant. *State v.*

4 *Rogers*, 44 Wn. App. 510, 515-16, 722 P.2d 1249 (1986). When the witness, an

5 elderly individual who was not wearing his glasses, arrived at his apartment,

6 he identified the defendant when the defendant came out of the building. *Id.*

7 There was a uniformed police officer in front of the defendant and another

8 uniformed police officer following behind him. *Id.*

9   Similarly, in *State v. Booth*, 36 Wn. App. 66, 70-71, 671 P.2d 1218 (1983),

10 the court held that the show-up was not impermissibly suggestive when the

11 police asked the witness to accompany them to the place where the defen-

12 dant had been arrested and the witness identified the defendant after seeing

13 him in the back of a police car. *Id.* at 67-68; *accord State v. Guzman-Cuellar*,

14 47 Wn.2d 326, 734 P.2d 966 (1987) (show-up not impermissibly suggestive

15 when eyewitnesses were shown the defendant, who was in handcuffs stand-

16 ing next to a police car.)

17   If Officer Yuen had not asked Martinez whether the pedestrian looked like

18 her assailant, he would not have been doing his job. If he was going to protect

19 others, Officer Yuen needed to know whether the pedestrian was Martinez's

20 assailant. The officer's question, "Is that the man?" was not enough to turn

21 a permissible show-up into one that was impermissibly suggestive.

22   B. <u>Martinez's identification was reliable: she had observed her assailant</u>
         <u>on two occasions, her attention was focused on her assailant, and,</u>
23   <u>except for her statement about her assailant's age, her description</u>
24   <u>was accurate.</u>

25   Even if the police procedures were suggestive, the identification is admis-

26 sible unless the procedures are "so impermissibly suggestive as to give rise

State's Brief in Opposition to
Defendant's Motion to Suppress   5

Mary Kingsburgh
Asst. Prosecuting Attorney
King County
Seattle, Washington 98122

1   to very substantial likelihood of irreparable misidentifications." *Simmons v.*

2   *United States*, 390 U.S. 377, 384, 88 S. Ct. 967, 19 L. Ed. 2d 402 (1968). In

3   deciding whether the identification is reliable, the courts consider the witness's

4   opportunity to view the criminal at the time of the crime, the witness's degree

5   of attention, the accuracy of the witness's description, the level of certainty

6   demonstrated by the witness at the confrontation, and the length of time

7   between the crime and the confrontation. *Neil v. Biggers*, 409 U.S. 188, 199-

8   200, 93 S. Ct. 375, 34 L. Ed. 2d 401 (1972).

9   The courts do not require that the witness have viewed the defendant for

10   an extended period of time. For example, in *Booth*, the court concluded that

11   the witness's identification was reliable when the witness had viewed the

12   defendant for less than a minute. Because the witness's attention had been

13   drawn to the fleeing man and because she viewed him in broad daylight, the

14   court held that the identification was reliable. Similarly, in our case, Martinez's

15   attention had been drawn to her assailant. Shortly before the assault, Martinez

16   watched as her assailant drove slowly by her. Consequently, when he drove

17   by her again, her attention was focused on him. She watched as he drove his

18   car in front of her, blocking her path. In addition, she watched as he got out

19   of his car and walked toward her. Thus, although she looked at him for only

20   two or three seconds once he pulled out the gun, before that time, she had a

21   good opportunity to view him and her attention had been focused on him.

22   The courts also do not require that the witness's description be completely

23   accurate. *State v. Kraus*, 21 Wn. App. 388, 584 P.2d 946 (1978). In *Kraus*, the

24   court held that the witness's identification was reliable despite the fact that

25   the witness had stated that the robber was wearing a dark jacket and the

26   defendant was wearing a light-colored jacket. *Id.* at 393. Similarly, in *State v.*

State's Brief in Opposition to
Defendant's Motion to Suppress   6

Mary Kingsburgh
Asst. Prosecuting Attorney
King County
Seattle, Washington 98122

1   *Maupin*, 63 Wn. App. 887, 892, 822 P.2d 355 (1992), the court held that the

2   witness's identification was reliable even though the witness was not able to

3   tell the police the rapist's race.

4   In this case, Martinez was able to give the police a detailed description of

5   her assailant. When she was interviewed, she told the police that her assail-

6   ant was a white male with blondish-brown hair, that he was approximately

7   5'7'' tall and weighed between 165 and 170 pounds, that he appeared to

8   be in his early forties, and that he was wearing a dark green jacket. This

9   description is accurate in all but one respect. Although Martinez misjudged

10   the defendant's age, she accurately described his car, his hair, his height and

11   weight, and his clothing.

12   In addition, Martinez's identification occurred shortly after the assault,

13   and Martinez was certain in her identification. Although she did not answer

14   Officer Yuen's question the first time that he asked her, as soon as she got

15   a better look at the defendant, she identified him as her assailant. As she

16   stated in the police report, "[O]nce I got a good look at him I was sure it was

17   him."

18   C.   <u>Because the show-up was not impermissibly suggestive, the court</u>
              <u>should not suppress Martinez's line-up identification or prevent Mar-</u>
19   <u>tinez or Clipse from making in-court identifications.</u>

20

21   The Court should not suppress Martinez's line-up identification, nor should

22   it prevent Martinez or Clipse from making an in-court identification. Because

23   the show-up was not impermissibly suggestive, see subsection IA, it did not

24   taint either the line-up or any potential in-court identifications.

25   Although Clipse may have seen the police talking with the defendant, such

26   an act by itself is not enough to make a show-up impermissibly suggestive.

State's Brief in Opposition to
Defendant's Motion to Suppress   7

Mary Kingsburgh
Asst. Prosecuting Attorney
King County
Seattle, Washington 98122

1   *See State v. Guzman-Cuellar*, 47 Wn.2d 326, 333, 734 P.2d 966 (1987); *State v.*

2   *Rogers*, 44 Wn. App. 510, 512, 722 P.2d 1249 (1986); *State v. Booth*, 36 Wn.

3   App. 66, 72, 671 P.2d 1218 (1983). In addition, like Martinez, Clipse had a

4   good opportunity to view Martinez's assailant. His attention was drawn to the

5   assailant because the man was pulling into his parking spot, and, except for

6   his description of the assailant's age, Clipse's description was accurate.

7   **Prayer for Relief**

8   For the reasons set out above, the State respectfully requests that the

9   Court deny the defendant's motion to suppress and admit Martinez's show-

10   up and line-up identifications and permit Martinez and Clipse to make an

11   in-court identification.

12   Dated this 28th day of September, 2006.

13   _____

14   Assistant Prosecuting Attorney
                                                    Washington Bar No. 00000

15

16

17

18

19

20

21

22

23

24

25

26

State's Brief in Opposition to   Mary Kingsburgh
Defendant's Motion to Suppress   8   Asst. Prosecuting Attorney
                                                    King County
                                                    Seattle, Washington 98122

Writing an
Appellate Brief

It is the stuff of movies and childhood fantasies. You are standing before the United States Supreme Court making an impassioned argument. You are arguing that the votes should, or should not, be recounted in a presidential election; that the defendant was, or was not, the victim of racial profiling; or that the government should, or should not, be allowed to restrict stem cell research.

Although such high-stakes oral advocacy is exciting and dramatic, in many cases the brief is as important, if not more important. Although Hollywood and authors like John Grisham might be more inclined to write a scene depicting oral advocacy, in the real legal world it is frequently the written brief that makes the difference.

In this chapter, we continue our discussion of written advocacy, which was begun in the last chapter on motion briefs, and take it to the next level: the appellate brief. Much of what we discussed about writing a motion brief applies to appellate briefs. Thus, this chapter focuses on those parts of writing a brief that are unique to writing an appellate brief: finding and applying the rules on appeal, types of appeal, scope of review, standard of review, and harmless error. In Chapter 3 we discuss oral advocacy, specifically how to prepare for and deliver an effective oral argument.

§ 2.1 Practicing Before an Appellate Court

In most jurisdictions, there are court rules that govern appellate practice. For example, appellate practice before the United States Supreme Court is governed by the Rules of the Supreme Court of the United States (Sup. Ct. R.), and appellate practice before the United States Courts of Appeal is governed by the Federal Rules of Appellate Procedure (Fed. R. App. P.). Similarly, many states have rules that govern appellate practice within that state.

In addition to locating and reading the jurisdiction's or court's rules, also look for local rules. For example, if you are writing a brief in a case that will be heard by the Ninth Circuit Court of Appeals, look at both the Federal Rules of Appellate Procedure and the Ninth Circuit's rules. If you do not comply with both the general and local rules, the court might refuse to hear your appeal or petition for review or reject your brief.

PRACTICE  The easiest place to find a particular jurisdiction's or court's rules is the jurisdiction's or court's website. For example, you can find the Rules of the Supreme Court of the United States at http://www.supremecourtus.gov/ctrules.html and the Ninth Circuit rules at http://www.ca9.uscourts.gov.

§ 2.1.1 Types of Appellate Review

In most jurisdictions, court rules provide for two types of appellate review: an appeal as of right (Fed. R. App. P. 4) and discretionary review (Fed. R. App. P. 5). For example, in both the federal and state systems, a defendant convicted of a crime has the right to appeal to an intermediate court of appeals or, if the state does not have an intermediate court of appeals, to the state's highest court. However, in the federal system and most states, review by the jurisdiction's highest court is discretionary. Thus, a defendant seeking review of a decision of an intermediate court of appeals would have to file a petition for review or a writ of certiorari. If the highest court grants review, the parties would then prepare briefs in which they argue the case on its merits. In determining whether to grant discretionary review, courts will generally look to whether the case involves a conflict between circuits or divisions, raises an important constitutional question, or raises an issue of great public import. See, for example, Supreme Court Rule 10.

PRACTICE  Different jurisdictions might use different labels to refer to the parties. For example, in cases involving an appeal as of right, the parties might be referred to as the appellant and appellee or as the appellant and respondent. In contrast, in a case involving discretionary review, the parties might be referred to as the petitioner and respondent.

Thus, before writing your brief, check the applicable rules to determine which labels apply.

§ 2.1.2 Time Limits for Filing the Notice of Appeal or Petition for Discretionary Review

In pursuing an appeal as of right or seeking discretionary review, a party must adhere to the timelines as set out in the applicable rules. For example, Fed. R. App. P. 4 sets out the time for filing an appeal as of right in a federal court of appeal, and the time limits differ depending on the nature of the case and the party seeking an appeal. In a civil case, the party filing the appeal must file its notice of appeal within thirty days of the date the judgment or order appealed was entered. Fed. R. App. P. (4)(a)(1)(A). However, if the United States, its officer, or its agency is a party, the party filing the appeal must file its notice of appeal within sixty days of the date the judgment or the order was entered. Fed. R. App. P. (4)(a)(1)(B).

In contrast, in a criminal case, the defendant must file his or her notice of appeal "within 10 days after the later of: (i) the entry of either the judgment or the order being appealed; or (ii) the filing of the government's notice of appeal." Fed. R. App. P. (4)(b)(1)(A). When the government is entitled to appeal, "its notice of appeal must be filed in the district court within 30 days after the later of: (i) the entry of the judgment or order being appealed; or (ii) the filing of the notice of appeal by any defendant." Fed. R. App. P. (4)(b)(1)(B).

If a party is seeking review by the United States Supreme Court, it must file its petition for review on certiorari within ninety days after the entry of judgment. Sup. Ct. R. 13.1.

§ 2.1.3 The Notice of Appeal or Notice for Discretionary Review

In addition, in most jurisdictions there is a court rule that sets out the procedure for filing a notice of appeal or a notice for discretionary review. For example, Fed. R. App. P. 3 sets out the rules for filing and serving the Notice of Appeal when a party has an appeal as of right. A sample template for a notice of appeal is set out in Form 1 of the appendix to the Federal Rules of Appellate Procedure. Supreme Court Rule 12 sets out the method of seeking review on certiorari.

§ 2.1.4 Scope of Review

In determining the scope of review, the courts consider two factors. First, as a general rule, an appellate court will review only those issues or decisions listed in the notice of appeal or in the petition for discretionary review or writ of certiorari. Second, as a general rule, an appellate court will review only those errors that were raised, or preserved, at trial. This second rule gives the trial court the opportunity to rule on alleged errors in the first instance and helps ensure that attorneys will not stay silent, hoping for a favorable result at trial while using an appeal as a "fallback" position. There are, however, exceptions to this rule. In some jurisdictions, the requirement that issues be preserved for appeal by raising them at trial and exceptions to the requirement are developed through case law. *See, e.g.,* Ulrich, Kessler, & Anger, P.C., et al., *Federal Appellate Practice: Ninth Circuit*, § 8.12 (West 2d ed. 1999), for a discussion of the Ninth Circuit's approach to these issues. In other jurisdictions, the rules and exceptions are set out in a statute or a court rule. For example, in North Carolina, this rule and its exceptions are set out in a statute:

> (a) Except as provided in subsection (d), error may not be asserted upon appellate review unless the error has been brought to the attention of the trial court by appropriate and timely objection or motion. . . .
> (b) Failure to make an appropriate and timely motion or objection constitutes a waiver of the right to assert the alleged error on appeal, but the appellate court may review such errors affecting substantial rights in the interest of justice if it determines it is appropriate to do so.

N. C. Gen. Stat. Ann. § 15A-1446 (2005).

Some of the errors that can be raised on appeal even absent an objection or motion are a lack of jurisdiction, a failure of the pleading to state the essential elements of a violation, and insufficient evidence. N. C. Gen. Stat. A. § 15A-1446(d)(1), (4) and (5). In contrast, in Washington State, this rule and its exceptions are set out in the Rules of Appellate Procedure (RAP) 2.5.

§ 2.1.5 The Record on Appeal

After filing the notice of appeal or notice for discretionary review, the appellant or petitioner must then "designate the record on appeal," that is, select the portions of the trial record that the appellate court needs to decide the issues on appeal. Generally, the record consists of the original papers and exhibits filed in the trial court and transcripts of the proceedings that are relevant to the issues on review. In addition, under Fed. R. App. P. 10(a)(3), the appellant needs to include a certified copy of the docket entries prepared by the United States District Court clerk. The appellant bears the burden of ensuring that the record is adequate for review of the issues raised, but the responding party can supplement the record.

PRACTICE POINTER Remember that there might be local rules that govern the record on appeal. For example, under a Ninth Circuit rule, if the appellant does not plan on ordering the entire transcript, either the parties have to agree on the portions that will be ordered, or the appellant must let the appellee know which portions it plans to order along with a statement of issues it plans to raise. Ninth Cir. R. 10-3.1(a).

In addition, "Because all members of the panel assigned to hear the appeal ordinarily will not have the entire record (*see* Ninth Cir. R. 11-4.1), the parties must prepare excerpts of the record pursuant to Ninth Cir. R. 30-1. The purpose of the excerpts is to provide each member of the panel with those portions of the record necessary to reach a decision."

§ 2.1.6 Types of Briefs

The next step in the process is the preparation of the brief. As a general rule, the party seeking review (the appellant or petitioner) files an opening brief and serves a copy of that brief on the appellate court and the opposing party. After reading the appellant's (or petitioner's) brief, the opposing party (the appellee or respondent) prepares its brief, in which it addresses and responds to the issues and arguments raised in the appellant's (or petitioner's) brief. After the appellee (or respondent) has completed its brief, it serves it on both the court and the appellant (or petitioner). The appellant (or petitioner) then has the opportunity to file a reply brief, which answers arguments made in the appellee's (or respondent's) brief. In some jurisdictions, the court rules also permit the appellee (or respondent) to file a reply brief, the defendant in a criminal case to file a *pro se* brief, and interested parties to file an amicus brief, which is a brief submitted by a group or individual who has a strong interest in the subject matter of the case, but who is not a party.

§ 2.2 Understanding Your Audience, Your Purpose, and the Conventions

Just as it is important to understand the audience and purpose of an objective memorandum, opinion letter, and motion brief, it is also important to understand the audience and purpose of an appellate brief. If you understand your audience and your purpose in writing to that audience, you will be able to make sound decisions about what to include and exclude or about how to best present your arguments.

§ 2.2.1 Audience

The primary audience for an appellate brief is the panel of judges who will be deciding the appeal. This means that if you are seeking review in an intermediate court of appeals, you will usually be writing to a panel of three judges, and if you are seeking review in the United States Supreme Court, to nine justices. When you are writing for your intermediate court of appeals, you might or might not know who your judges will be: in the

United States Courts of Appeal and in many state intermediate courts, there are more than three judges on the court, and you are not told which judges will be on your panel until all of the briefs are filed and your case has been set on the court's docket. In contrast, when you are writing to the United States Supreme Court or your state supreme court, you will know who will be hearing your case (although there might be instances in which a justice recuses him- or herself or an intervening election or appointment changes the makeup of the court).

Even if you do not know which judges will be hearing your case, research your court before writing. You can do this research by reading recent decisions issued by the court or by talking with other attorneys who are familiar with the court. In addition, you can usually locate information about individual judges on the court's homepage or on other websites. Often these pages will provide a photograph of each judge and information about his or her education and legal experience.

The judges are not, however, your only audience. In most appellate courts, each appeal is assigned to a particular judge, who then assigns the case to one of his or her law clerks. After reading the briefs and independently researching the issues, the clerk prepares a memo to the judge (usually called a "bench memo" or a "prehearing memo") that summarizes the law and each side's arguments and, in some courts, recommends how the appeal should be decided. Because law clerks can shape how the judges view the appeal, they are some of your most significant readers. For more on writing prehearing memos, see section 4.5 in *Just Memos, Second Edition.*

In addition, you are writing for your client and for opposing counsel. You want to write your brief in such a way that your client feels that his or her story is being told and that opposing counsel knows that he or she is up against a well-prepared, thoughtful, and vigorous advocate.

As you write, you also need to keep in mind that most appellate judges have substantial workloads. Many intermediate appellate judges hear between 100 and 150 cases a year, and write opinions in approximately one-third of those cases. If each party submits a thirty-page brief, each judge would have to read between 6,000 and 9,000 pages in the course of a year. Thus, although you might think that a longer brief is a better brief, most appellate judges would disagree. For most appellate judges, the best briefs are those that make their points clearly and concisely.

Also keep in mind that appellate judges must work within certain constraints, the most significant of which is the standard of review. Although in some cases the court's review is *de novo,* in most cases the review is more limited: instead of deciding the case on its merits, the appellate court reviews only the trial court's decision to see if the trial judge abused his or her discretion or if there is substantial evidence to support the jury's verdict. (For more on standard of review, see section 2.4.2c in this book.)

Finally, in some cases the appellate court is itself bound by mandatory authority. State intermediate courts of appeal are bound by the decisions of the state's highest court, and both the state courts and the United States

Courts of Appeal are bound by decisions of the United States Supreme Court interpreting and applying the United States Constitution.

§ 2.2.2 Purpose

In writing an appellate brief, you want to accomplish two things. You want to educate the judges about the facts of your case and the applicable law, and you want to persuade a majority of the judges to rule in your client's favor. Thus, in addition to explaining the underlying facts, the relevant procedural history, and the law, you must also persuade the appellate court either that the decision of the trial court was correct and should be affirmed, or that the trial court's decision was wrong and should be reversed or reversed and remanded.

§ 2.2.3 Conventions

Just as the process of bringing an appeal is governed by rules, so is the format of an appellate brief. These rules are usually quite specific, governing everything from the types of briefs that can be filed to the sections that must be included, the order of the required sections, and how to reference the parties and the record. See Fed. R. App. P. 28.

PRACTICE    Remember to check local rules. For example, in the Ninth Circuit, an appendix containing the record is not included with the brief. Instead, excerpts of the record are filed. *See* Ninth Cir. R. 10-2 (b). References to the excerpts of the record are referred to by "ER" followed by a page number.

Also, a brief filed in the Ninth Circuit must contain a statement regarding the defendant's bail status, Ninth Cir. R. 28-2.4, and a statement of any known related cases pending before the court. Ninth Cir. R. 28-2.6. Moreover, the appellee cannot omit the jurisdictional statement section; an appellee must include either a statement of jurisdiction or a statement agreeing with the appellant's statement of jurisdiction. Ninth Cir. R. 28-2.2(c).

Although these rules are representative, some jurisdictions have other requirements. For example, in Washington State, the appellant must include assignments of error. Wash. RAP 10.3.(g).

In addition to rules governing the content of briefs, there are rules governing the format of the briefs, including length, typeface, and paper size. For example, with the advent of word processing programs, the courts have enacted very specific rules about length to avoid having attorneys try to skirt the length limits by changing typefaces, font sizes, and margins. See Fed. R. App. P. 32.

In addition to the rules, there might be other, unwritten conventions governing the format of the brief. For example, in some jurisdictions, attorneys may use a particular format for the table of authorities or for the questions presented, or there might be conventions regarding the capitalization of words like "court." Therefore, in addition to reading and following the rules, always check with the court clerk and other attorneys to find out what is expected.

§ 2.3 Getting the Case: *United States v. Josephy*

For the rest of this chapter, presume that it is your second year in law school and you are working as an intern at the Office of the Federal Public Defender in Seattle, Washington. One of the cases the office is handling is *United States v. Josephy*. The facts of the case are as follows.

At about 9:30 a.m. on June 25, 2007, an individual placed a 911 call from a pay phone at the Bellis Fair Mall in Bellingham, Washington, which is about a five-minute drive from the Travel House Inn. The individual, who said that his name was Zachary Dillon, told the 911 operator that Peter Josephy was involved in drug trafficking between Canada and the United States and that Josephy was currently at the Travel House Inn, where he was going to sell a large amount of marijuana to a man named Oliver. Dillon also told the operator that police should go to the Travel House Inn right away because Josephy would only be there for another hour or two.

When the 911 operator asked Dillon to describe Josephy, Dillon stated that Josephy was a Native American, had black hair, was in his mid to late twenties, and was driving a blue Chevy Blazer. Dillon also told the operator that he did not know Oliver's last name but that Oliver was in his thirties, that he was six feet tall, and that he had brown hair and a beard. Dillon was not able to give the operator the license number of the Blazer, and he said that he did not know what the men were wearing. In addition, Dillon would not tell the operator where he lived or give the operator his home or cell phone number.

After the 911 operator conveyed the information from the phone call to a Bureau of Alcohol, Tobacco, and Firearms (ATF) agent, Agent Bhasin, the agent checked several databases, trying to locate a Zachary Dillon. Agent Bhasin was not, however, able to find anyone by that name in the greater Bellingham area.

At about 10:00 a.m., Agent Bhasin drove to the Travel House Inn to investigate. When he arrived at 10:15 a.m., Agent Bhasin located a blue Chevy Blazer parked in the parking lot. After running the license plate number and determining that the Blazer was registered to Peter Jason Josephy and that Josephy was registered at the motel, Agent Bhasin requested a K-9 unit (an agent and a dog trained to alert to the presence of drugs) as backup.

At about 10:45 a.m., Mr. Josephy and a man later identified as Oliver Preston walked out of one of the rooms and went into the office, where Mr.

Josephy paid the bill. The two men left the office, talked for two or three minutes just outside the office, and then parted ways. Mr. Josephy walked to his vehicle and got in. As Mr. Josephy started his car, Agent Bhasin pulled behind Mr. Josephy's car and another agent, Agent O'Brien, pulled in front.

Agent Bhasin then got out of his car, approached the driver's side of Mr. Josephy's vehicle, and asked Mr. Josephy to get out of the car. Although Mr. Josephy complied with this request, he refused Agent Bhasin's request for permission to search the vehicle. Agent Bhasin then instructed the agent with the dog to walk the dog around the outside of the vehicle. After the dog alerted to the vehicle, Agent Bhasin searched the vehicle and located four kilos of marijuana in the wheel well. Agent Bhasin then arrested Mr. Josephy.

Before trial, Mr. Josephy moved to suppress the marijuana on the grounds that (1) a seizure occurred when Agent Bhasin pulled behind Mr. Josephy's vehicle and Agent O'Brien pulled in front and (2) the tip was not sufficient to provide the agents with a reasonable suspicion that Mr. Josephy had possession of a controlled substance with intent to sell. Although the trial court agreed with Mr. Josephy that a seizure occurred when the agents blocked Mr. Josephy's vehicle with their own vehicles, the trial court denied the motion to suppress on the grounds that the tip was sufficient to provide the agents with a reasonable suspicion that Mr. Josephy was in Unlawful Possession of a Controlled Substance with the Intent to Deliver in violation of 21 U.S.C. § 841(a)(1) (2006).

The case proceeded to trial, and during jury selection, the judge asked whether any jurors had concerns regarding their ability to serve as jurors for the duration of the trial. Juror No. 12, Mr. Williams, stated that his tribal council was scheduled to meet the following Thursday and Friday, that he would like to attend the meeting, but that he could skip the meeting if he needed to do so. Juror No. 2, Mr. Feldman, stated that he was flying to Africa on the next Saturday and that his boss was unhappy that he was missing work. However, Mr. Feldman stated that his boss would just have "to live with it." Juror No. 18, Mr. Woods, stated that his eighty-seven-year-old mother had a massive heart attack, that she was given a 20 percent chance to live, and that he did not know whether he needed to go out of town the following week. No other jurors mentioned a problem regarding the trial schedule.

The prosecutor then asked whether anyone had had bad experiences with law enforcement officers. Juror No. 5, Ms. Whitefish, stated that she had been pulled aside for questions each time she crossed the border. Ms. Whitefish attributed the extra questioning to her age and her belief that college students are stopped more frequently than others. Juror No. 11, Mr. Martin, said he that he had been stopped on a number of occasions for routine problems with his car, for example, a taillight that was not working. On further questioning Mr. Martin stated that the police stopped people with long hair more often than they did people with short hair and that he was bothered by the fact that the police tended to target people with long hair.

After the questioning ended, and both the prosecutor and the defense counsel accepted the panel for cause, the parties used their peremptory challenges. The prosecutor excused Juror No. 2, Mr. Feldman; Juror No. 5, Ms. Whitefish; and Juror No. 12, Mr. Williams.

Although the prosecutor then accepted the panel, defense counsel made a *Batson*[1] objection, arguing at sidebar that the Government's exclusion of Ms. Whitefish and Mr. Williams, the only two Native Americans on the panel, violated Mr. Josephy's right to equal protection.

The district court concluded that Mr. Josephy had made a prima facie case of discrimination regarding race and asked whether the prosecutor had neutral reasons for excluding Ms. Whitefish and Mr. Williams.

The prosecutor offered the following reasons: (1) he excused Ms. Whitefish because he believed that she would have difficulty being impartial given her personal experiences at the border, and (2) he excused Mr. Williams because he believed that Mr. Williams would have difficulty focusing on the facts of the case because he needed to attend the tribal council meeting the following Thursday and Friday. The trial court held that these reasons were neutral reasons.

Defense counsel then argued that, given the fact that the prosecutor had used his peremptory challenges to excuse the only Native Americans in the jury pool, the Government's proffered reasons were pretexts for purposeful discrimination. The district court concluded that the Government had not engaged in purposeful discrimination and denied Mr. Josephy's *Batson* challenge. At the close of the trial, the jury found Mr. Josephy guilty.

Soon after the entry of judgment and sentence, Ms. Elder, Mr. Josephy's attorney, met with Mr. Josephy to explain his options. She described the appeals process, telling him how long he had to file an appeal, how long it would take for his case to be heard by the court of appeals, and the provisions for staying his sentence while his case was on appeal. In addition, she explained that if he did not appeal or if his appeal was denied, his current convictions might affect his sentence for any future crimes.

After considering his options, Mr. Josephy decided that he wanted to appeal. As a result, Ms. Elder filed a notice of appeal within the required time limits and ordered the relevant portions of the record.

§ 2.4 Preparing to Write the Brief

§ 2.4.1 Reviewing the Record for Error

Like many attorneys, Ms. Elder uses a four-step process to review the record for errors. First, she reviews her trial notes, writing down the errors that

---

[1] *Batson v. Kentucky*, 476 U.S. 79, 86-7 (1986). A *Batson* violation occurs when (1) the defendant establishes a prima facie case of purposeful discrimination in the government's use of peremptory challenges by showing that the challenged juror is a member of a cognizable class and that the circumstances raise an inference of discrimination; (2) the government fails to meet its burden to provide a race-neutral explanation for its strike; or (3) the government offers a race-neutral reason, but the defense meets its burden of showing that a review of all relevant circumstances shows purposeful discrimination. *Id.; see also Johnson v. California*, 545 U.S. 162, 169 (2005).

she identified during the trial. Second, Ms. Elder goes through the record, document by document, page by page, and exhibit by exhibit, noting the following:

- Each motion that she made that was denied.
- Each motion that the prosecutor made that was granted.
- Each objection that she made that was overruled.
- Each objection that the prosecutor made that was granted.
- Each request for a jury instruction that she made that was denied.
- Each request for a jury instruction that the prosecutor made that was granted.

For example, during this step, Ms. Elder notes the following *Batson* objection, which the court overruled.

EXAMPLE   **EXCERPT FROM THE TRANSCRIPT OF A SIDEBAR DURING VOIR DIRE**

THE COURT:	Does the defendant have an objection?
DEFENSE:	Unfortunately, we do, Your Honor. As you know, Mr. Josephy is Native American, and the prosecutor improperly excluded both Juror No. 5, Ms. Whitefish, and Juror No. 12, Mr. Williams, the only two Native Americans on the panel.
THE COURT:	Under *Batson*, the defendant is required, of course, to make a prima facie showing of purposeful discrimination based on race. Because the defendant has established a prima facie case, the prosecutor has the burden of showing that he had a neutral explanation for the striking the juror. Can I hear from the prosecutor?
PROSECUTOR:	Yes, Your Honor. I excused Ms. Whitefish because I think that her experiences at the border would make it difficult for her to judge this case fairly and impartially. I excused Mr. Williams because I think that his other obligation may make it difficult for him to focus on the trial. These are neutral reasons for excluding these people from this panel.
THE COURT:	I agree. Defense Counsel, would you like to respond?
DEFENSE:	The reasons stated are not neutral; they are only a mask for unconstitutional race discrimination. Mr. Williams said that it would not be a problem for him to be on the jury, and Ms. Whitefish indicated that she was not bothered by the fact that all college students seemed to be subjected to tighter screening. Given the pattern of strikes, the reasons that the prosecutor has given are pretexts.
THE COURT:	Your objection is noted, Counsel, but the Court finds no purposeful discrimination here.

Third, Ms. Elder looks for the other, less obvious types of errors.

- Were Mr. Josephy's constitutional rights violated? (Was he read his *Miranda* rights? Was he represented by counsel at all significant stages in the process?)
- Was Mr. Josephy tried within the appropriate time period? Was he given the right to confront the witnesses against him? Is his sentence cruel and unusual?
- Is the statute under which Mr. Josephy was charged constitutional?
- Was there misconduct on the part of the judge, opposing counsel, or the jury?

Finally, Ms. Elder examines her own actions. Did she fail to raise a viable defense or fail to make an objection that she should have made? If she did, Mr. Josephy might be able to argue that he was denied effective assistance of counsel.

Having identified the potential errors, Ms. Elder moves to the next step in the process: researching the potential errors to determine which errors she should raise in her brief.

§ 2.4.2 Selecting the Issues on Appeal

As an appellate judge, whom would you find more credible: the attorney who alleges twenty-three errors or the one who alleges three?

Most appellate judges take the attorney who lists two, three, or four errors more seriously than the attorney who lists a dozen or more. Instead of describing the attorney who lists numerous errors as "thorough" or "conscientious," judges use terms such as "inexperienced," "unfocused," and "frivolous." When so many errors are listed, the appellate court is likely to think that the problem is not the trial court but the attorney bringing the appeal.

How do you decide which errors to discuss in your brief? Once again, Ms. Elder uses a four-step process. She determines (1) whether there was in fact an error, (2) whether that error was preserved, (3) the standard of review, and (4) whether the error was harmless.

a. Was There an Error?

The first question is whether there was in fact an error. Does the Constitution, a statute, or case law allow you to make a credible argument that the trial court erred? To answer this question, you usually need to do some research. For example, in *United States v. Josephy*, Ms. Elder needs to do some preliminary research to determine whether she can make a good faith argument that the tip was not sufficient to establish a reasonable suspicion that Mr. Josephy was in possession of drugs with intent to sell them and whether she can make a good faith argument that the district court improperly overruled her *Batson* objection. Because her research indicates there are arguments to be made on both issues, she continues with her analysis. In contrast, the other research that Ms. Elder did is not as fruitful. For example, after doing some preliminary research, Ms. Elder determines that she cannot make a good faith argument that the district court erred in denying her objection to one of the statements that Agent Bhasin made during direct examination. As a result, Ms. Elder abandons that issue. Without a good faith basis for raising the issue, she risks, at a minimum, annoying the court and, at worst, a potential Rule 11 action for making a frivolous claim.

PRACTICE

Under Fed. R. Civ. P. 11(b) an attorney signing a brief "certifies that to the best of the attorney's knowledge, information or belief, formed after an inquiry reasonable under the circumstances" that "the claims, defenses, and other legal contentions therein are warranted by existing law or by a nonfrivolous argument for the extension, modification, or reversal of existing law or the establishment of new law[.]" A violation of Rule 11 can lead to sanctions, including monetary sanctions, sufficient to deter the repetition of such conduct. Fed. R. Civ. P. 11(c).

---

b. Was the Error Preserved?

It is not enough that there was an error. Unless the error involved an issue of constitutional magnitude, that error must have been preserved. Defense counsel must have objected or in some other manner brought the alleged error to the attention of the trial court and given the trial court the opportunity to correct the error. As noted in section 2.1.3, in some jurisdictions the rules regarding preservation of error for appeal are developed through case law; in others they are addressed explicitly in a statute or court rule.

In *United States v. Josephy*, both issues were preserved for appeal: Ms. Elder preserved the issue relating to the search incident to arrest through the motion to suppress and the issue relating to jury selection by making a *Batson* objection.

c. What Is the Standard of Review?

The next step relates to the standard of review. In deciding whether there was an error, what standard will the appellate court apply? Will it review the issue *de novo,* making its own independent determination, or will it defer to the trial court, affirming the trial court unless, for example, the trial court's finding was clearly erroneous or the trial court judge abused his or her discretion.

As a general rule, an appellate court will review questions of law *de novo.* As a consequence, when the issue is whether the jury was properly instructed, the appellate court will make its own independent determination. The standard is different when the question is one of fact. In most circumstances, an appellate court will not disturb factual findings unless such findings are "clearly erroneous" or "contrary to law." Similarly, an appellate court will give great deference to the trial court's evidentiary rulings and will not reverse the trial court unless the judge abused, or manifestly abused, his or her discretion. Because very few issues are pure questions of law or pure questions of fact, you might be able to argue the standard of review. The appellant (or petitioner) will usually want to argue that the appellate court should review the question *de novo,* but the appellee (or respondent) will usually want to argue that the appellate court should affirm unless the trial court's ruling was clearly erroneous or the trial court abused its discretion.

PRACTICE POINTER   The standard of review can also be affected by the case's procedural posture. For example, the standard of review a federal circuit court uses in deciding a direct appeal will differ from the standard of review the court uses in deciding a case in which a party is seeking habeas relief from a state court ruling.

These rules are general; for specific issues, you must research the standard of review. Sometimes this research will be easy. In one of its opinions, the court will set out the standard that is to be applied. At other times, the research is much more difficult. Although the court decides the issue, it does not explicitly state what standard it is applying. In such cases, read between the lines. Although the court does not explicitly state that it is reviewing the issue *de novo,* is that what the court has done? Also, look for helpful secondary sources. For example, if your appeal is in the Ninth Circuit, look at *Standards of Review/Ninth Circuit Court of Appeals,* United States Court of Appeals (9th Circuit), Chambers of O.R. Scopil, Jr. (2006) available at http://www.ca9.uscourts.gov/ under "rules and changes."

PRACTICE POINTER   One way to research the standard of review is to use one or more standards as a search term. For example, search for "de novo" or "abuse! /3 discretion."

---

d. Was the Error Harmless?

The final question that must be asked is whether an alleged error was harmless, that is, whether the error, even if established, would not warrant a reversal. As the courts have often said, an appellant is entitled to a fair trial, not a perfect one.

> The reversal of a conviction entails substantial social costs: it forces jurors, witnesses, courts, the prosecution, and the appellants to expend further time, energy, and other resources to repeat a trial that has already once taken place. . . . These societal costs of reversal and retrial are an acceptable and often necessary consequence when an error . . . has deprived the appellant of a fair determination of the issue of guilt or innocence. But the balance of interest tips

decidedly the other way when the error has had no effect on the outcome of the trial.

William Rehnquist, *Harmless Error, Prosecutorial Misconduct, and Due Process: There's More to Due Process Than the Bottom Line,* 88 Colum. L. Rev. 1298, 1301 (1988).

As a consequence, as an advocate, you will usually not want to assign error to a decision that, although incorrect, was harmless. For instance, although the court might have acted improperly when it admitted a particular piece of evidence or testimony, that error might not be prejudicial if that same evidence or testimony was properly elicited from another witness.

In some instances, the court does not do a harmless error analysis; persuading the appellate court that a trial error occurred is all that is needed to obtain a reversal. For example, in *United States v. Josephy*, if Ms. Elder can persuade the Court of Appeals that the district court erred in denying her motion to suppress, reversal would be required because the conviction for possession of a controlled substance with intent to deliver cannot stand if the marijuana is inadmissible. Similarly, if she is able to persuade the Court of Appeals that the district court erred in overruling her *Batson* objection, the remedy would be a new trial (*see Gray v. Mississippi*, 481 U.S. 648, 668 (1987) (holding that there is no harmless error analysis when there has been a *Batson* violation)).

Generally, however, you will need to consider whether the error was harmless. In so doing, keep in mind that the courts apply different tests for different types of errors. For example, as a general rule, the courts apply one test for nonconstitutional errors and a different, more stringent, test for constitutional errors. In addition, different jurisdictions can apply different tests: when reviewing a nonconstitutional error, some courts look to whether the error had a substantial and injurious effect on the verdict, and others look to whether, within reasonable probabilities, the outcome of the trial would have been materially affected had the error not occurred.

In contrast, when reviewing a constitutional error, most courts apply either the contribution test or the overwhelming untainted evidence test. Under the contribution test, the appellate court looks at the tainted evidence to determine whether that evidence could have contributed to the fact finder's determination of guilt. If it could have, reversal is required. The courts that apply the overwhelming untainted evidence test take a different approach. Instead of looking at the tainted evidence, they look at the untainted evidence. If the untainted evidence is sufficient to support a finding of guilt, reversal is not required. Note, however, that in a criminal case, the government has the burden of showing the error was harmless.

PRACTICE  An argument that the erroneous admission or exclusion of evidence requires reversal necessarily rests on how the evidence related to the specific elements of the cause of action or charge. However, arguments can also be developed by looking to how the evidence was addressed in closing arguments: How much weight was it given? Was it emphasized, repeated, or touched on only briefly? Was it characterized as being a small piece in a larger puzzle or as being critical to the case?

Having gone through these four steps, Ms. Elder is ready to select the issues on appeal. She does, in fact, decide to challenge the district court's denial of her motion to suppress and the district court's decision to overrule her *Batson* objection.[2] The first issue, whether the investigatory stop was supported by a reasonable articulable suspicion, is a question of law; thus, review is *de novo*. However, for the second issue, whether the court correctly overruled the defense's *Batson* objection, the appellate court will give deference to the district court's finding that defense counsel did not establish unlawful discrimination in the prosecutor's use of peremptory challenges even though those findings relate to a constitutional issue.

§ 2.4.3 Preparing an Abstract of the Record

Before beginning to write, Ms. Elder does one last thing: she creates an abstract of the record by going through the trial transcript and taking notes on each piece of relevant testimony. For each piece of relevant testimony, she notes the name of the individual who gave the testimony, she writes down the page number on which the testimony appears, and she summarizes the testimony.

EXAMPLE   **EXCERPT FROM MS. ELDER'S ABSTRACT OF THE RECORD**

Direct Examination of Gregory Bhasin.

P. 4:	Gregory Bhasin, ATF agent; several years experience investigating cross-border drug cases; 1-1/2 years in Blaine office.
P. 30-31:	At about 9:30 received a call from 911 operator in Bellingham. Man who said his name was Zachary Dillon had called and said that a man called Peter Josephy was involved in selling drugs that had been brought into the U.S. from Canada.
P. 32-33:	Dillon says that Josephy will be at Travel House Inn for another hour or so. Gives physical description of Josephy's car, Josephy, and the man Josephy is selling the drugs to.
P. 32-35:	Dillon would not give 911 operator his address or a phone number. Records check does not indicate that anyone by the name of Zachary Dillon lives in the greater Bellingham area.

---

[2] As noted earlier, Ms. Elder will not need to include a harmless error analysis for either of these issues. Therefore, sample harmless error arguments from other briefs have been included at the end of this chapter after the sample briefs in *United States v. Josephy*.

P. 42:	Agent Bhasin goes to the Travel House Inn and finds a blue Blazer in the parking lot. Checks license plate — car registered to Peter Josephy.

Although preparing such an abstract is time-consuming, the process forces Ms. Elder to go through the record carefully, identifying each piece of relevant testimony. It also makes brief writing and preparation for oral argument easier. Instead of having to search through the entire record looking for the testimony she needs, Ms. Elder can refer to her abstract.

§ 2.4.4 Preparing the Record on Appeal

After having determined which issues she will raise on appeal, Ms. Elder goes back through the trial record, identifying those parts that she wants included as the record on appeal. She selects pleadings and documents filed with the district court: the charging document, the Motion to Suppress, the Findings of Fact and Conclusions of Law and Order Denying the Motion to Suppress, the jury's Verdict Form, the Judgment and Sentence, and the Notice of Appeal. In addition, she includes the transcript of the evidentiary hearing on the motion to suppress and the transcript of voir dire.

Because she is not assigning error to anything that happened during the trial, Ms. Elder does not have the trial record transcribed. In addition, because there were no relevant exhibits, she does not include any of them in the record on appeal.

§ 2.5 Researching the Issues on Appeal

How an individual researches an issue depends in large part on that individual's familiarity with the area of law. For example, in this case, Ms. Elder is an experienced criminal defense lawyer with extensive trial experience who knows the law relating to a *Batson* analysis. As a consequence, when she starts her research, she already knows the names of the key cases, for example, *Batson v. Kentucky*, 476 U.S. 799 (1986) and *Johnson v. California*, 545 U.S. 162, 169 (2005). Ms. Elder rereads these and other cases and then cite checks the cases that are most on point to locate more recent cases. In contrast, attorneys who are less familiar with criminal law would have to take a different approach: they would need to begin their research by doing some background reading on a free website, in a hornbook, or in a federal practice book that discusses the analysis the Ninth Circuit court uses to determine if a *Batson* violation has occurred. Using the citations that they obtain while doing this background reading, these attorneys would need to locate, read, and cite check the key cases. In addition, they might want to look for a law review or bar journal article that specifically discusses *Batson*.

For more on researching issues involving constitutional issues, see Chapter 9 in *Just Research*.

§ 2.6 Planning the Brief

Having researched the issues, Ms. Elder is ready to begin drafting the brief. She does not, however, start writing until she has spent several hours analyzing the facts and the law, developing a theory of the case, and selecting an organizational scheme.

§ 2.6.1 Analyzing the Facts and the Law

To write an effective brief, Ms. Elder must have mastered both the facts of the case and the law. For example, before she begins drafting the arguments relating to the motion to suppress, she needs to know what each witness said, and did not say, at the suppression hearing and every finding of fact and conclusion of law that the court entered. Similarly, before she begins drafting the arguments related to the *Batson* challenge, she needs to know what questions the potential jurors were asked during voir dire, needs to read carefully all of the relevant cases and think not only about how she might be able to use them to support her argument but also about how the government might use them in its arguments.

Ms. Elder also needs to think about what relief she wants and the various ways in which she might persuade the court to grant that relief. Here, ends–means reasoning often works well. In doing an ends–means analysis for the *Batson* issue, Ms. Elder starts with the conclusion that she wants the court to reach and then works backward through the steps in the analysis. Although the *Batson* analysis involves a three-step process, Ms. Elder does not address the first step in her ends–means analysis. She knows from her research of Ninth Circuit cases that the issue of whether defense counsel established a prima facie case of discrimination is moot because the government proffered reasons for the use of the peremptory challenges to excuse the two Native Americans. *See United States v. Esparza-Gonzalez*, 422 F.3d 897, 906 (9th Cir. 2007).

- *Relief wanted:* Conviction reversed.
- *How to have conviction reversed:* Have the appellate court reverse the district court.
- *How to have the appellate court reverse the district court:* Show the district court improperly overruled her *Batson* objection.
- *How to show that the district court erred:* Show the prosecutor's reasons were not race neutral.
- *If the court determines the reasons were race neutral,* show the district court erred in not finding that the reasons were a pretext for discrimination.

- *How to show the district court erred in not finding the reasons were a pretext for discrimination:*
  - Show the reasons were not supported by the record.
  - Use a comparative analysis to show the prosecutor did not use peremptory challenges to excuse similarly situated non-Native Americans by comparing the answers given by Native Americans with answers given by non-Native Americans.
  - Show the court failed to do the required analysis when it made a cursory ruling without setting out its reasons clearly on the record.

In contrast, the prosecutor's ends–means analysis for the *Batson* issue would look like this:

- *Relief wanted:* Jury verdict affirmed.
- *How to get the jury verdict affirmed:* Show that the district court did not err when it overruled defense counsel's *Batson* objection.
- *How to show district court did not err:* Show that the government met its burden of offering a race-neutral reason for excusing Mr. Williams and Ms. Whitefish and that the defendant did not carry his burden of showing discrimination.
- *How to show that the prosecution met its burden of offering a race-neutral reason for excusing Ms. Whitefish and Mr. Williams:* Show the reasons are not based on stereotypes about Native Americans, but are based on specific responses from Ms. Whitefish based on her experiences at the border and from Mr. Williams based on his outside obligations the following week.
- *How to show defense did not carry its burden of showing that the prosecutor's reasons were a pretext for discrimination:* Dismissing only two jurors of the defendant's race does not, by itself, establish pretext.
- *How to show using peremptory challenges to excuse the two Native American jurors was not racially based in this case:* Show that the defendant's comparative analysis does not satisfy his burden of showing the government's reasons were a pretext for discrimination.
- Show that the court did the required analysis on the record by specifically addressing each of the three steps.

Each side would do a similar ends–means analysis for each of the issues the parties will address.

§ 2.6.2 Developing a Theory of the Case

Having thoroughly mastered both the facts and the law, Ms. Elder is ready to develop her theory of the case. At its simplest, a theory of the case is the legal theory that the attorney relies on in arguing the case to the court. A good theory of the case, however, goes beyond a legal theory or legal argument. It becomes the lens through which the attorney and, if the attorney is effective, the court views the case. For more on theory of the case, see section 1.4 in this book.

Developing the legal theory is relatively easy. Simply research the points that you set out in your ends–means analysis and, based on that research, discard the weak arguments and keep the strong ones. When Ms. Elder did her ends–means analysis for the *Batson* issue, she thought that she could make alternative arguments based on the second and third parts of the *Batson* analysis. Under the second part of the analysis, she could argue that the district court erred when it concluded that the reasons the prosecutor gave for striking Mr. Williams and Ms. Whitefish were not neutral on their face and, under the third part of the analysis, she could argue that even if the reasons were neutral on their face, those reasons were a pretext for discrimination. However, in doing her research, Ms. Elder discovered that the argument based on the second part of the *Batson* analysis was very weak: after looking at the case law, Ms. Elder concluded that she had little or no chance of persuading the Ninth Circuit Court of Appeals that the reasons that the prosecutor gave were not neutral on their face. Thus, Ms. Elder decided not to rely on this legal theory.

There was, though, some good news. Based on her research, Ms. Elder concluded that the argument based on the third part of the *Batson* analysis was a strong argument. In addition, in doing her research, she found cases that say that the trial court must do a "sensitive analysis" and "set out its reasoning on the record." Because the district court's only statement was, "Your objection is noted, Counsel, but the Court finds no purposeful discrimination here," Ms. Elder thinks that she has a strong argument that the district court did not do the required analysis and, even if it did the required analysis, the record is not sufficient. Therefore, she decides to make this argument. Consequently, in arguing that the district court erred in denying Mr. Josephy's motion to suppress, Ms. Elder has two legal theories: she will argue that the district court erred in denying her *Batson* challenge (1) because the reasons that the government gave were a pretext for discrimination and (2) because the district court did not do the required "sensitive analysis."

Having identified her legal theories, Ms. Elder then thinks about the lens that she wants to use in arguing those legal theories. Does she want a narrow focus, emphasizing that Mr. Josephy's rights were violated when the government used a peremptory strike to excuse Ms. Whitefish and again when the government used a peremptory strike to excuse Mr. Williams, or does she want a wider focus, emphasizing that this case is not just about Mr. Josephy but about the integrity of the jury system itself and Ms. Whitefish's and Mr. Williams's right not to be excluded from participation because they are Native Americans? Peremptory challenges serve an important function, but they cannot be a mask for discrimination.

In the end, Ms. Elder decides to keep the narrower focus, emphasizing the violation of Mr. Josephy's rights, rather than the integrity of the jury system as a whole. She believes this is her best approach for two reasons. First, she will be arguing that Mr. Josephy's constitutional rights were violated both before trial when his suppression motion was denied, and in the jury selection at the start of trial. Second, the fact that both the struck jurors and Mr. Josephy are Native American makes the violation seem that much more egregious.

§ 2.6.3 Selecting an Organizational Scheme

Because there has to be a one-to-one correspondence between the issue statements and the argumentative headings (see sections 2.11 and 2.14.3), the last thing that Ms. Elder does before she begins writing is select an organizational scheme. She needs to decide how many issue statements and, thus, how many main headings she wants to have, and she needs to decide how to order those issue statements and main headings.

a. Deciding on the Number of Issues and Headings

In almost every brief, there is more than one way to organize the arguments. As a consequence, before you begin writing, you need to decide whether you want to set out only one issue statement and one main argumentative heading, or whether you want to set out several issue statements and a corresponding number of main argumentative headings. In addition, if you have more than one issue statement, you need to decide how to order those issues. Finally, you need to decide whether you want to use subheadings and, if you do, how many.

In *United States v. Josephy*, Ms. Elder decides to argue both that the district court erred when it denied her motion to suppress and that the district court erred in overruling her *Batson* objection. Because these two errors are not closely related, Ms. Elder decides to have at least one issue statement and one main argumentative heading that relate to the motion to suppress and at least one issue statement and one main argumentative heading that relate to the *Batson* challenge. In deciding whether she should have one or more than one issue statement for each of these two errors, Ms. Elder thinks strategically: which organizational scheme will allow her to set out her arguments clearly and concisely, and which organizational scheme will improve her chances of persuading the appellate court that the district court erred?

For example, in organizing her discussion of the suppression issue, Ms. Elder has at least three options:

1. Ms. Elder could have three issue statements and three main argumentative headings.
2. Ms. Elder could have one issue statement, one main argumentative heading, and no subheadings.
3. Ms. Elder could have one issue statement, one main argumentative heading, and three subheadings.

The following examples illustrate these options.

EXAMPLE 1   **OPTION 1**

Three issue statements and three main headings. The first issue statement and main heading would relate to whether the tip was or was not anonymous, the second issue statement and main heading would relate to whether the tip had sufficient indicia of reliability, and the third issue statement and main heading would relate to whether the police corroborated more than innocuous details.

Issues

1. Did the ATF agents lack a particularized objective suspicion that Mr. Josephy was engaged in criminal activity when the tip came from an unknown informant who gave the 911 operator his name but refused to give his address or phone number?

2. Did the ATF agents lack a particularized objective suspicion that Mr. Josephy was engaged in criminal activity when the tip included only general physical descriptions of the people and vehicle, it omitted any description of clothing, and the only action it predicted was that Mr. Josephy would be leaving a motel shortly before checkout time?

3. Did the ATF agents have a particularized objective suspicion that Mr. Josephy was engaged in criminal activity when the police corroborated only innocuous details, for example, Mr. Josephy's physical appearance, his vehicle, and his departure from a motel shortly before checkout time?

Argument

A. THE ATF AGENTS DID NOT HAVE A PARTICULARIZED OBJECTIVE SUSPICION THAT MR. JOSEPHY WAS ENGAGED IN CRIMINAL ACTIVITY BECAUSE THE TIP CAME FROM AN UNKNOWN INFORMANT AND, ALTHOUGH THE INFORMANT GAVE THE 911 OPERATOR HIS NAME, HE REFUSED TO GIVE HIS ADDRESS OR PHONE NUMBER.

[The law and arguments relating to this issue go here.]

B. THE ATF AGENTS DID NOT HAVE A PARTICULARIZED OBJECTIVE SUSPICION THAT MR. JOSEPHY WAS ENGAGED IN CRIMINAL ACTIVITY BECAUSE THE TIP INCLUDED ONLY GENERAL PHYSICAL DESCRIPTIONS, IT OMITTED ANY DESCRIPTION OF CLOTHING, AND THE ONLY ACTION IT PREDICTED WAS THAT MR. JOSEPHY WOULD BE LEAVING A MOTEL SHORTLY BEFORE CHECKOUT TIME.

[The law and arguments relating to this issue go here.]

C. THE ATF AGENTS DID NOT HAVE A PARTICULAR-
IZED OBJECTIVE SUSPICION THAT MR. JOSEPHY
WAS ENGAGED IN CRIMINAL ACTIVITY BECAUSE
THE POLICE CORROBORATED NO MORE THAN
INNOCUOUS DETAILS, FOR EXAMPLE, MR. JOSE-
PHY'S PHYSICAL APPEARANCE, HIS VEHICLE, AND
HIS DEPARTURE FROM A MOTEL SHORTLY BEFORE
CHECKOUT TIME.

[The law and arguments relating to this issue go here.]

EXAMPLE 2   **OPTION 2**

One issue statement, one main heading, no subheadings.

Issue

Did the district court err in concluding that a telephone tip created an objective particularized suspicion when the informant declined to give more than his name; the informant called from a public pay phone and gave only a general physical description of Mr. Josephy, his vehicle, and his location; and the police merely corroborated that Mr. Josephy left a motel shortly before checkout time and got into his vehicle?

Argument

A. THE ATF AGENTS VIOLATED MR. JOSEPHY'S FOURTH
AMENDMENT RIGHTS BECAUSE THEY DID NOT HAVE
A PARTICULARIZED OBJECTIVE SUSPICION THAT MR.
JOSEPHY WAS ENGAGED IN CRIMINAL ACTIVITY.

[Introductory paragraph and all of the law and arguments go here.]

EXAMPLE 3   **OPTION 3**

One issue statement, one main heading, and three subheadings. The first subheading relates to the argument that the tip should be treated as being anonymous, the second subheading relates to the argument that the tip lacked sufficient indicia of reliability, and the third subheading relates to the argument that the police failed to corroborate anything more than innocuous details.

Issue

Did the district court err in concluding that a telephone tip created an objective particularized suspicion when the informant declined to give more than his name; the informant called from a public pay phone and gave only a general physical description of Mr. Josephy, his vehicle, and his location; and the police merely corroborated that Mr. Josephy left a motel shortly before checkout time and got into his vehicle?

Argument

A. THE ATF AGENTS VIOLATED MR. JOSEPHY'S FOURTH AMENDMENT RIGHTS BECAUSE THEY DID NOT HAVE A PARTICULARIZED OBJECTIVE SUSPICION THAT MR. JOSEPHY WAS ENGAGED IN CRIMINAL ACTIVITY.

[Introductory paragraphs go here.]

1. The ATF agents did not have a particularized objective suspicion that Mr. Josephy was engaged in criminal activity because the tip came from an unknown informant: although the informant gave the 911 operator his name, he refused to give his address or phone number.

   [Arguments relating to first subheading go here.]

2. The ATF agents did not have a particularized objective suspicion that Mr. Josephy was engaged in criminal activity because the tip included only general physical descriptions, it omitted any description of clothing, and the only action it predicted was that Mr. Josephy would be leaving a motel shortly before checkout time.

   [Arguments relating to second subheading go here.]

3. The ATF agents did not have a particularized objective suspicion that Mr. Josephy was engaged in criminal activity because the police corroborated only innocuous details, for example, Mr. Josephy's physical appearance, his vehicle, and his departure from a motel shortly before checkout time.

   [Arguments relating to the third subheading go here.]

Although in *United States v. Josephy*, all three of these options could work, Ms. Elder chooses the third option. Ms. Elder rejects the first option (three issue statements and three main headings) because such an organizational scheme suggests that each of the issues and headings can stand on its own when, in fact, it cannot. Although the court will consider whether the tip came from a known or unknown informant, whether there are sufficient indicia of reliability, and whether law enforcement officers corroborated more than innocuous details, in the end, the test is a totality of the circumstances test. In addition, under the first option, there is no place to set out the general rules, in this instance, the totality of the circumstances test and the factors that the courts consider. Finally, given that Ms. Elder plans to argue *Batson*, it will be easier for the appellate court to see that there are two different independent bases for reversal if the brief has one issue statement and one main heading relating to the motion to suppress and one issue statement and one main heading relating to the *Batson* objection.

Ms. Elder also rejects the second option (one issue statement and one main heading but no subheadings). The advantage of this second option is that it makes clear that the arguments relating to whether the tip came from a known or unknown informant, whether there are sufficient indicia of reliability, and whether law enforcement officers corroborated more than innocuous details are all related to the larger issue of whether the district court erred in denying Mr. Josephy's motion to suppress. The disadvantage of this second organizational scheme is that it does not allow Ms. Elder to emphasize that there are three reasons why the district court erred in denying Mr. Josephy's motion to suppress. Thus, the government might want to use this organizational scheme to emphasize that the test is a totality of the circumstances test, but Ms. Elder does not.

The third option has all of the advantages with no disadvantages. By having a single issue statement and a single argumentative heading, Ms. Elder makes it clear that all of the pieces of her arguments are related to her main assertion: that the district court erred in denying Mr. Josephy's motion to suppress. In addition, by using three subheadings, Ms. Elder can emphasize that there are three reasons why the district court erred, and she can divide her argument into manageable chunks. Most importantly, though, the third option is consistent with Ms. Elder's theory of the case: the third option allows Ms. Elder to argue both of her legal theories through a narrow lens. For more on theory of the case, see section 2.6.2 in this book.

Like Ms. Elder, the government's attorney rejects the first option. Because the government wants the Court of Appeals to affirm the district court, it wants to limit and not expand the number of alleged errors. Deciding between the second and third options is more difficult. Although the second option allows the government to emphasize that the test is a totality of the circumstances test, the lack of subheadings means that the entire argument will need to be set out in one large chunk. On the flip side, although Option 3 allows the government to present its arguments in more manageable chunks, dividing the argument into three parts feeds into Ms. Elder's argument that any one reason is sufficient to support a conclusion that the district court erred. After weighing the pros and cons, the government's attorney settles on the second option because that option is more consistent with its theory of the case. He does, however, make presenting the government's argument concisely a high priority. See the appellee's brief set out at the end of this chapter.

b. Ordering the Issues and Arguments

In many cases, logic dictates the order in which you set out the issues and the arguments related to those issues. Threshold questions—for example, issues relating to subject matter jurisdiction, service of process, and the statute of limitations—must be discussed before questions relating to the merits of the case. Similarly, the parts of a test should usually be discussed in order and, when one argument builds on another, the foundation argument should be set out first.

When logic does not dictate the order of the issues and arguments, you will usually want to start with your strongest argument. By doing so, you ensure that the judges will read your strongest argument and that your strongest argument is in a position of emphasis. You can then go through the rest of your issues and arguments in the order of their strength, or you can begin and end with strong issues and arguments, sandwiching your weaker arguments in the middle.

PRACTICE POINTER   The appellant files its brief first, and the appellee needs to respond to the issues raised by the appellant, but the appellee does not need to, and usually will not want to, use the appellant's organizational scheme. Instead, the appellee will usually want to select an organizational scheme that allows him or her to set out his or her strongest argument first.

In *United States v. Josephy*, both logic and strategy dictate the ordering of the issues and arguments related to those issues. If the appellate court determines that the evidence should have been suppressed, it will not reach the *Batson* issue. In addition, a "win" on the *Batson* issue would result in a remand for a new trial, but, more likely than not, a win on the suppression issue would end up with the charges being dismissed.

Having thoroughly analyzed the facts and the law, developed a theory of the case, and selected an organizational scheme, Ms. Elder is now ready to write. For the purpose of this chapter, we discuss the sections in the order in which they appear in the brief. However, many attorneys do not draft the sections in that order. Instead, many start with the statement of the case or with the arguments. However, no matter how you decide to draft the brief, keep in mind that writing an appellate brief is a recursive process, with the completion of one section often requiring revision of another section. For example, once she drafts the arguments, Ms. Elder might find she needs to include additional facts in her statement of the facts or that she needs to revise her issue statements.

§ 2.7   Preparing the Cover

The first page of a brief is the title page, or cover. As in most other jurisdictions, in the federal courts, there are rules that govern the cover. For instance, the rules prescribe the types of information that must be on the cover, the order of that information, and the color. *See* Fed. R. App. P. 32 (2). The briefs at the end of the chapter comply with the rule for briefs submitted to the Ninth Circuit Court of Appeals.

§ 2.8 Preparing the Table of Contents

The second page of the brief should be the table of contents. Once again, the rules specify the information that should be included and the format that should be used. *See* Fed. R. App. P. 28(a)(2) and the sample briefs at the end of this chapter.

If you are writing a brief to the United States Supreme Court, the questions presented would be set out, by themselves, on the page directly after the cover. *See* Sup. Ct. R. 24(1)(a).

§ 2.9 Preparing the Table of Authorities

Immediately following the table of contents is the table of authorities. In this section, list each of the cases, constitutional provisions, statutes, rules, and secondary authorities cited in the brief. As a general rule, cases are listed first, in alphabetical order, followed by constitutional provisions, statutes, court rules, and secondary authorities. *See* Fed. R. App. P. 28(a)(3).

In listing the authorities, use the citation form prescribed by your court rules (your jurisdiction might or might not have adopted the *ALWD Citation Manual* or *The Bluebook*) and include references to each page in the brief where the authority appears. Both LexisNexis™ and Westlaw have programs that you can use to check your citations and prepare the table of authorities.

If you use a program to create your table of authorities, make sure the table the program generates is complete, accurate, and in compliance with the applicable rules. For example, some programs might not catch citations embedded in parentheticals, where one case cites to another case. In addition, make sure that the citations are in proper order (cases before secondary authorities) and in proper form (case names in italics or underlined) and make sure that the table of authorities is easy to read: use white space between each citation and make sure that the citation does not run up against the page references. Finally, do not finalize your table of authorities until you have finished editing, revising, and proofreading the body of your brief so that the page references are accurate.

§ 2.10 Drafting the Jurisdictional Statement

Under Fed. R. App. P. 28(4), briefs filed in federal courts must have a jurisdictional statement setting out the following:

> (A) the basis for the district court's or agency's subject matter jurisdiction, with citations to applicable statutory provisions and stating relevant facts establishing jurisdiction;
>
> (B) the basis for the court of appeals' jurisdiction, with citations to applicable statutory provisions and stating relevant facts establishing jurisdiction;

(C) the filing dates establishing the timeliness of the appeal or petition for review; and

(D) an assertion that the appeal is from a final order or judgment that disposes of all parties' claims, or information establishing the court of appeals' jurisdiction on some other basis[.]

PRACTICE POINTER   Under the federal rules, an appellee's brief need not include a jurisdictional statement unless the appellee disagrees with the appellant's jurisdictional statement. *See* Fed. R. App. P. 28(b)(1). However, in the Ninth Circuit, the appellee cannot omit the jurisdictional statement section; an appellee must include either a statement of jurisdiction or a statement agreeing with the appellant's statement of jurisdiction. Ninth Cir. R. 28-2.2(c).

---

§ 2.11 Drafting the Statement of Issues Presented for Review

The Federal Rules of Appellate Procedure require that the appellant include a statement of the issues presented for review. Fed. R. App. P. 28(a)(5). The Federal Rules of Appellate Procedure do not require the appellee to include a statement of the issues. Fed. R. App. P. 28(b)(2). However, in most instances, the appellee will want to set out the issues in such a way that they support its theory of the case.

Look, for example, at the following issue statements from *Hishon v. King & Spaulding*, a case in which the United States Supreme Court was asked to decide whether law firms were subject to federal civil rights laws prohibiting discrimination in employment on the basis of sex, race, religion, or national origin.

EXAMPLE 1   **PETITIONER'S STATEMENT OF THE ISSUE**

Whether King and Spaulding and other large institutional law firms that are organized as partnerships are, for that reason alone, exempt from Title VII of the Civil Rights Act of 1964, and are free (a) to discriminate in the promotion of associate lawyers to partnership on the basis of sex, race or religion; and (b) to discharge those associates whom they do not admit to partnership based on reasons of sex, race or religion under an established "up-or-out" policy.

EXAMPLE 2   **RESPONDENT'S STATEMENT OF THE ISSUES**

1. Whether law partners organized for advocacy are entitled to constitutionally protected freedom of association.

2. Whether Congress intended through Title VII of the Civil Rights Act of 1964 to give the Equal Employment Opportunity Commission, a

> politically appointed advocacy agency engaged in litigation, jurisdiction over invitations to join law firm partnerships.

The petitioner's issue statement sets out its theory of the case: according to the petitioner, the issue is whether law firms are free to discriminate on the basis of sex, race, religion, or national origin. Similarly, the respondent's issue statements set out its theory. To the respondent, this is not a case about discrimination. Instead, it is a case about whether the partners in a law firm are entitled to their constitutionally protected right of freedom of association and about whether members of a politically appointed advocacy agency have the right to determine who is invited to join a law firm.

§ 2.11.1 Select a Format

Most court rules do not prescribe the format that should be used for the issue statement. As a consequence, in writing your issue statement or statements, you can use the under-does-when format, the whether format, or a multisentence format. *See* section 1.7.2.

EXAMPLE 1 **"UNDER-DOES-WHEN" FORMAT**

Did the district court err in denying Mr. Josephy's *Batson* challenge when the prosecutor used his peremptory challenges to excuse both Mr. Williams and Ms. Whitefish, the only two Native Americans in the jury pool and, in overruling the objection, the trial judge's only statement was "Your objection is noted, Counsel, but the Court finds no purposeful discrimination here"?

EXAMPLE 2 **"WHETHER" FORMAT**

Whether the district court erred in denying Mr. Josephy's *Batson* challenge when the prosecutor used his peremptory challenges to excuse both Mr. Williams and Ms. Whitefish, the only two Native Americans in the jury pool and, in overruling the objection, the court's only statement was "Your objection is noted, Counsel, but the Court finds no purposeful discrimination here"?

EXAMPLE 3 **MULTISENTENCE FORMAT**

The prosecutor excused a Native American juror who assured the Court he could miss a scheduled meeting, but he did not excuse a white juror who might have had to leave town because the doctors had given his mother a 20 percent chance of living. In addition, the prosecutor excused a Native American juror who said she was not bothered by searches at the border that she attributed to her age, but he did not excuse a white juror with long hair who admitted being bothered by police officers who targeted individuals who had long hair. The judge's only ruling was, "Your objection is noted, Counsel, but the Court finds no purposeful discrimination here." Given the fact that Mr. Josephy is a Native American, did the district court err when it overruled Mr. Josephy's *Batson* objection?

Although you can use any format, once you select a format, use it for each of your issues. Do not write one issue using the under-does-when format and another using the whether format. Also, remember that you are not bound by opposing counsel's choices. You do not need to use the format that he or she used, and you do not need to have the same number of issues. Select the format and number of issues that work best for your client.

PRACTICE POINTER   Some issues statements work equally well under any of the three formats; others do not. Consequently, although you might have a preferred format, if you have an issue that just does not work with that particular format, don't force it. Use the format that will work for all of the issues raised.

---

§ 2.11.2 Make the Issue Statement Subtly Persuasive

A good issue statement is subtly persuasive: not only does your issue statement set out your theory of the case, but it also subtly suggests the conclusion you want the court to reach and provides support for that conclusion.

In writing the issue statements for an appellate brief, you can use three techniques to make your statements subtly persuasive: (1) you can state the question so that it suggests the conclusion you want the court to reach; (2) you can emphasize the facts that support your theory of the case; and (3) you can emphasize or de-emphasize the burden of proof or standard of review.

a. State the Question So that It Suggests the Conclusion You Want the Court to Reach

Begin by framing the legal question so that it suggests the conclusion you want the court to reach. For example, in writing the issue statement for *United States v. Josephy*, Ms. Elder frames the question so that it suggests that the district court erred in overruling her *Batson* objection, but the government frames the question so that it suggests that the district court acted properly when it overruled the objection.

EXAMPLE 1   APPELLANT'S STATEMENT OF THE LEGAL QUESTION

Did the district court err in denying Mr. Josephy's *Batson* challenge . . . ?

| EXAMPLE 2 | APPELLEE'S STATEMENT OF THE LEGAL QUESTION |

Whether the district court properly overruled Mr. Josephy's *Batson* objection . . . ?

| PRACTICE POINTER | Note that the appellant uses "denying" and "*Batson* challenge," but the appellee uses "overrule" and "*Batson* objection." Because some courts use one phrase and other courts use the |

other phrase, each side could select the phrase that is most favorable to its position. In this instance, the appellee uses "overrule" and "objection" because appellate courts usually defer to a trial court's decision to sustain or overrule an objection. In contrast, the appellant uses "denying" and "*Batson* challenge" because that phrase suggests that the case involves more than just a routine evidentiary issue.

Similarly, the attorneys think carefully about the language they will use in connection with the suppression issue. The appellee uses a general statement of the rule courts apply: whether the officers had a reasonable suspicion that the defendant was involved in criminal activity. However, although Ms. Elder includes this language, she frames her argument in more favorable specific language from Ninth Circuit cases, which define a reasonable suspicion as a "particularized and objective basis for suspecting the particular person stopped of criminal activity."

For more on word choice, see pages 19-20. One way to see what phrase the courts use in a particular situation is to run a search for the possible alternative terms in a fee-based service like Westlaw or LexisNexis® or a free service that has copies of opinions.

There are of course, other ways of framing the legal question: instead of always using the same format, select the one that works best with your theory of the case.

| EXAMPLE 3 | OTHER WAYS THAT THE APPELLANT COULD SET OUT THE LEGAL QUESTION THAT SUGGEST THE CONCLUSION THE APPELLANT WANTS THE COURT TO REACH |

Under the Equal Protection Clause, was Mr. Josephy denied his right to a jury trial when . . . ?

Were the reasons that the prosecutor gave for excusing the only two Native Americans in the jury pool a pretext for discrimination when . . . ?

Did the prosecutor violate Mr. Josephy's constitutional rights when . . . ?

EXAMPLE 4   **OTHER WAYS THAT THE APPELLEE COULD SET OUT THE LEGAL QUESTION THAT SUGGEST THE CONCLUSION THE APPELLEE WANTS THE COURT TO REACH**

Did the government properly exercise its right to use peremptory challenges when . . . ?

Did the defendant fail to prove purposeful discrimination when . . . ?

Given that the district court was in the best position to judge the prosecutor's action, did the district court properly overrule the *Batson* objection when . . . ?

---

b. Emphasize the Facts that Support Your Theory of the Case

In addition to stating the question so that it suggests a favorable conclusion, also emphasize the facts that support your theory of the case. For instance, in the following example, Ms. Elder has emphasized the facts that suggest the prosecutor's proffered reasons were a pretext for discrimination by including the jurors' names and stating that these two jurors were the only two Native Americans in the jury pool. In addition, Ms. Elder has emphasized the facts that suggest that the district court did not do the required "sensitive analysis" by stating that the district court's ruling consisted of a single statement and quoting that statement.

EXAMPLE 1   **APPELLANT'S USE OF FACTS**

Did the district court err in denying Mr. Josephy's *Batson* challenge when the prosecutor used his peremptory challenges to excuse both Mr. Williams and Ms. Whitefish, the only two Native Americans in the jury pool and, in denying the challenge, the judge's only statement was "Your objection is noted, Counsel, but the Court finds no purposeful discrimination here"?

In contrast, in drafting its issue statement, the government emphasizes the facts that support its theory of the case. In particular, in the first part of its issue statement, the government sets up its argument that it excused Ms. Whitefish because of her age and her experiences, and not because she is a Native American, by including in its issue statement references to Ms. Whitefish's age and the problems that she encountered at the border. Similarly, the government sets up its argument that it did not engage in purposeful discrimination when it excused Mr. Williams by highlighting the fact that the government excused both a Native American and a white juror for similar reasons. Finally, note that Ms. Elder refers to the jurors by name, which allows her to include a name that appears to be a Native American name (Ms. Whitefish) in her issue statement, but the government does not refer to the jurors by name.

EXAMPLE 2 **APPELLEE'S USE OF FACTS**

Whether Mr. Josephy failed to prove that the government engaged in purposeful discrimination when (1) the government excused a twenty-one-year-old Native American juror who volunteered that she had experienced problems each time she had crossed from the United States into Canada and (2) the government excused both a Native American juror who told the judge that he had a tribal council meeting the following week and a white juror who was worried about missing work.

---

c. Emphasize or De-Emphasize the Burden of Proof and Standard of Review

Another way to make your issue statement subtly persuasive is to use the burden of proof and standard of review to your advantage. As a general rule, if the other side has the burden of proof, emphasize that fact. In contrast, if you have the burden of proof, de-emphasize that fact. Similarly, if the standard of review favors your client, include a reference to it in your issue statement; if it does not, do talk about the standard of review in the argument, but not in the issue statement.

EXAMPLE 1 **BECAUSE THE APPELLANT HAS THE BURDEN OF PROOF, MS. ELDER DOES NOT MENTION THE BURDEN OF PROOF IN HER ISSUE STATEMENT**

Did the district court err in denying Mr. Josephy's *Batson* challenge when . . . ?

EXAMPLE 2 **BECAUSE THE APPELLANT HAS THE BURDEN OF PROOF, THE GOVERNMENT EMPHASIZES THAT FACT IN ITS ISSUE STATEMENT**

Whether Mr. Josephy failed to prove that the government had engaged in purposeful discrimination when . . . .

PRACTICE

In some jurisdictions the courts or individual judges have stated that the parties should not be referred to as appellant/petitioner or appellee/respondent. Instead, the courts or judges have stated that the parties should be referred to by name, by a label that identifies their relationship to other parties (for example, employer and employee

or doctor and patient), or by the label that describes their status at the trial court (for example, plaintiff and defendant). Thus, before deciding what to call the parties, check your local rules.

§ 2.11.3 Make Sure the Issue Statement Is Readable

An issue statement that is not readable is not persuasive. Thus, during the revising process, check your issue statement to make sure a judge can understand it after reading it just once. First, look at length. If your issue statement is more than four or five lines long, try to shorten it. The longer the statement, the more difficult it becomes to read. Second, make sure that you have presented the information in manageable "chunks." One way to make a long issue statement easier to read is to use the three slots in a sentence:

_____,	_____	_____.
introductory phrase	main clause	modifier(s)

Another way is to use enumeration: in listing the key facts, use numbers or letters to introduce each item in the list of facts. Finally, make sure your statement of the issue does not contain any grammatical errors. In particular, make sure that your subject and verb agree and that, in listing the facts, you have used parallel constructions for all of the items in the list.

See sections 8.4.1 and 8.7 in *Just Writing, Second Edition*. See section 1.7.4 in this book for a checklist for critiquing issue statements.

§ 2.12 Drafting the Statement of the Case

Over and over again, judges emphasize the importance of the facts. At both the trial and appellate court levels, judges want to know what the facts are and how the law should be applied to them.

Because the facts are so important, good advocates spend considerable time crafting their statement of the case. They think carefully about which facts they want to include, how those facts should be organized, and how the facts can be presented in the light most favorable to their client.

§ 2.12.1 Check the Rules

Just as there are rules governing the cover, tables, and statement of issues, there is also a rule governing the statement of the case. Under the federal rules, an appellant's brief must contain the following:

Fed. R. App. P. 28(a)

* * *

(6) a statement of the case briefly indicating the nature of the case, the course of proceedings, and the disposition below;

(7) a statement of facts relevant to the issues submitted for review with appropriate references to the record (see Rule 28(e))[.]

Although the rules do not require that an appellee include a statement of the case and statement of facts, Fed. R. App. P. 28(b)(3)-(4), most attorneys include them so that they can set out the procedure and facts in the light that is most favorable to their clients.

§ 2.12.2 Draft the Statement of the Case

Under the federal rules, the statement of the case precedes the statement of facts. Fed. R. App. P. 28(a)(6). In most instances, you will want to include the following facts in your statement of the case: (1) a statement describing the nature of the action, (2) a description of any relevant motions and their disposition, and (3) a statement telling the court whether the case was heard by a judge or by a jury. For example, in *United States v. Josephy*, the statement of the case would look something like this.

EXAMPLE   **APPELLANT'S STATEMENT OF THE CASE**

STATEMENT OF THE CASE

On June 26, 2007, Peter Jason Josephy was charged with one count of Unlawful Possession of a Controlled Substance with the Intent to Deliver under 21 U.S.C. § 841(a)(1) (2006). (CR 7). After an evidentiary hearing, the district court denied Mr. Josephy's motion to suppress evidence obtained during a warrantless search. (CR 26; ER 30).

The case proceeded to jury trial, the Honorable Alesha J. Moore presiding. (CR 28). During voir dire, Mr. Josephy challenged the government's use of two of its peremptory challenges to excuse the only two Native Americans on the jury panel. (ER 123-24). The district court concluded that while Mr. Josephy had established a prima facie case of discrimination, the reasons given by the government were race neutral and that Mr. Josephy had not established purposeful discrimination. (ER 124). Thus, the court denied Mr. Josephy's *Batson* challenge.

Notice that each statement is supported by a reference to the rule. CR stands for Clerk's Record—that is, a document filed with the trial court; ER stands for Excerpt of Record—that is, those portions of the record filed in connection with the appeal.

§ 2.12.3 Select the Facts

Like the statement of facts in an objective memo and a motion brief, the statement of facts in an appellate brief contains three types of facts: legally significant facts, emotionally significant facts, and background facts.

a. Legally Significant Facts

Because the court rules require that the statement of the case include the facts relevant to the issues being raised, in writing the statement of facts you must include all of the legally significant facts, both favorable and unfavorable. Thus, in *United States v. Josephy*, the parties must include all of the facts that will be relevant in determining whether ATF agents had a reasonable suspicion that Mr. Josephy was engaged in criminal activity and all of the facts that will be relevant in determining whether the district court erred in overruling Ms. Elder's *Batson* challenge. For example, in setting out the facts relating to the *Batson* challenge, Ms. Elder must include the fact that the prosecutor used one of his peremptory challenges to excuse a white juror who had scheduling problems, and the prosecutor must include the fact that he excused all of the Native Americans in the jury pool.

b. Emotionally Significant Facts

Although you must include all of the legally significant facts, you do not need to include all of the emotionally significant facts. Although as a defensive move you might sometimes include an emotionally significant fact that is unfavorable, recharacterizing it or minimizing its significance, most of the time you will not. It is more common to include only those emotionally significant facts that favor your client.

The harder question is how to handle emotionally significant facts that are unfavorable to the other side. Should you sling mud, or should you take a higher road and omit any reference to those facts? The answer is that it depends: it depends on the fact, on the case, and on the attorney. If the case is strong and the fact's connection to the case is tenuous, most attorneys would not include the fact. If, however, the case is weak and the fact's connection is closer, many attorneys will include it, some using it as a sword, others using it much more subtly.

c. Background Facts

Background facts play a different role in persuasive writing than they do in objective writing. In an objective statement of facts, the writer includes only those facts that are needed for the story to make sense. However, in drafting a persuasive statement of facts, you want to do more. You want to use background facts to create a favorable context. *See* section 2.12.5a.

§ 2.12.4 Select an Organizational Scheme

After selecting the facts, the next step is to select an organizational scheme. Should the facts be presented chronologically, topically, or using an organizational scheme that combines the two?

Unlike an objective statement of facts in which the only selection criterion was logic, in writing a persuasive statement of facts there are three criteria: (1) you want to select a scheme that is logical, (2) you want to select a scheme that is consistent with the order in which you set out the arguments, and (3) you want to select a scheme that allows you to present the facts in a light favorable to your client.

In *United States v. Josephy*, logic dictates that Ms. Elder start with the facts relating to the seizure and not with the facts relating to the *Batson* challenge: the seizure occurred before the jury selection. In addition, starting with the facts relating to the search is consistent with the way in which Ms. Elder has decided to order the arguments: because the charges would be dismissed if the court concludes that the search was illegal, Ms. Elder has decided to discuss the search before she discusses the *Batson* challenge. Finally, starting with the facts that relate to the seizure allows Ms. Elder to present the facts in a light favorable to Mr. Josephy. Although in some ways the facts relating to the *Batson* objection are more compelling than the facts relating to the search, Ms. Elder decides that, on balance, it works best to start with the facts relating to the search. However, instead of starting with the tip, she decides to start with the seizure, which allows her to tell the story from her client's perspective.

In contrast, for the prosecutor, the best choice is to set the facts out in chronological order because this is logical and consistent with the order in which the prosecutor plans to discuss the issues. In addition, setting out the facts in chronological order allows the prosecutor to start with the facts that are most favorable to the government: the fact that Zachary Dillon called and told the police that Mr. Josephy was involved in selling drugs that had been brought into the United States from Canada.

§ 2.12.5 Present the Facts in the Light Most Favorable to the Client

Although the statement of facts must be accurate, it need not be objective. Therefore, as an advocate, you want to present the facts in the light most favorable to your client. In doing so, you can use the following strategies.

Strategies for Writing
a Persuasive Statement of Facts

a. Create a favorable context.
b. Tell the story from the client's point of view.

c. Emphasize the facts that support your theory of the case and de-emphasize those that do not.
   1. Airtime
   2. Detail
   3. Positions of emphasis
   4. Sentence and paragraph length
   5. Main and dependent clauses
   6. Active and passive voice
d. Choose words carefully.
e. Be subtly persuasive.

PRACTICE POINTER   Although the statement of the facts should be persuasive, do not misstate, mischaracterize, or overstate the facts. Because one of your greatest tools as an advocate is your professional reputation, do not do anything that might damage it or undermine your credibility.

---

a. Create a Favorable Context

The opening paragraph or paragraphs of your statement of facts are like the opening scenes in a movie. They create both a context and a "mood" for the story that you are about to tell and for the arguments that you want to make. Thus, think carefully about where you want to start the story and about the language that you use.

For instance, in the example problem set out in Chapter 1, Mr. Patterson's attorney wanted to start the story by creating a picture of Mr. Patterson and his activities on the day that the assault occurred. In doing so, the attorney hoped to present her client as a young and attentive husband who could not, and would not, have assaulted the victim, Ms. Martinez.

EXAMPLE 1   OPENING PARAGRAPHS OF THE DEFENDANT'S STATEMENT OF FACTS IN *PATTERSON*

At 7:30 on Monday morning, August 14, 2006, twenty-two-year-old Dean Patterson finished his shift as a security guard and walked to his apartment. After having breakfast with his wife, Patterson went to bed and slept until about 1:00 p.m. At about 2:30 p.m., Patterson's wife received a phone call asking her to work at the local hospital, where she is employed as a nurse. She got ready, and Patterson dropped her off at the hospital at about 3:10 p.m.

At about 3:30 p.m., Patterson called his wife to find how long she would have to work: they had plans to go to a movie that evening, and he wanted to know whether he should change those plans. At about 3:50 p.m., Patterson took a load of laundry to the apartment complex's laundry room. When he returned to his apartment, Patterson watched part of an old movie. At about 4:20, Patterson went back to the laundry room to put the clothes in the dryer.

In contrast, in *Patterson*, the State started its statement of facts where the story started for the victim. In the first paragraph of its statement of facts, the State described the assault and then the show-up and line-up.

EXAMPLE 2   **OPENING PARAGRAPH OF THE STATE'S STATEMENT OF FACTS IN *PATTERSON***

On Monday, August 14, 2006, Beatrice Martinez was assaulted with a deadly weapon. At a show-up held thirty to forty minutes after the attack, Martinez identified the defendant, Dean E. Patterson, as her assailant. Four days after the assault, Ms. Martinez picked Patterson out of a line-up, once again identifying him as her assailant.

For more on the statement of facts in *Patterson*, see section 1.6.3 in this book.

Although the differences are more subtle, context is equally important in *United States v. Josephy*. For example, in drafting the opening paragraph, Ms. Elder wants to present Mr. Josephy in a favorable light by creating the impression that Mr. Josephy was engaged in a lawful activity when two ATF agents pulled behind and in front of his car. The following examples show two different ways in which Ms. Elder can create this favorable context.

EXAMPLE 3   **ONE WAY OF STARTING THE STATEMENT OF FACTS IN THE APPELLANT'S BRIEF**

On the evening of June 24, 2007, Peter Jason Josephy checked into the Travel House Inn in Bellingham, Washington. (ER 44). When he checked in, Mr. Josephy filled out a registration form, which included a description and the license number of his blue Chevy Blazer. (ER 44).

Hotel guests were required to check out no later than 11:00 a.m. (ER 40). Shortly before 11:00 on the morning of June 25, Mr. Josephy paid his bill and checked out. (ER 22). After a brief conversation with an acquaintance, Oliver Preston, both men walked out of the hotel; the men parted ways at the front of the hotel. Mr. Josephy walked to his vehicle and got in. (ER 43).

Mr. Josephy started his engine, but he was unable to move. His vehicle was suddenly blocked from the front and from behind by ATF vehicles. (ER 44).

EXAMPLE 4   **ANOTHER WAY OF STARTING THE STATEMENT OF FACTS IN THE APPELLANT'S BRIEF**

At 10:45 a.m. on June 25, 2007, Peter Josephy left his room at the Travel House Inn in Bellingham, checked out, and, after talking to a friend for three or four minutes, walked to his car and got in. (ER 22, 43). As Mr. Josephy started his car, one Alcohol, Tobacco, and Firearms (ATF) agent pulled behind Mr. Josephy's car, and another ATF agent pulled in front, preventing Mr. Josephy from leaving the parking lot. (ER 44).

In contrast, the government wants to start its statement of the facts by portraying Mr. Josephy as a drug dealer. The following examples show two ways of creating this favorable context.

EXAMPLE 5   ONE WAY OF STARTING THE STATEMENT OF FACTS IN THE APPELLEE'S BRIEF

At about 9:30 a.m. on June 25, 2007, Zachary Dillon called 911 and reported that Peter Josephy was involved in selling drugs that had been brought into the United States from Canada. (ER 30). Two hours later, Alcohol, Tobacco, and Firearms (ATF) agents searched Mr. Josephy's vehicle and found four kilos of marijuana in the wheel well. (ER 49).

EXAMPLE 6   ANOTHER WAY OF STARTING THE STATEMENT OF FACTS IN THE APPELLEE'S BRIEF

At 9:30 a.m. on June 25, 2007, the Bellingham Police Department received a tip that Peter Josephy was involved in selling marijuana that had been brought into the United States from Canada. (ER 30). During the 911 call, which was recorded, the caller identified himself as Zachary Dillon. (ER 31). Although Mr. Dillon did not know where Josephy lived, he said that Josephy was currently at the Travel House Inn, a local motel. (ER 32).

> **PRACTICE POINTER**
>
> In the preceding *Patterson* examples, the authors did not include references to the record because, at the time that they drafted their briefs, there was no record. In contrast, in the *Josephy* examples, the authors did include references to the record because there was a record and the appellate rules require citations to that record.

b. Tell the Story from the Client's Point of View

One of the most powerful persuasive devices is point of view: as a general rule, you will want to present the facts from your client's point of view. You can do this by telling the story as your client would tell it and by using your client's name as the subject in most sentences. Look at the following examples. In the first example, Mr. Josephy's name is used as the subject in five of the seven sentences. In contrast, in the second example, Ms. Elder used Mr. Josephy as the subject in the first sentence but the ATF agents as the subjects in the second sentence. Although Ms. Elder wanted to emphasize that Mr. Josephy was engaged in lawful activities, she also wanted to emphasize that Mr. Josephy was the victim of what she will argue were the agents' unlawful acts. Thus, in the second sentence, she puts the agents in the subject slots of the sentence and Mr. Josephy in the object slot.

In the following examples, the subjects are in boldface type.

| EXAMPLE | **ONE WAY OF STARTING THE STATEMENT OF FACTS IN THE APPELLANT'S BRIEF** |

On the evening of June 24, 2007, **Peter Jason Josephy** checked into the Travel House Inn in Bellingham, Washington. (ER 44). When he checked in, **Mr. Josephy** filled out a registration form, which included a description and the license number of his blue Chevy Blazer. (ER 44).

Hotel guests were required to check out no later than 11:00 a.m. (ER 40). Shortly before 11:00 on the morning of June 25, **Mr. Josephy** paid his bill and checked out. After a brief conversation with an acquaintance, Oliver Preston, **both men** walked out of the hotel; **the men** parted ways at the front of the hotel. **Mr. Josephy** walked to his vehicle and got in. (ER 43).

Mr. Josephy started his engine, but he was unable to move. **His vehicle** was suddenly blocked from the front and from behind by ATF vehicles. (ER 44).

| EXAMPLE | **ANOTHER WAY OF STARTING THE STATEMENT OF FACTS IN THE APPELLANT'S BRIEF** |

At 10:45 a.m. on June 25, 2007, **Peter Josephy** left his room at the Travel House Inn in Bellingham, checked out, and, after talking to a friend for three or four minutes, walked to his car and got in. (ER 43). As Mr. Josephy started his car, **one Alcohol, Tobacco, and Firearms (ATF) agent** pulled behind Mr. Josephy's car, and **another ATF agent** pulled in front, preventing Mr. Josephy from leaving the parking lot. (ER 44).

Defense counsel in a criminal case usually tells the story from the client's point of view, but the government has more options: if there is a victim, the government can tell the story from the victim's point of view or, if there is not a victim, it can tell the story from the point of view of government agents. In addition, when the defendant did something egregious, the prosecutor can use the defendant as the actor. In Example 1, the prosecutor uses the informant as the subject in the first sentence and the ATF agents as the subjects in the second sentence. In Example 2, the prosecutor has written the first sentence using the passive voice: the Bellingham Police Department *received* a tip. By using the passive voice, the prosecutor is able to use the Police Department as the subject of the first sentence. The prosecutor then uses the "caller" and "he" as the subjects of the second and third sentences.

| EXAMPLE 1 | **ONE WAY OF STARTING THE STATEMENT OF FACTS IN THE APPELLEE'S BRIEF** |

At about 9:30 a.m. on June 25, 2007, **Zachary Dillon** called 911 and reported that Peter Josephy was involved in selling drugs that had been brought into the United States from Canada. Two hours later, **ATF agents** searched Mr. Josephy's vehicle and found four kilos of marijuana in the wheel well. (ER 49).

EXAMPLE 2   ANOTHER WAY OF STARTING THE STATEMENT
OF FACTS IN THE APPELLEE'S BRIEF

At 10:00 a.m. on June 25, 2007, **the Bellingham Police Department** received a tip that Peter Josephy was involved in selling marijuana that had been brought into the United States from Canada. (ER 30). During the 911 call, which was recorded, the **caller** identified himself as Zachary Dillon. (ER 31). Although Mr. Dillon did not know where Josephy lived, **he** said that Josephy was currently at the Travel House Inn, a local motel. (ER 32).

---

c. Emphasize Those Facts that Support Your Theory of the Case and De-emphasize Those that Do Not

In addition to presenting the facts from the client's point of view, good advocates emphasize those facts that support their theory of the case and de-emphasize those that do not. They do this by using one or more of the following techniques.

1. Airtime

Just as listeners remember best the songs that get the most radio airtime, readers remember best the facts that get the most words. Consequently, if you want the judges to remember a fact, give that fact as much airtime as possible.

For example, in *United States v. Josephy*, Ms. Elder wants to emphasize the facts that support her argument that the tip should be treated as an anonymous tip because the person called the 911 operator from a public pay telephone and, other than giving the operator a name, the person making the call did not provide the operator with information that the agents could use to locate the caller. The facts that Ms. Elder has emphasized by giving them airtime are in bold. In contrast, Ms. Elder wants to de-emphasize the fact that the caller told the 911 operator that Mr. Josephy was selling drugs that had been brought into the United States from Canada. Thus, Ms. Elder gives these facts, which are underlined, very little airtime.

EXAMPLE 1   EXCERPT FROM THE APPELLANT'S BRIEF

Agent Bhasin had gone to the Travel House Inn after **receiving a phone call from a 911 operator who reported that she had received a call from a public pay telephone located in the Bellis Fair Mall,** which is about a five-minute drive from the Travel House Inn. (ER 30, 34). <u>The informant claimed that a Mr. Josephy was at the Travel House Inn to sell drugs to a man named Oliver.</u> (ER 30). In addition, the informant told that 911 operator that, if the police wanted to catch Mr. Josephy, they should go the Travel House Inn soon because Mr. Josephy would be there for only another hour or two. (ER 32-33).

When asked to describe Mr. Josephy, the informant told the 911 operator that Mr. Josephy was a Native American with black hair in his mid to late twenties and that he was driving a blue Chevy Blazer. (ER 32). When asked about Oliver's last name, the informant said that he did not know Oliver's last name. When pushed for a description, the informant told the 911 operator that Oliver was about six feet tall, that he had brown hair and a beard, and that he was in his thirties. (ER 32).

The 911 operator then asked the informant for his name, address, and a phone number so that the police or ATF agents could recontact him. Although the informant told the 911 operator that his name was Zachary Dillon, he then became uncooperative and refused to give the 911 operator his address, his home telephone number, or a cell phone number. (ER 32, 35).

In contrast, the prosecutor wants to de-emphasize the fact that the 911 call came from a pay phone and that the caller did not provide the 911 operator with any information about himself other than his name and that Agent Bhasin was not able to locate anyone by the name of Zachary Dillon in the databases that he checked. Thus, the prosecutor gives these facts very little airtime. Instead, he gives airtime to the facts that support the government's position: that Mr. Dillon gave the operator his name and that he gave the 911 operator a description of both Mr. Josephy and Oliver and that call was made from a phone that is very close to the Travel House Inn. The facts that the prosecutor has emphasized are in bold and the facts that he has de-emphasized are underlined.

EXAMPLE 2 EXCERPT FROM THE APPELLEE'S BRIEF

During the 911 call, which was recorded, Mr. Dillon told the operator that Mr. Josephy was at the Travel House Inn to meet with, and deliver marijuana to, a man named Oliver. (ER 30-31). <u>Although Mr. Dillon declined to give the 911 operator his address or phone number,</u> **Mr. Dillon did tell the 911 operator that Mr. Josephy was a Native American, that Josephy had black hair, and that Josephy was in his mid to late twenties. (ER 32). Mr. Dillon also told the operator that Mr. Josephy owned, and was driving, a blue Chevy Blazer. (ER 32). Although Mr. Dillon did not know Oliver's last name, he described Oliver as being in his thirties, about six feet tall, and with brown hair and a beard. (ER 32). Finally, Mr. Dillon told the police not to wait too long because Mr. Josephy would be leaving the motel in the next hour or two. (ER 33).**

The 911 operator relayed the information from Mr. Dillon to Agent Bhasin, an ATF agent with more than ten years of service. (ER 4). <u>Not finding anyone by the name of Zachary Dillon in the ATF databases,</u> Agent Bhasin drove to the Travel House Inn in an unmarked car to determine whether there was a blue Chevy Blazer in the parking lot. (ER 35, 40). **When he arrived at the motel at approximately 10:15 a.m., Agent Bhasin located a blue Chevy Blazer in the parking lot; when he ran the license plates, he was told that the Blazer was registered to Peter Jason Josephy. (ER 42).**

2. Detail

Just as readers tend to remember best those facts that get the most airtime, they also tend to remember best those things that are described in detail.

Thus, one way to emphasize a favorable fact is to describe it in detail. Use concrete subjects, action verbs, adjectives, and adverbs to create vivid pictures. In contrast, if you want to de-emphasize a particular fact, use more general language. In the following examples, compare the ways in which the attorneys describe Ms. Whitefish's and Mr. Martin's statements during voir dire.

EXAMPLE 1 **EXCERPT FROM THE APPELLANT'S STATEMENT OF FACTS**

Later, the prosecutor asked if anyone had ever had negative experiences with law enforcement personnel. (ER 119). Ms. Whitefish, a Native American who was a junior majoring in history at Western Washington University, responded that each time she crossed the border she had been "pulled aside for additional questions." (ER 119). However, when the prosecutor asked Ms. Whitefish whether she was bothered by the fact that she had been pulled over for additional questions, she stated, "Not particularly. I am a college student, and all of us have had similar experiences. They seem to stop young people more . . . ." (ER 119).

Similarly, Mr. Martin, a white man with long hair, told the prosecutor that he had had a number of negative experiences with police officers. (ER 120). For example, Mr. Martin told the prosecutor that on one occasion a police officer had stopped him because one of his taillights was out but that the police had not stopped other individuals who had one of their taillights out. (ER 120). In addition, Mr. Martin told the prosecutor that on two occasions he had been given tickets for jaywalking when other individuals on the same street who had short hair jaywalked but did not get tickets. (ER 120). When the prosecutor asked whether he was bothered by the police officers' actions, Mr. Martin said, "You bet I am." (ER 121).

EXAMPLE 2 **EXCERPT FROM THE APPELLEE'S STATEMENT OF FACTS**

During voir dire, the prosecutor asked the members of the jury panel whether anyone had had a negative experience with a law enforcement officer. (ER 119). Juror No. 5, a young Native American, responded that she had negative experiences each time she crossed the border between the United States and Canada. (ER 119). Although Juror No. 5 stated that she was not bothered by her experiences at the border, she also stated that she had been pulled aside for additional questioning every time that she had crossed the border. (ER 119.)

In contrast, Juror No. 11, Mr. Martin, a white man in his forties with long hair, told the prosecutor that he had been stopped by the police on one occasion because he had a taillight out and on two other occasions because he was jaywalking. (ER 120). Although Mr. Martin said that he was bothered by the fact that he had been stopped by the police, he also said he felt that police officers tended to stop people with long hair more often than people with short hair. (ER 120).

Note that in her statement of facts, Ms. Elder goes into detail in describing Ms. Whitefish: Ms. Elder tells the court that Ms. Whitefish is a Native American, Ms. Elder refers to Ms. Whitefish by name and not by her jury number, and Ms. Elder tells the court that Ms. Whitefish is a junior majoring in history at Western Washington University. In contrast, the prosecutor refers to Ms. Whitefish by her jury number, Juror No. 5, and only tells the court that Juror No. 5 is a young Native American. Also note that Ms. Elder goes into very little detail in describing Ms. Whitefish's experiences at the border, and the prosecutor does just the opposite. Because Ms. Elder does not want to emphasize that Ms. Whitefish had negative experiences crossing the border, she is more general and concise about Ms. Whitefish's experiences at the border. In contrast, the prosecutor emphasizes these facts, specifically stating that Juror No. 5 had been pulled aside for additional questioning every time that she had crossed the border. Finally, note that although Ms. Elder goes into detail in describing Mr. Martin's negative experiences with the police, the prosecutor does not go into detail. Thus, although both Ms. Elder and the prosecutor have included all of the legally significant facts (for example, that Ms. Whitefish is a Native American and that Mr. Martin is white), when possible, they have described more favorable facts in more detail and less favorable facts in less detail.

3. Positions of Emphasis

Another technique that can be used to emphasize favorable facts is to place favorable facts in positions of emphasis. Because readers remember better those things that they read first and last, favorable facts should be placed at the beginning and end of the statement of facts, at the beginning and end of paragraphs, and at the beginning and end of sentences. Unfavorable facts should be "buried" in the middle: in the middle of the statement of facts, in the middle of a paragraph, or in the middle of a sentence.

In *United States v. Josephy*, the attorneys used the positions of emphasis to emphasize favorable facts. For instance, Ms. Elder puts some of the facts that favor her client in the first paragraph of her statement of facts. In addition, in constructing that opening paragraph, she puts the most favorable fact, that the ATF agents pulled behind and in front of Mr. Josephy's vehicle, preventing him from leaving, at the very end of the paragraph.

EXAMPLE 1   **EXAMPLE FROM THE APPELLANT'S BRIEF**

At 10:45 a.m. on June 25, 2007, Peter Josephy left his room at the Travel House Inn in Bellingham, Washington; checked out; and, after talking to a friend for three or four minutes, walked to his car and got in. (ER 22, 43). As Mr. Josephy started his car, Agent Bhasin, an Alcohol, Tobacco, and Firearms (ATF) agent, pulled behind Mr. Josephy's car, and another ATF agent, Agent O'Brien, pulled in front. **As a result, Mr. Josephy could not move his car. (ER 44).**

The prosecutor does the same thing. He puts some of the facts that favor the government in the opening paragraph of his statement of facts, and he puts the most favorable fact from that group of facts—that the police found four kilos of marijuana in the wheel well of Mr. Josephy's vehicle—in the last sentence.

EXAMPLE 2   **EXCERPT FROM THE APPELLEE'S BRIEF**

At about 9:30 a.m. on June 25, 2007, Zachary Dillon called 911 and reported that Peter Josephy was involved in selling drugs that had been brought into the United States from Canada. (ER 30). Two hours later, Alcohol, Tobacco, and Firearms (ATF) agents searched Mr. Josephy's vehicle and found four kilos of marijuana in the wheel well. (ER 49).

---

4. Sentence and Paragraph Length

Because readers tend to remember information placed in shorter sentences better than information placed in longer sentences, good advocates place favorable facts in shorter sentences. Similarly, because readers tend to remember information placed in short paragraphs better than information placed in longer paragraphs, when they can, good advocates place their most favorable facts in short paragraphs. In contrast, when they can, good advocates try to bury unfavorable facts in longer sentences and in longer paragraphs.

In the next example, Ms. Elder places a favorable fact, that the agents parked their vehicles in such a way that Mr. Josephy could not move his car, in a short sentence in a position of emphasis. The favorable fact is in bold.

EXAMPLE 1   **EXCERPT FROM APPELLANT'S BRIEF**

At 10:45 a.m. on June 25, 2007, Peter Josephy left his room at the Travel House Inn in Bellingham, Washington; checked out; and, after talking to a friend for three or four minutes, walked to his car and got in. (ER 22, 43). As Mr. Josephy started his car, Agent Bhasin, an Alcohol, Tobacco, and Firearms (ATF) agent, pulled behind Mr. Josephy's car, and another ATF agent, Agent O'Brien, pulled in front. **As a result, Mr. Josephy could not move his car.** (ER 44).

In contrast, in the following example, the prosecutor buried an unfavorable fact, that Mr. Dillon would not give the 911 operator his address or phone number, in a long sentence in the middle of a long paragraph. The unfavorable fact is underlined.

EXAMPLE 2   **EXCERPT FROM THE APPELLEE'S BRIEF**

During the 911 call, which was recorded, Mr. Dillon told the operator that Mr. Josephy was at the Travel House Inn to meet with, and deliver marijuana to, a man named Oliver. (ER 30-31). <u>Although Mr. Dillon declined to give the 911 operator his address or phone number</u>, Mr. Dillon did tell the 911 operator that Mr. Josephy was a Native American, that Josephy had black hair, and that Josephy was in his mid- to late twenties. (ER 32). Mr. Dillon also told the operator that Mr. Josephy owned, and was driving, a blue Chevy Blazer. (ER 32). Although Mr. Dillon did not know Oliver's last name, he described Oliver as in being his thirties, about six feet tall, and with brown hair and a beard. (ER 32). Finally, Mr. Dillon told the police not to wait too long because Mr. Josephy would be leaving the motel in the next hour or two. (ER 33).

5. Sentence Construction

Because information that is placed in a main, or independent clause, is more likely to be remembered than information that is placed in a dependent, or subordinate clause, try to put favorable facts in the main clause and unfavorable ones in the dependent clause. For example, in the next sample paragraph, Ms. Elder makes two points in the second sentence: (1) that the caller gave the 911 operator his name and (2) that the caller would not give the 911 operator his address or a telephone number. Because the fact that the caller gave the 911 operator his name is unfavorable, Ms. Elder puts that fact in a dependent clause. In contrast, because the facts that the caller would not give the 911 operator his address or his phone number are favorable facts, Ms. Elder sets out those facts in the main clause and gives them a fair amount of airtime. Note also how Ms. Elder buries the unfavorable fact in the middle of the paragraph and how she uses airtime and detail to emphasize the favorable facts. The unfavorable facts are underlined and the favorable facts are in bold.

EXAMPLE 1   **EXCERPT FROM THE APPELLANT'S BRIEF**

The 911 operator then asked the informant for his name, address, and a phone number so that the police or ATF agents could recontact him. <u>Although the informant told the 911 operator that his name was Zachary Dillon,</u> **he then became uncooperative and refused to give the 911 operator his address, his home telephone number, or a cell phone number.** (ER 32, 35).

If the prosecutor wanted to make the same two points, he would flip the order, putting the fact that the caller did not give the operator his address or phone number in the dependent clause and the fact that he did give the operator his name in the main clause. Also note that the prosecutor would not set out the unfavorable facts in any detail and that he would choose his words carefully. Once again, the unfavorable facts are underlined and the favorable fact is in bold.

EXAMPLE 2   **HOW THE APPELLEE WOULD PRESENT THE SAME FACTS**

<u>Although the caller did not give the 911 operator his address or phone number,</u> **he did give his name.** (ER 32).

PRACTICE
POINTER

Putting favorable facts in the main clause often allows you to take advantage of the positions of emphasis: the unfavorable fact is in a dependent clause in the middle of the paragraph, and the favorable fact is in the main clause at the end of the paragraph.

6. Active and Passive Voice

Good advocates use the active voice when they want to emphasize the actor and the passive voice when they want to draw the reader's attention away from who performed an action. For instance, in setting out the facts relating to the *Batson* challenge, Ms. Elder uses the active voice to describe the prosecutor's use of his peremptory challenges to strike the only Native Americans in the jury pool.

EXAMPLE 1   EXCERPT FROM THE APPELLANT'S BRIEF

At the end of voir dire, the government used two of its peremptory challenges to remove Mr. Williams and Ms. Whitefish.

If the prosecutor were to make the same point, he would use the passive rather than the active voice.

EXAMPLE 2   HOW THE PROSECUTOR MIGHT MAKE THE SAME POINT

Both Mr. Williams and Ms. Whitefish were excused.

In addition, more likely than not, the prosecutor would combine the use of the passive voice with another persuasive technique. For example, the prosecutor might put the fact that he used his peremptory challenges to excuse the only Native Americans in the jury pool in a dependent clause and the more favorable fact in the main clause. Note that in the following sentence the dependent clause is written using the passive voice, and the main clause is written using the active voice. The dependent clause, which uses the passive voice, is underlined, and the main clause, which uses the active voice, is in bold.

EXAMPLE 3   HOW THE PROSECUTOR MIGHT USE THE ACTIVE AND PASSIVE VOICE IN CONJUNCTION WITH THE MAIN AND DEPENDENT CLAUSES

<u>Although both Native Americans were excused</u>, **the prosecutor also excused a white juror who had similar commitments.**

d. Choose Words Carefully

Because words create powerful images, select your words carefully. In addition to selecting the word that conveys the right meaning, select the word that creates the right image. Look, for example, at words that Ms. Elder uses in the following paragraphs.

EXAMPLE 1   EXCERPT FROM THE APPELLANT'S BRIEF

Agent Bhasin had gone to the Travel House Inn after receiving a phone call from a 911 operator who reported that she had received a call from a public pay telephone located in the Bellis Fair Mall, which is about a five-minute drive from the Travel House Inn. (ER 30, 34). The informant claimed that a Mr. Josephy was at the Travel House Inn to sell drugs to a man named Oliver. (ER 30). In addition, the informant told the 911 operator that, if the police wanted to catch Mr. Josephy, they should go the Travel House Inn soon because Mr. Josephy would be there for only another hour or two. (ER 32-33).

Instead of using "claimed," which suggests that the caller might be lying, Ms. Elder could have used "stated," which is neutral, or "advised," "informed," "notified," or "reported," which suggest that the caller was a credible source telling the truth. Similarly, in the following paragraph, the prosecutor chooses his words carefully. For example, the prosecutor could have said that Mr. Dillon "refused" to give the operator his address or phone number, but instead the prosecutor uses the word "declined," which has a softer feel and a more positive connotation.

EXAMPLE 2   EXCERPT FROM THE APPELLEE'S BRIEF

During the 911 call, which was recorded, Mr. Dillon told the operator that Mr. Josephy was at the Travel House Inn to meet with, and deliver marijuana to, a man named Oliver. (ER 30-31). Although Mr. Dillon **declined** to give the 911 operator his address or phone number, Mr. Dillon did tell the 911 operator that Mr. Josephy was a Native American, that Josephy had black hair, and that Josephy was in his mid- to late twenties. (ER 32). Mr. Dillon also told the operator that Mr. Josephy owned, and was driving, a blue Chevy Blazer. (ER 32). Although Mr. Dillon did not know Oliver's last name, he described Oliver as being in his thirties, about six feet tall, and with brown hair and a beard. (ER 32). Finally, Mr. Dillon told the police not to wait too long because Mr. Josephy would be leaving the motel in the next hour or two. (ER 33).

P R A C T I C E   POINTER   If you are having trouble coming up with just the right word, use a thesaurus. Most popular word processing programs include an electronic thesaurus.

e. Be Subtly Persuasive

Most beginning attorneys make one of two mistakes. They either present the facts objectively or, in an attempt to be persuasive, they go over the line, including arguments in their statement of facts, setting out facts that are not supported by the record, or using "purple prose." *Just Writing, Second Edition,* at 159-161.

EXAMPLE   **EXCERPT FROM AN APPELLEE'S BRIEF WITH NOVICE MISTAKES**

> Based on this reliable tip, Agent Bhasin drove to the Travel House Inn, where he immediately located a blue Chevy Blazer in the parking lot. (ER 40, 42). Not surprisingly, when Agent Bhasin ran the plates, he discovered that the Blazer belonged to Peter Josephy. (ER 42). Expecting trouble, Agent Bhasin immediately called for backup. (ER 43).

In this example, the writer makes a number of serious mistakes. First, in the opening sentence, the writer sets out a legal conclusion: that the tip was reliable. Although the writer might want to include this statement in his argument, he should not set out legal conclusion or arguments in the statement of facts. Second, in drafting the second sentence, the writer sets out his own "take" on the facts when he says "not surprisingly." Finally, in the last sentence, the writer misrepresents the testimony. There is nothing in the record that indicates that Agent Bhasin called for backup because he was "expecting trouble."

For a checklist for critiquing the statement of facts, see section 1.6.4.

§ 2.13 Drafting the Summary of the Argument

The summary of the argument is what the title implies: a summary of the advocate's argument. Although some courts do not require a summary of the argument, the federal rules require "a summary of the argument, which must contain a succinct, clear, and accurate statement of the arguments made in the body of the brief, and which must not merely repeat the argument headings[.]" Fed. R. App. P. 28(a)(8).

However, even when the rules do not require a summary of the argument, consider including one. For those judges who read the entire brief, such a summary provides an overview of the arguments; for those judges who do not read everything, it sets out the key points.

You might want to write two drafts of your summary of the argument. By preparing a first draft before you write the argument section, you will force yourself to identify the most important points in your argument. If you truly understand your arguments, you should be able to set out each of them in a paragraph or two. If you can't, more thinking, charting, outlining, or writing is needed.

Preparing a second draft after you have written the argument section is equally useful. This version can serve as a check on your arguments: when read together, the opening sentences of your paragraphs or paragraph blocks should provide the judges with a summary of the argument. If they don't, it is the argument section itself, and not the summary, that needs work.

The most common problem attorneys have with the summary of the argument is length. They write too much. The summary of the argument should be no more than one or two pages long, with one or two paragraphs for each argument. Citations to authority should also be kept to a minimum. Although you might want to refer to key cases and statutes, the focus should be on the arguments, not the citations. Another common problem is that attorneys do not make clear the connections between their arguments. Use transitions to make clear when one argument is a continuation of another argument and when an argument is an alternative argument. For examples of summaries of the argument, see the sample briefs at the end of this chapter.

§ 2.14 Drafting the Argumentative Headings

Argumentative headings serve two functions in an appellate brief. They provide the court with an outline of the argument, and they help persuade.

§ 2.14.1 Use the Argumentative Headings to Outline the Argument for the Court

When properly drafted, the argumentative headings provide the court with an outline of the arguments. By reading the headings set out in the table of contents, the judges can see your assertions, your support for those assertions, and relationships between your various assertions and arguments.

Argumentative headings also serve several other purposes. They help the judges by dividing the argument into manageable sections. In addition, they help the writer. Because attorneys like Ms. Elder seldom have large blocks of time available for writing, the brief must usually be written in sections. By drafting the headings first, an attorney can write one section or subsection at a time, putting the pieces together at the end.

PRACTICE POINTER   Although you might write your argumentative headings before the related arguments, do not let the headings "lock you in" to an analytical approach. The content of the arguments should drive the organization, and thus, the focus of the headings. Be willing to revise the content or location of headings.

§ 2.14.2 Use the Argumentative Headings to Persuade

Good attorneys use argumentative headings in the same way good politicians use sound bites—to catch their reader's attention and to help their reader see the issue as they see it.

Most good argumentative headings have four characteristics: (1) they are framed as positive assertions, (2) they set out both the assertion and the support for that assertion, (3) they are specific, and (4) they are easy to read and understand. In addition, in a good argumentative heading, the writer uses the same persuasive techniques that he or she used in drafting the issue statements and statement of facts.

a. Write Headings as Positive Assertions

In general, a heading is easier to understand and more persuasive if it is in the form of a positive assertion. For example, instead of writing, "The district court did not act properly when it denied Mr. Josephy's *Batson* challenge," Ms. Elder would write, "The district court erred when it denied Mr. Josephy's *Batson* challenge." The following example sets out the appellant's main headings and subheadings. Note first that each heading contains an assertion. Second, note that although Ms. Elder begins each of the subheadings relating to the motion to suppress with the same assertion, she does not use this technique in the subheadings relating to the *Batson* issue. Although the technique works for the first set of headings, it does not work for the second set. Third, note that Ms. Elder uses dovetailing to make it clear how the subheadings are related to the main headings. For example, she ends her first main heading with the phrase "did not have a particularized objective suspicion that Mr. Josephy was engaged in criminal activity" and then uses that same phrase in the assertion that begins each of the subheadings. For more on dovetailing, see section 4.3.1 in *Just Writing, Second Edition*.

EXAMPLE 1   **ARGUMENTATIVE HEADINGS FROM THE APPELLANT'S BRIEF**

A. THE ATF AGENTS VIOLATED MR. JOSEPHY'S FOURTH AMENDMENT RIGHTS BECAUSE THEY DID NOT HAVE A PARTICULARIZED OBJECTIVE SUSPICION THAT MR. JOSEPHY WAS ENGAGED IN CRIMINAL ACTIVITY.

   1. The ATF agents did not have a particularized objective suspicion that Mr. Josephy was engaged in criminal activity because the tip came from an unknown informant: although the informant gave the 911 operator his name, he refused to give his address or phone number.

   2. The ATF agents did not have a particularized objective suspicion that Mr. Josephy was engaged in criminal activity because the tip included only general physical descriptions, it omitted any descrip-

tion of clothing, and the only action it predicted was that Mr. Josephy would be leaving a motel shortly before checkout time.

3. The ATF agents did not have a particularized objective suspicion that Mr. Josephy was engaged in criminal activity because the police corroborated only innocuous details, for example, Mr. Josephy's physical appearance, his vehicle, and his departure from a motel shortly before checkout time.

B. THE DISTRICT COURT ERRED IN DENYING MR. JOSEPHY'S *BATSON* CHALLENGE BECAUSE THE PROSECUTOR STRUCK THE ONLY TWO NATIVE AMERICANS IN THE JURY POOL, AND THE COURT'S ENTIRE RULING CONSISTED OF A SINGLE SENTENCE.

1. The reasons the prosecutor gave for striking the only two Native Americans in the jury pool were a pretext for discrimination because they were not supported by the record and the prosecutor did not excuse white jurors who had similar obligations and experiences.

2. In addition, the district court erred by not conducting the required sensitive inquiry and by not stating its reasoning on the record.

Likewise, the government sets out its positive assertions. The assertions are in bold.

EXAMPLE 2   **ARGUMENTATIVE HEADINGS FROM THE APPELLEE'S BRIEF**

A. **THE *TERRY* STOP WAS PERMISSIBLE** BECAUSE THE ATF AGENTS HAD A REASONABLE SUSPICION THAT MR. JOSEPHY WAS INVOLVED IN CRIMINAL ACTIVITY.

B. **THE DISTRICT COURT PROPERLY EXERCISED ITS DISCRETION** IN OVERRULING MR. JOSEPHY'S *BATSON* OBJECTION.

     1. **Mr. Josephy has not met his burden of proving** that the reasons that the prosecutor gave for the peremptory challenges were a pretext for purposeful discrimination.

     2. **The record establishes** that the district court conducted the required sensitive inquiry because the court ensured that both parties had the opportunity to respond at each of the three steps of the *Batson* analysis.

---

b. Provide Support for Your Assertions

By itself, though, an assertion is not persuasive. Therefore, in most instances, you will want to support your assertions. One way to provide this support is to add a "because" clause.

Assertion   +   because   +   support for assertion

For example, instead of just stating that the ATF agents violated Mr. Josephy's Fourth Amendment rights, the prosecutor should include the reason why. Similarly, instead of just saying that the *Terry* stop was permissible, the prosecutor needs to add the support for that assertion. In the following examples, the support for each of the assertions is set out in bold.

EXAMPLE 1   **APPELLANT'S ASSERTION FOLLOWED BY A "BECAUSE" CLAUSE**

A. THE ATF AGENTS VIOLATED MR. JOSEPHY'S FOURTH AMENDMENT RIGHTS BECAUSE **THEY DID NOT HAVE A PARTICULARIZED OBJECTIVE SUSPICION THAT MR. JOSEPHY WAS ENGAGED IN CRIMINAL ACTIVITY.**

1. The ATF agents did not have a particularized objective suspicion that Mr. Josephy was engaged in criminal activity because **the tip came from an unknown informant: although the informant gave the 911 operator his name, he refused to give his address or phone number.**

2. The ATF agents did not have a particularized objective suspicion that Mr. Josephy was engaged in criminal activity **because the tip included only general physical descriptions, it omitted any description of clothing, and the only action it predicted was that Mr. Josephy would be leaving a motel shortly before checkout time.**

3. The ATF agents did not have a particularized objective suspicion that Mr. Josephy was engaged in criminal activity because **the police corroborated only innocuous details, for example, Mr. Josephy's physical appearance, his vehicle, and his departure from a motel shortly before checkout time.**

You do not, however, always need to include a "because" clause. In some instances, it might work better to set out your assertion in the main clause and then the support for that assertion in the subheadings. In other instances, it might work better to save the support for the argument. For instance, in the following example, look at the second subheading. Because Ms. Elder thought that it was more important to emphasize that the argument was an alternative argument than to set out facts, she sets out her assertion but no "because" clause.

EXAMPLE 2   **HEADINGS FROM THE APPELLANT'S BRIEF**

B. THE DISTRICT COURT ERRED IN DENYING MR. JOSEPHY'S *BATSON* CHALLENGE BECAUSE THE PROSECUTOR STRUCK THE ONLY TWO NATIVE AMERICANS IN THE JURY POOL,

AND THE COURT'S ENTIRE RULING CONSISTED OF A SINGLE SENTENCE.

1. <u>The reasons the prosecutor gave for striking the only two Native Americans in the jury pool were a pretext for discrimination because they were not supported by the record and the prosecutor did not excuse white jurors who had similar obligations and experiences.</u>

2. <u>In addition, the district court erred by not conducting the required sensitive inquiry and by not stating its reasoning on the record.</u>

c. Make Sure that Your Headings Are Neither Too Specific nor Too General

As a general rule, make your headings case specific. Instead of writing statements that are so broad that they could apply to a number of different cases, write statements that talk specifically about the parties and facts in your case. Do not, however, be so specific that the headings are not broad enough to cover all of the points that you make in that section. Compare the following examples. The headings set out in Example 1 are too broad because they could apply equally to any number of cases. In contrast, the headings set out in Example 2 are too narrow because they cover only one of the government's two peremptory challenges.

EXAMPLE 1 **HEADINGS ARE TOO GENERAL**

THE TRIAL COURT ERRED.

THE TRIAL COURT PROPERLY OVERRULED THE DEFENDANT'S *BATSON* OBJECTION.

EXAMPLE 2 **HEADINGS ARE TOO SPECIFIC**

THE DISTRICT COURT ERRED WHEN IT DENIED THE DEFENDANT'S *BATSON* CHALLENGE BECAUSE THE PROSECUTOR DISMISSED A NATIVE AMERICAN JUROR WHO HAD HAD NEGATIVE EXPERIENCES WITH LAW ENFORCEMENT OFFICERS BUT NOT A WHITE JUROR WHO HAD SIMILAR EXPERIENCES.

THE DISTRICT COURT PROPERLY OVERRULED THE DEFENDANT'S *BATSON* OBJECTION BECAUSE THE GOVERNMENT EXCUSED BOTH A NATIVE AMERICAN JUROR AND A WHITE JUROR WHO HAD WORK COMMITMENTS.

d. Make Your Headings Readable

A heading that is not readable is not persuasive. For example, even though the following heading is in the proper form, it is not persuasive because it is so long that very few judges would read it.

EXAMPLE 1   **ARGUMENTATIVE HEADING THAT IS DIFFICULT TO READ**

A.   THE DISTRICT COURT ERRED IN DENYING MR. JOSEPHY'S *BATSON* CHALLENGE BECAUSE (1) THE PROSECUTOR EXCUSED A NATIVE AMERICAN JUROR WHO HAD HAD A NEGATIVE EXPERIENCE WITH LAW ENFORCEMENT OFFICERS BUT DID NOT EXCUSE A WHITE JUROR WHO HAD HAD SIMILAR NEGATIVE EXPERIENCES AND (2) THE PROSECUTOR EXCUSED A NATIVE AMERICAN JUROR WHO HAD A TRIBAL COUNCIL MEETING THE FOLLOWING WEEK BUT WHO WAS WILLING TO MISS THAT MEETING BUT DID NOT EXCUSE A WHITE JUROR WHO MIGHT HAVE TO GO OUT OF TOWN TO CARE FOR HIS MOTHER WHO HAD ONLY A 20 PERCENT CHANCE OF LIVING.

Thus, in drafting your headings, you need to balance two competing pieces of advice: advice about trying to make your headings fact specific and advice about keeping your headings short. Ideally your headings would be both fact specific and short, but sometimes you cannot write a fact-specific short heading, and you will have to choose between a longer fact-specific heading and a shorter more general heading. Compare the following two examples. In Example 1, Ms. Elder has chosen to write a longer heading that is fact specific. In contrast, in Example 2, the prosecutor has chosen to write a shorter heading that is more general.

EXAMPLE 1   **SUBHEADING FROM THE APPELLANT'S BRIEF THAT IS LONGER BUT MORE FACT SPECIFIC**

1.   The reasons the prosecutor gave for striking the only two Native Americans in the jury pool were a pretext for discrimination because they were not supported by the record and the prosecutor did not excuse white jurors who had similar obligations and experiences.

EXAMPLE 2   **SUBHEADING FROM THE APPELLEE'S BRIEF THAT IS SHORTER BUT MORE GENERAL**

1.   Mr. Josephy has not met his burden of proving that the reasons that the prosecutor gave for the peremptory challenges were a pretext for purposeful discrimination.

When you choose to write a longer heading, use sentence constructions that make the headings easier to read. Use parallel constructions (for more on parallel constructions see section 8.7 in *Just Writing, Second Edition*) and, when appropriate, repeat the words that highlight the parallel structure (for example, "that" or "because"). Finally, when appropriate, use commas, semicolons, and colons to divide the sentence into more manageable units of meaning. See Chapter 9 in *Just Writing, Second Edition.*

e. Use the Same Persuasive Techniques You Used in Drafting the Issue Statements and Statement of Facts

In drafting their argumentative headings, good advocates use many of the same persuasive techniques that they used in drafting their issue statements and statements of facts: when possible, they create a favorable context, they set out the facts from the client's point of view, they give more airtime to favorable facts than to unfavorable facts, they describe favorable facts in more detail than unfavorable facts, they take advantage of the positions of emphasis, and they choose words carefully. In Example 1, the writer has set out her assertion and her support for that assertion, but she has not emphasized the favorable facts. In contrast, in Example 2, the writer has emphasized the favorable facts: she has added the word "only"; she has used the phrase "*Batson* challenge" rather than "*Batson* objection"; she has used the harsher word, "struck," rather than the softer word, "excused"; and instead of saying that the district court did not go into detail in explaining its reasoning she states that the court's entire ruling consisted of a single sentence.

EXAMPLE 1   **APPELLANT HAS NOT USED PERSUASIVE TECHNIQUES**

A. THE DISTRICT COURT ERRED IN DENYING MR. JOSEPHY'S *BATSON* OBJECTION BECAUSE THE PROSECUTOR EXCUSED TWO NATIVE AMERICAN JURORS AND THE DISTRICT COURT DID NOT GO INTO DETAIL IN EXPLAINING ITS REASONING.

EXAMPLE 2   **APPELLANT HAS USED PERSUASIVE TECHNIQUES**

A. THE DISTRICT COURT ERRED IN DENYING MR. JOSEPHY'S *BATSON* CHALLENGE BECAUSE THE PROSECUTOR STRUCK THE ONLY TWO NATIVE AMERICANS IN THE JURY POOL, AND THE COURT'S ENTIRE RULING CONSISTED OF A SINGLE SENTENCE.

---

§ 2.14.3 Use the Conventional Formats for Headings

Although seldom set out in rules, in most jurisdictions there are conventions governing the number, type, and typeface for argumentative headings. For example, as we noted in section 1.8.4, convention dictates that you should have a main heading for each of your issue statements. Thus, if you have one issue, you should have one main heading; if you have two issues, two main headings; and so on. The issue sets out the question, and the heading gives your answer to that question.

In addition to main headings, you can also use subheadings and sub-subheadings and, rarely, sub-sub-subheadings. There are, however, some things to keep in mind if you use additional headings. First, if you include one subheading, you need to have at least two headings at that same level. As a consequence, if you find that you have only one subheading in a section, either delete that heading or add at least one additional heading. Second, although you are not required to put text between the main heading and the first subheading, it is usually a good idea to do so: use this space to set out the general rule and a roadmap for that section of your brief. Finally, keep in mind the typefaces that attorneys use for the various levels of headings. These typefaces provide the judges with signals about where they are in the argument.

See section 1.8.5 for a checklist for critiquing the argumentative headings.

§ 2.15 Drafting the Arguments

Although it is relatively easy to tell someone how to draft the statement of the case, the statement of facts, the issue statements, and the argumentative headings, it is very difficult to tell someone how to draft the arguments. Although experienced attorneys can offer newer attorneys some general advice, by necessity, that advice is just that, general advice. Because the law and facts of each case are different, the arguments are also different, and there is no foolproof recipe for how to draft a persuasive argument. The starting point is a mastery of the facts of your case, a solid understanding of the governing law, and the ability to write clearly and concisely, but by themselves, this mastery, understanding, and ability are not enough. Writing a persuasive brief also requires some things that are much harder to describe and impossible to teach: insight, creativity, and confidence. Thus, although this chapter can get you started, it cannot give you all of the answers. Instead we will remind you of the overriding question when it comes to any argument: is it persuasive? When in doubt, use that question as your touchstone for determining what is and is not an effective argument.

§ 2.15.1 Knowing What You Need, and Want, to Argue

One of the first steps is knowing what you need, and want, to argue. You cannot just throw out a number of assertions, rules, and cases and hope that the court will make sense of them for you.

As a consequence, before you begin to write, you need to determine what type of argument you are making. Are you arguing an issue of first impression, that is, are you asking the court to make new law by adopting a new rule or test, or are you arguing that the trial court improperly applied existing law? If you are arguing that the trial court improperly applied existing law, are you arguing that the trial court abused its discretion when it ruled on a motion or objection, or are you arguing that there is insufficient evidence to support the jury's verdict?

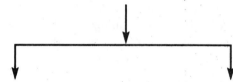

Are you asking the appellate court to apply an existing rule or test or to adopt a new rule or test?

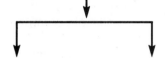

If you are asking the appellate court to apply an existing rule or test, is the standard of review *de novo* or something more deferential?

If the standard of review is *de novo,* you need to set out the rule or test and then walk the court through it, showing why each part is or is not met.

If the standard of review is more deferential, for example, abuse of discretion, you need to show the appellate court why the trial court did or did not abuse its discretion.

If you are asking the appellate court to adopt a new rule or test, you need to establish (1) that the appellate court is not bound by mandatory authority, (2) that the rule that you are advocating is a better rule than the rule your opponent is advocating, and (3) that under your rule, you win. In addition, in the alternative, you may want to argue that you are entitled to relief under the rule that your opponent is advocating.

§ 2.15.2 Selecting an Organizational Scheme

Once you have determined what type of argument you want to make, select the organizational scheme that will work best for that argument.

If you are arguing an issue of first impression, you will usually use a version of the blueprint set out in Example 1. You will start by establishing that there is no existing rule or test, then persuade the court that the rule or test you are proposing is "better" than the rule or test being proposed by your opponent, and end by applying your proposed rule or test to the facts of your case. In addition, sometimes you will argue in the alternative: even if the court adopts the rule or test being advocated by opposing counsel, you still win under that test.

EXAMPLE 1 **ORGANIZATIONAL SCHEME FOR ISSUES OF FIRST IMPRESSION**

A. MAIN HEADING
Introduction establishing that the issue is one of first impression
1. <u>Subheading setting out first assertion</u>
    • Paragraph setting out the rule that you want the court to adopt
    • Arguments relating to why the court should adopt your proposed rule rather than the rule being proposed by your opponent
    • Application of your proposed rule to the facts of your case
2. <u>Subheading setting out additional or alternative argument</u>
    • If appropriate, argue that even under the rule being proposed by your opponent your client wins

In contrast, if you are arguing that the trial court incorrectly applied the existing law, you have more options. For example, if your case involves an elements analysis or a multi-part test, you will usually want to include an introductory section in which you set out the general rules, that is, the standard of review and the applicable statutory language, the applicable regulations, the applicable court rule, or the applicable common law rule. However, once you begin your discussion of the elements or the multi-part test, you can start with an assertion, a statement of the rule, the facts of your case, or even an analogous case. The following examples show some of the options for an issue involving an elements analysis.

EXAMPLE 1 **ELEMENTS ANALYSIS IN WHICH THE AUTHOR BEGINS THE DISCUSSION OF EACH ELEMENT WITH AN ASSERTION**

A. ARGUMENTATIVE HEADING
Paragraph setting out a favorable statement of the standard of review, the applicable statutory language, regulation, court rule, or common law rule and listing or identifying the elements
1. <u>Argumentative heading for first element</u>
    • Assertion
    • Statement of the rule
    • Descriptions of analogous cases
    • Your argument, including your response to your opponent's arguments
    • Conclusion
2. <u>Argumentative heading for second element</u>
    • Assertion
    • Statement of the rule
    • Descriptions of analogous cases
    • Your argument, including your response to your opponent's arguments

      • Conclusion
  3. <u>Argumentative heading for third element</u>
      • Assertion
      • Statement of the rule
      • Descriptions of analogous cases
      • Your argument, including your response to your opponent's arguments
      • Conclusion

EXAMPLE 2 **ELEMENTS ANALYSIS IN WHICH THE AUTHOR BEGINS THE DISCUSSION WITH A FAVORABLE STATEMENT OF THE RULE**

A. ARGUMENTATIVE HEADING

Paragraph setting out a favorable statement of the standard of review and the applicable statutory language, regulation, court rule, or common law rule and listing or identifying the elements

  1. <u>Argumentative heading for first element</u>
      • Statement of the rule
      • Descriptions of analogous cases
      • Your argument, including your response to your opponent's arguments
      • Conclusion
  2. <u>Argumentative heading for second element</u>
      • Statement of the rule
      • Descriptions of analogous cases
      • Your argument, including your response to your opponent's arguments
      • Conclusion
  3. <u>Argumentative heading for third element</u>
      • Statement of the rule
      • Descriptions of analogous cases
      • Your argument, including your response to your opponent's arguments
      • Conclusion

EXAMPLE 3 **ELEMENTS ANALYSIS IN WHICH THE AUTHOR STARTS THE DISCUSSION WITH A FAVORABLE STATEMENT OF THE FACTS**

A. ARGUMENTATIVE HEADING

Paragraph setting out a favorable statement of the standard of review and the applicable statutory language, regulation, court rule, or common law rule and listing or identifying the elements

  1. <u>Argumentative heading for first element</u>
      • Statement of key facts
      • Statement of the rule

- Descriptions of analogous cases
- Your argument, including your response to your opponent's arguments
- Conclusion

2. <u>Argumentative heading for second element</u>
   - Statement of key facts
   - Statement of the rule
   - Descriptions of analogous cases
   - Your argument, including your response to your opponent's arguments
   - Conclusion

3. <u>Argumentative heading for third element</u>
   - Statement of key facts
   - Statement of the rule
   - Descriptions of analogous cases
   - Your argument, including your response to your opponent's arguments
   - Conclusion

EXAMPLE 4   **ELEMENTS ANALYSIS IN WHICH THE AUTHOR STARTS THE DISCUSSION WITH A FAVORABLE STATEMENT OF THE ANALOGOUS CASES**

A. ARGUMENTATIVE HEADING

Paragraph setting out a favorable statement of the standard of review and the applicable statutory language, regulation, court rule, or common law rule and listing or identifying the elements

1. <u>Argumentative heading for first element</u>
   - Description of the analogous cases
   - Statement of the rule
   - Your argument, including the application of the law to your facts and your response to your opponent's arguments
   - Conclusion

2. <u>Argumentative heading for second element</u>
   - Description of the analogous cases
   - Statement of the rule
   - Your argument, including an application of the law to your facts and your response to your opponent's arguments
   - Conclusion

3. <u>Argumentative heading for third element</u>
   - Description of the analogous cases
   - Statement of the rule
   - Your argument, including your response to your opponent's arguments
   - Conclusion

In selecting one of the these organizational schemes, keep the following in mind. First, you do not need to use the same organizational scheme for each element. For instance, it might work best to start your discussion of one element with an assertion, your discussion of another element with the facts, and your discussion of yet another element with a rule. Second, in selecting an organizational scheme for a particular element, make sure that you pick one that will work not only for you but also for the judges who will be reading your brief. Thus, select an organizational scheme that highlights your theory of the case and allows you to set out your points clearly and concisely.

Third, make sure that you don't get into a rut. Although there is always a temptation to use the organizational scheme with which you are most comfortable, as an advocate this is a temptation you need to resist. If you are to persuade the court, you need to pick the scheme that allows you to emphasize the strongest parts of your argument. For example, if the rule strongly favors your client, you will usually want to select an organizational scheme that allows you to put the rule at the beginning, in the position of emphasis. Conversely, if the facts are very favorable, you will usually want to use an organizational scheme that allows you to put them at the beginning. At other times, when there are a number of steps to the analysis, it works best to select an organizational scheme that allows you to begin your argument with your assertions, which can then act as a roadmap for the rest of the argument. Fourth, keep in mind that you are not bound by your opponent's organizational scheme. Instead, use the organizational scheme that allows you to make your points effectively.

Finally, make sure that you do not make one of the most common errors that attorneys make in writing briefs: setting out one case and then comparing the facts in that case to the facts in your case, setting out a second case and then comparing the facts in that second case to the facts in your case, and so on. Instead of organizing your arguments around individual cases, organize them around assertions.

EXAMPLE 5 POOR WAY OF ORGANIZING THE ARGUMENTS

A. Argumentative Heading
    Statement of rule
        Description of Case A
            Comparison of the facts in your case to the facts in Case A
        Description of Case B
            Comparison of the same facts in your case to the facts in Case B
        Description of Case C
            Comparison of the same facts in your case to the facts in Case C
        Description of Case D
            Comparison of the same facts in your case to the facts in Case D
    Conclusion

EXAMPLE 6   **BETTER WAY OF ORGANIZING THE ARGUMENTS**

   A. Argumentative Heading
      Statement of rule
      Assertion 1
      Principle
         Description of Case A
         Description of Case B
            Argument using Case A and Case B
      Assertion 2
      Principle
         Description of Case C
         Description of Case D
            Argument using Case C and Case D
      Conclusion

---

§ 2.15.3 Presenting the Rules, Descriptions of Analogous Cases, and Arguments in the Light Most Favorable to Your Client

Although the organizational schemes for the argument section in a brief are similar to the organizational schemes for the discussion section in an objective memorandum, the method of presentation is different. In an objective memorandum you present the rules, cases, and arguments as objectively as possible; in a brief you present them persuasively.

a. Presenting the Rules

Good advocacy begins with a favorable statement of the rule. Although you do not want to misstate a rule, quote a rule out of context, or mislead a court, you do want to present the rule in such a way that it favors your client. There are a number of ways in which you can do this. You can present the rule in a favorable context, you can state the rule broadly or narrowly, you can state the rule so that it suggests the conclusion you want the court to reach, and you can emphasize who has the burden of proof.

The following example sets out an objective statement of a rule.

EXAMPLE 1   **OBJECTIVE STATEMENT OF THE RULE**

To determine if a *Batson* violation has occurred, the courts engage in a three-step analysis. First, the defendant must make out a prima facie case "by showing that the totality of the relevant facts gives rise to an inference of discriminatory purpose." *Batson v. Kentucky*, 476 U.S. 79, 93-94 (citing *Washington v. Davis*, 426 U.S. 229, 239-42 (1976)). Second, if the defendant has made out a prima facie case, the "burden shifts to the Government to explain adequately the racial exclusion" by offering permissible race-neutral justifications for the strikes. *Batson*, 476 U.S. at 93-94. Third, "[i]f a race-neutral explanation is tendered, the trial court must then decide . . . whether the opponent of the strike has proved purposeful racial discrimination." *Johnson v. California*, 125 U.S. 2410, 2416 (2007).

In the next example, Ms. Elder has rewritten the objective statement of the rule so that the rule is presented in way that highlights her theory of the case and that is favorable to her client. Instead of beginning with the rule itself, she begins by creating a favorable context: in the first paragraph Ms. Elder reminds the Court that the United States Supreme Court has "consistently and repeatedly . . . reaffirmed that racial discrimination by the State in jury selection offends the Equal Protection Clause." Then, in setting out the three-step test, Ms. Elder sets out the rules so that they suggest the conclusions that Ms. Elder wants the court to reach. For example, in setting out the test, Ms. Elder de-emphasizes the defendant's burden of proof and emphasizes the government's burden: "the defendant need only establish a prima facie case of purposeful discrimination," "the burden shifts to the government," and "the government must provide a race-neutral reason . . . ." In addition, Ms. Elder uses language that suggests that Mr. Josephy will be able to meet his burden: "once the defendant establishes a prima facie case." Finally, Ms. Elder sets up her "sensitive analysis" argument by using that language in the rule section.

EXAMPLE 2 **EXCERPT FROM THE APPELLANT'S BRIEF WITH PERSUASIVE PRESENTATION OF THE RULES**

For more than a century, the United States Supreme Court has "consistently and repeatedly . . . reaffirmed that racial discrimination by the State in jury selection offends the Equal Protection Clause." *Miller-El v. Dretke*, 125 U.S. 2317, 2324 (2005) (quoting *Georgia v. McCollum*, 505 U.S. 42 (1992)); *see also* U.S. Const. amend. XIV. Racial discrimination in jury selection denies defendants their right to a jury trial, denies jurors the right to participate in public life, and undermines public confidence in the fairness of our justice system. *Batson v. Kentucky*, 476 U.S. 79, 86-87 (1986); *Williams v. Runnels*, 432 F.3d 1102, 1108 (9th Cir. 2006). Therefore, the "Constitution forbids striking even a single prospective juror for a discriminatory purpose." *United States v. Vasquez-Lopez*, 22 F.3d 900, 902 (9th Cir. 1992).

In *Batson*, the Court developed a three-step test to uncover discrimination masked by peremptory challenges. 476 U.S. at 96-97. Under the first step of the test, the defendant need only establish a prima facie case of purposeful discrimination by showing that the prosecutor has struck a member of a cognizable class and that the circumstances raise an inference of discrimination. *Id.* at 96. Once the defendant establishes a prima facie case, the burden shifts to the government: the government must provide a race-neutral explanation for striking a member of a cognizable class. *Id.* at 97. If the government does meet its burden, the court must do a sensitive analysis to determine whether the government has engaged in purposeful discrimination. *See Johnson v. California*, 545 U.S. 162, 169 (2005).

Similarly, the prosecutor has rewritten the neutral statement of the rule so that the rules are presented in a light that is more favorable to the government's position. In the following example, the prosecutor starts his statement of the rule by creating a favorable context: he reminds the Court that peremptory challenges are an important tool available to both prosecutors and defense counsel. In the second sentence, the prosecutor de-emphasizes the United States Supreme Court's statements about the difficulty of balancing the need to protect constitutional rights with the proper use of peremptory challenges by placing that point in a dependent clause in the middle of a relatively long paragraph. The prosecutor then ends the paragraph with a favorable point: that the United States Supreme Court has not indicated a willingness to deprive parties of their right to use peremptory challenges or to change the *Batson* test.

EXAMPLE 3   EXCERPT FROM THE APPELLEE'S BRIEF WITH PERSUASIVE PRESENTATION OF THE RULES

Peremptory challenges are an important trial tool that permits both parties' counsel to use their professional judgment and educated hunches about individual jurors to select a fair and impartial jury. *United States v. Bauer*, 84 F.3d 1549, 1555 (9th Cir. 1996). While the Supreme Court has acknowledged difficulties in balancing the need to protect constitutional rights with the proper use of peremptory challenges, the Court has not indicated a willingness to deprive the parties of their right to use peremptory challenges. *See Miller-El v. Dretke*, 545 U.S. 231, 239-40 (2005). Indeed, Justice Breyer's concurrence, in which he posited that the Court should reconsider the *Batson* test and the peremptory system as a whole, failed to garner a single co-signer. *Id.* at 266-67 (Breyer, J. concurring).

Thus, the courts continue to apply the three-step test set out in *Batson*. *Batson*, 476 U.S. at 89, 96-98. Under the test, a defendant's rights are not violated unless (1) the defendant establishes a prima facie case of purposeful discrimination in the government's use of peremptory challenges by showing that the challenged juror is a member of a cognizable class and that the circumstances raise an inference of discrimination; and (2) the government fails to meet its burden to provide a race-neutral explanation for its strike; or (3) the government offers a race-neutral reason, but the defendant meets his burden of showing that a review of all relevant circumstances shows purposeful discrimination. *See Johnson v. California*, 545 U.S. 162, 169 (2005); *Batson*, 746 U.S. at 89, 96-98.

For additional examples, see section 1.9.3.

b. Presenting the Cases

In drafting your brief, you will use cases in two ways: (1) as citations for rules, for example, a citation for a common law rule or rules that the courts have created in interpreting statutes, regulations, or court rules; and (2) as illustrations of how the courts have applied statutes, regulations, court rules, or common law rules in cases that are factually analogous to your case. What you do not want to do is to set out case descriptions just to set out case descriptions. Therefore, before you include a case description in your brief, ask yourself the following questions:

- Does the case illustrate how the courts have applied a statute, regulation, court rule, or common law rule in a case that is factually analogous to your case?
- Does the case or a group of cases illustrate how a particular rule has developed or is developing?
- Do you need to distinguish the case because the other side has relied on it or is likely to rely on it?
- As an officer of the court, are you obligated to bring the case to the court's attention?

Unless you have answered "yes" to one or more of these questions, do not include the case description in your brief.

PRACTICE POINTER   Remember that you can use a case as authority for a rule without setting out its facts, holdings, and rationale.

When you do include descriptions of analogous cases, be clear about why you have included those descriptions. One way to do this is to set out the principle that you are using the case or cases to illustrate and then the case descriptions. The following example illustrates this type of "principle-based" analysis, that is, analysis in which the cases are used to illustrate how the courts have applied a rule or principle.

EXAMPLE 1   **EXCERPT FROM APPELLANT'S BRIEF DEMONSTRATING PRINCIPLE-BASED ANALYSIS**

2. <u>The ATF agents did not have a particularized objective suspicion that Mr. Josephy was engaged in criminal activity because the tip included only general physical descriptions, it omitted any description of clothing, and the only action it predicted was that Mr. Josephy would be leaving a motel shortly before checkout time.</u>   Subheading

A tip from an unknown informant that does no more than describe an individual's readily observable location and appearance does not have sufficient indicia of reliability to support a stop. *Florida v. J.L.*, 529 U.S. 266, 272 (2000). Although such a tip might help the police identify the person whom the informant means to accuse, such a tip does not establish that the informant has knowledge of concealed criminal activity. *Id.* at 272.   Rules

In the cases in which the courts have held that the tip lacked sufficient indicia of reliability, the tip lacked predictive information and included only a general description of the defendant   Principle that Ms. Elder has drawn from the cases in which the and his location, and the informant did not explain how he had acquired the information. *See, e.g., Florida v. J.L.*, 529 U.S. at 272. For instance, in *J.L.*, an anonymous caller reported to police that "a young black male standing at a particular bus stop and wearing a plaid shirt was carrying a gun." *Id.* at 269. In concluding that this tip was not sufficient to establish a reasonable suspicion of criminal activity, the Court said that "[t]he anonymous call concerning J.L. provided no predictive information and therefore left the police without means to test the informant's knowledge or credibility." *Id.* at 270. The Court went on to say that the fact that the allegation about the gun turned out to be true did not establish a reasonable basis for suspecting J.L. of engaging in unlawful conduct:

> The reasonableness of official suspicion must be measured by what the officers knew before they conducted their search. All the police had to go on in this case was the bare report of an unknown, unaccountable informant who neither explained how he knew about the gun nor supplied any basis for believing he had inside information about J.L.

Id. at 271.

In contrast, in most of the cases in which the courts have held that the tips had sufficient indicia of reliability to support a *Terry* stop, the callers were reporting what they had recently seen or experienced, *see, e.g., United States v. Terry-Crespo*, 356 F.3d 1170, 1172 (9th Cir. 2004), or the callers provided the police with not only details about the defendant and his or her current location but also information about what the defendant was about to do, *see, e.g., United States v. Fernandez-Castillo*, 324 F.3d 1114, 1119 (9th Cir. 2003). For example, in *Terry-Crespo*, the court held that a 911 call contained sufficient indicia of reliability for four reasons: (1) the call was not anonymous because the caller provided the 911 operator with his name and the call was recorded; (2) the caller was the victim of a crime, and the police must be able to take seriously, and respond promptly to, emergency 911 calls; (3) the caller jeopardized any anonymity he might have had by calling 911 and providing his name to an operator during a recorded call; and (4) the caller was giving first-hand information about an event that had just occurred. *Terry-Crespo* 356 F.3d at 1172-77. Similarly, in *Fernandez-Castillo*, the court held that a tip had sufficient reliability because it came from a Montana Department of Transportation (MDOT) employee and there are relatively few MDOT employees; the MDOT employee who reported the erratic driving not only provided the dispatcher with the make and model of the car but also told the dispatcher that the car

Sidebar annotations (right margin):

courts have held the tips lacked sufficient indicia of reliability

Description of case that illustrates the principle and illustrates the types of cases in which the courts have held that the tips lacked sufficient indicia of reliability

Principle that Ms. Elder has drawn from the cases in which the courts have held that the tips had sufficient indicia of reliability followed by descriptions of cases that illustrate that principle had North Dakota license plates; the MDOT employee made the report almost immediately after he observed the defendant driving erratically; and the report contained predictive information: that the car was driving eastbound near milepost 116. *Fernandez-Castillo*, 324 F. 3d at 1119.

Although most of the time you will want to start your case description or descriptions by setting out the principle that you are using the case or cases to illustrate, there are times when it works to start with a citation to the case. For example, in the following excerpt, which is taken from the appellee's brief, the prosecutor starts the paragraph with a cite to *Alabama v. White*. In this instance, starting with a citation to a case is effective because it allows the prosecutor to emphasize that *Alabama v. White* is a United States Supreme Court case. When you use this technique, it usually works best to set out the court's holding in the topic sentence.

EXAMPLE 2 EXCERPT FROM APPELLEE'S BRIEF IN WHICH THE PROSECUTOR HAS STARTED A PARAGRAPH WITH A CITATION TO A CASE

Similarly, in *Alabama v. White*, 496 U.S. 325, 330 (1990), the United States Supreme Court held that the police had a reasonable suspicion that the defendant, White, was engaged in criminal activity. In *White*, an anonymous caller phoned 911 and told the operator that Vanessa White would be leaving the Lynnwood Terrace Apartments at a particular time in a brown Plymouth station wagon with a broken taillight to go to Dobey's Motel. *Id.* at 327. In addition, the caller told the 911 operator that White would have about "an ounce of cocaine inside a brown attaché case." *Id.* Although the two police officers who went to the apartment complex saw White get into a brown Plymouth station wagon with a broken taillight, they did not see anything in White's hands. *Id.* Moreover, although White appeared to be driving to Dobey's Motel, the officers had a patrol unit stop the vehicle before it reached the motel. *Id.* The Court held that the officers had a reasonable suspicion despite failing to verify White's predicted destination. *Id.* at 330.

Another way to make it clear why you have included a particular case description is to state explicitly that the facts in the analogous case are similar to the facts in your case or to say that facts in the analogous case can be distinguished from the facts in your case. Example 3 shows how Ms. Elder sets up a case description by stating that the case be distinguished. In reading this example, also note the order in which Ms. Elder sets out information. Instead of putting the description of the analogous case between the rules and the arguments, Ms. Elder sets out the rules, her arguments based on those rules, and then the description of the case, which she then distinguishes.

| EXAMPLE 3 | **EXCERPT FROM APPELLANT'S BRIEF DEMONSTRATING DISTINGUISHING A CASE** |

1. <u>The ATF agents did not have a particularized objective suspicion that Mr. Josephy was engaged in criminal activity because the tip came from an unknown informant: although the informant gave the 911 operator his name, he refused to give his address or phone number.</u>   Subheading

Where an informant declines to be identified, there is a risk the tip has been fabricated, undercutting its reliability. *Florida v. J.L.*, 529 U.S. 266, 269-70, 272 (2000). The unknown informant's reputation cannot be accessed, nor can the informant be held responsible for a false accusation. *Id.* This possibility that the informant might be lying outweighs the value of the information provided unless there are other factors that establish that the informant is reliable, for example, the informant provides law enforcement officers with information about the suspect's future actions, which law enforcement officers then independently verify. *United States v. Morales*, 253 F.3d 1070, 1075 (9th Cir. 2001).   Rules

In *United States v. Josephy*, the Court should treat the tip as a tip from an unknown informant. Although the informant gave the 911 operator a name, "Zachary Dillon," he called from a public pay phone in a large mall, and he refused to give the 911 operator his address or phone number. (ER 32, 35). In addition, when Agent Bhasin tried to locate an individual by the name of Zachary Dillon in his databases, he was not able to find anyone by that name in the greater Bellingham area. (ER 42). Consequently, neither Agent Bhasin nor any other law enforcement officer was able to contact Zachary Dillon to determine how he obtained the information that he gave to the 911 operator or to hold him accountable if the statements that he made turned out to be false.   Argument

Thus, the facts in this case can be distinguished from the facts in *United States v. Terry-Crespo*, 356 F.3d 1170, 1172 (9th Cir. 2004), a case in which the court held that information provided by an individual who had called 911 to report that the defendant had threatened him with a firearm was sufficient to support a *Terry* stop even though the police were not able to locate anyone by the caller's name in their databases. Unlike the caller in *Terry-Crespo*, who was the victim of a crime, in this case the informant, "Dillon," was not the victim of a crime. In addition, unlike the caller in *Terry-Crespo*, who made the call from the scene of the crime, in this case, "Dillon" made the call from a mall five minutes from the motel where the drug buy was allegedly occurring. Finally, in *Terry-Crespo* the caller did not give the 911 operator his phone number because he did not know the number of the   Argument distinguishing a case cell phone that he had borrowed to make the emergency call, but in this case "Dillon" refused to give the operator his address, home phone number, or a cell phone number. Consequently, in *Terry-Crespo* the facts supported the court's conclusion that the caller was not trying to hide his identity, but in this case the facts suggest just the opposite.

Thus, because "Dillon" appears to have taken steps to hide his identity, this Court should treat his tip as a tip from an unknown informant. However, even if this Court does not treat the tip as coming from an unknown informant, the tip is not reliable because it lacks sufficient indicia of reliability.

     Conclusion

Just as there are a number of techniques that you can use to present a rule in a light favorable to your client, there are also a number of techniques you can use to present a case in a light favorable to your client. You can set out the court's holding more broadly in cases that support your client's position and more narrowly in cases that support the other side's position; you can emphasize or de-emphasize particular facts or rules through the use of airtime, detail, the positions of emphasis, sentence length, and sentence construction; and you can choose words not only for their denotation but also for their connotation.

For instance, in the following example, the prosecutor uses detail, the positions of emphasis, and word choices to set out his description of *United States v. Terry-Crespo* in a light favorable to the government.

EXAMPLE 4 **EXCERPT FROM THE APPELLEE'S BRIEF SHOWING FAVORABLE PRESENTATION OF A CASE**

In determining whether a *Terry* stop was permissible, the courts do a de novo review, looking at the totality of the circumstances and considering all relevant factors, including those factors that "in a different context, might be entirely innocuous." *Florida v. J.L.*, 529 U.S. at 277-78; *accord United States v. Terry-Crespo*, 356 F.3d 1170, 1172 (9th Cir. 2004). For example, in *Terry-Crespo*, this Court held that the informant's preliminary phone call was, by itself, sufficient to establish a reasonable suspicion that the defendant, Terry-Crespo, was engaged in criminal activity. *Id.* at 1172. In doing so, this Court rejected Terry-Crespo's argument that the informant, Mr. Domingis, should be treated as an anonymous informant because he was not able to provide the 911 operator with the number of the phone from which he placed the call; he changed the subject when the operator asked him to provide another number; and,

The prosecutor begins the paragraph by setting out the rule that he is using *Terry-Crespo* to illustrate.

The prosecutor uses the active voice and the phrase "this Court" to emphasize that *Terry-Crespo* is a Ninth Circuit case. In addition, by using the phrase "this Court rejected Terry-Crespo's argument" the prosecutor suggests that the court should do the same thing in this case.

when asked for his location, he gave the operator a nonexistent intersection. *Id.* at 1174-75. As this Court stated in its opinion,

> [d]uring the course of the 911 call, the operator asked Mr. Domingis for his telephone number. Mr. Domingis explained that he did not know the return number because he was calling from someone else's cellular telephone. When the operator asked if there was another number where she could reach him, he did not answer her question but returned to discussing the subject of the suspect's location. The operator asked Mr. Domingis for his location. Initially, he responded by providing a nonexistent intersection on Portland's grid system and then stammeringly told the operator that "I don't want . . . I don't want . . . I don't want . . . ." Although not certain, it appears that Mr. Domingis did not want police contact.

Id. at 1172.

The Court then went on to note that although the police tried to locate Mr. Domingis in a number of different databases, including the Yahoo! Databases, they were not able to locate anyone by that name. *Id.* However, the Court concluded that the tip had sufficient indicia of reliability because Mr. Domingis was reporting that he had just been the victim of a crime and because Mr. Domingis risked any anonymity that he might have enjoyed by giving the 911 operator his name during a recorded call. *Id.* at 1174-76. As the Court stated, "Merely calling 911 and having a recorded telephone conversation risks the possibility that the police could trace the call or identify Mr. Domingis by his voice." *Id.* at 1176. Thus, even though the police did not independently verify any of the information contained in the tip, this Court held that, under the totality of the circumstances, the tip was sufficient to support a finding that Terry-Crespo was engaged in criminal activity.

By setting out the facts in detail and using a quotation, the prosecutor emphasizes the facts in *Terry-Crespo.*

Instead of putting the fact that the police tried to locate Mr. Domingis in a number of different databases in the same paragraph as the quote, the prosecutor starts a new paragraph, which allows him to emphasize this fact by putting it in a position of emphasis.

The prosecutor buries an unfavorable fact, that Mr. Domingis was the victim of a crime, in the middle of the paragraph.

By putting the dependent clause at the end of the sentence rather than at the beginning, the prosecutor is able to put a favorable fact, that the police did not independently verify any of the information in the tip, in a position of emphasis.

Although you will want to include full descriptions of the most important cases, avoid the temptation to describe all or even most of the cases that you found while researching the issue. By being selective, you will keep your brief shorter, something that will please almost every judge, and your preparation for oral argument will be easier. (Remember, for every case you cite, you need to know that case, inside and out, for oral argument.) When it is important to cite more than a few cases, set out the best case or cases in text and then reference the other cases using parentheticals.

EXAMPLE 5 **EXCERPT FROM APPELLANT'S BRIEF DEMONSTRATING FULL CASE DESCRIPTION AND USE OF A PARENTHETICAL**

Under this comparative analysis, a defendant meets his burden of proving the reason the prosecutor gave for striking a juror was a pretext for discrimination when the reason given applies equally to a juror of another race, but the prosecutor strikes only one of the jurors. *McClain v. Prunty*, 217 F.3d 1209, 1221 (9th Cir. 2000). For instance, in *McClain*, this Court concluded that the reason the prosecutor gave for striking a black juror was a pretext for discrimination when the reason given applied equally to a white juror, but the prosecutor did not strike the white juror. Although the prosecutor stated that he had struck a black juror because the juror lacked experience making decisions, the prosecutor did not strike a white juror who also lacked decision-making experience. As the Court stated, the fact that the prosecutor did not treat jurors of different races in the same way "fatally undermine[d] the credibility of the prosecutor's stated justification." *Id.* at 1221-22; *see also United States v. Chinchilla*, 874 F.2d 695 (9th Cir. 1989) (reversing a conviction because the prosecutor's stated reason for striking a Hispanic juror—that the juror lived in La Mesa—applied equally to a juror who was not Hispanic and who was not struck).

Principle that Ms. Elder wants to illustrate

Full description of first case

Description of second case using a parenthetical

Finally, remember that if you describe a case you need to use that case in your argument. Do not describe a case and then leave the judge to figure out why you included a description of that case in your brief.

PRACTICE POINTER   In choosing the cases on which to rely, you need to be aware of your jurisdiction's rule on citing to unpublished opinions. In December 2006, the United States Supreme Court amended Fed. R. App. P. 32.1 to allow citation to unpublished federal opinions issued on or after January 1, 2007. However, some state jurisdictions still prohibit citation to unpublished cases. *See, e.g.*, Wash. R. of App. P. 10.4(h).

c. Constructing and Presenting the Arguments

For many attorneys, the most enjoyable part of drafting the brief is constructing and presenting the arguments: it is in constructing and presenting the arguments that attorneys get to use their insights and creativity to pull together, into a coherent and persuasive package, the facts, rules, and cases that they have set out in the earlier sections of their brief.

In constructing the arguments, think first about the standard types of arguments: factual arguments in which you apply the plain language of a statute, regulation, court rule, or common law rule to the facts of your case; analogous case arguments in which you compare and contrast the facts in your case to the facts in analogous cases; and policy arguments.

Although factual arguments are very common in trial briefs, they are less common in appellate briefs. In most instances, the appellate courts defer to the trial court's findings of fact or the jury's verdict, only overturning those findings or the verdict if they are not supported by the evidence. There are, however, times when you can make an effective factual argument, either letting that factual argument stand by itself or combining it with an analogous case or policy argument. For example, in *United States v. Josephy*, Ms. Elder makes a factual argument that the tip is from an unknown rather than a known informant. In reading the following example, examine the way in which Ms. Elder uses the facts to support her assertion the courts should treat the tip as a tip from an unknown informant. Ms. Elder puts unfavorable facts, for example, the fact that the informant gave the 911 operator a name, in a dependent clause; she uses the phrase "gave the operator a name" rather than the phrase "gave the operator his name" to suggest that the informant might not have given the operator his real name. She places her strongest argument, that neither Agent Bhasin nor any other law enforcement officer was able to contact the informant to determine how he obtained the information or to hold him accountable if the statements turned out to be false, in a position of emphasis at the end of the paragraph.

EXAMPLE 1 **EXCERPT FROM THE APPELLANT'S BRIEF SHOWING HOW TO PRESENT A FACTUAL ARGUMENT**

Where an informant declines to be identified, there is a risk the tip has been fabricated, undercutting its reliability. *Florida v. J.L.*, 529 U.S. 266, 269-70, 272 (2000). The unknown informant's reputation cannot be accessed, nor can the informant be held responsible for a false accusation. *Id.* This possibility that the informant might be lying outweighs the value of the information provided unless there are other factors that establish that the informant is reliable, for example, the informant provides law enforcement officers with information about the suspect's future actions, which law enforcement officers then

Rules

independently verify. *United States v. Morales*, 253 F.3d 1070, 1075 (9th Cir. 2001).

In this case, the Court should treat the tip as a tip from an unknown informant. Although the informant gave the 911 operator a name, "Zachary Dillon," he called from a public pay phone in a large mall, and he refused to give the 911 operator his address or phone number. (ER 32, 35). In addition, when Agent Bhasin tried to locate an individual by the name of Zachary Dillon in his databases, he was not able to find anyone by that name in the greater Bellingham area. (ER 42). Consequently, neither Agent Bhasin nor any other law enforcement officer was able to contact Zachary Dillon to determine how he obtained the information that he gave to the 911 operator or to hold him accountable if the statements that he made turned out to be false.

Assertion

Factual argument

If a factual argument is the least common type of argument in appellate briefs, the most common type is an analogous case argument, that is, an argument in which a party either compares its case to analogous cases or distinguishes its case from the cases that the other side says are analogous.

In constructing and presenting analogous case arguments, keep five things in mind. First, as a general rule, begin your argument by setting out your assertion. Second, be explicit in making the comparisons. Third, in addition to making comparisons, explain why those comparisons are legally significant. Fourth, make sure that you compare like things; for example, make sure that you compare cases to cases, people to people, and facts to facts. Finally, keep in mind that you can do more than just compare and contrast facts: you can also compare and contrast the arguments that the parties make and the courts' reasoning.

In the following excerpt from the appellant's brief, Ms. Elder begins her analogous case argument by setting out her assertion: like the tip in *J.L.*, the tip in this case lacks the required indicia of reliability. Ms. Elder is then explicit in comparing the facts in *J.L.* to the facts in her case: like the informant in *J.L.*, who called from a borrowed cell phone and did not give the 911 operator either his own phone number or his own address, "Dillon" called from a public pay phone and refused to give the operator his phone number or address. Ms. Elder does, however, do more than just tell the judge how the cases are similar. She also explains why that similarity is important: because neither of the informants provided the 911 operator with contact information, law enforcement officers were not able to contact either informant to determine the basis for the allegations or to hold them accountable if the information that they provided turned out to be false. Finally, Ms. Elder is precise in comparing the analogous case and her case. In the first sentence, she compares a tip to a tip, a case to a case, and facts to facts. In addition, in the second sentence, Ms. Elder compares a case to a case: *J.L.* to *United States v. Josephy*.

| EXAMPLE 2 | **EXCERPT FROM THE APPELLANT'S BRIEF SHOWING AN ANALOGOUS CASE ARGUMENT** |

In the case before this Court, the tip lacked the required indicia of reliability. Like the informant in *J.L.*, who called from a borrowed cell phone and did not give the 911 operator either his own phone number or his own address, Dillon called from a public pay telephone and refused to give the operator his phone number or his address. (ER 30). As a consequence, in both cases, law enforcement officers were not able to contact the informants to determine the basis for their allegations or to hold them accountable if the information that they provided turned out to be false.

PRACTICE POINTER

When you italicize a name, you are telling your reader that you are citing to a case. In contrast, when you do not italicize a name, you are telling your reader that you are referring to the party or person. Thus, "*J.L.*" is a reference to *Florida v. J.L.*; "J.L." is a reference to the defendant, a juvenile with the initials J. and L.

Although you might incorporate policy statements into your presentation of the rules and your descriptions of analogous cases on a fairly regular basis, typically you will not make a policy argument unless you are asking the court to modify an existing rule or adopt a new rule. Our example case, *United States v. Josephy*, illustrates this point. If Ms. Elder had argued that the court should eliminate peremptory challenges because they can mask discrimination, her primary argument would have been a policy argument, and the government's primary argument would have been a policy argument. Ms. Elder would have argued that, as a matter of public policy, the courts should eliminate peremptory challenges, and the government would have argued that, as a matter of public policy, the courts should not deprive parties of their right to use such challenges. However, given the fact that the United States Supreme Court rejected a request to eliminate peremptory challenges in a relatively recent opinion, *see Miller-El v. Dretke*, 545 U.S. 231, 239-40 (2005), Ms. Elder decided not to pursue this line of argument. As a consequence, although both Ms. Elder and the prosecutor refer to policy in their statements of the rules and their descriptions of the cases, neither Ms. Elder nor the prosecutor makes a policy argument in her or his brief.

d. Using Quotations

Some attorneys and judges will tell you that you should not include quotations, and particularly long quotations, in your brief. Other attorneys and judges will tell you that quotations are one of the advocate's most valuable tools. Both groups have legitimate points.

In drafting your brief, do not use quotations as a crutch. For example, do not use a quotation to cover up the fact that you do not understand a rule or a court's holding or reasoning. Instead, take the time to figure out the rule and the court's decision. Similarly, do not use a quotation because you lack confidence in your writing skills or because you do not want to take the time to construct your own language.

Do, however, use quotations in the following circumstances. First, as a general rule, quote the relevant portions of governing statutes, regulations, and court rules, and quote applicable sections of contracts, wills, and similar documents. Second, as a general rule, quote from the record when the specific language that the judge, attorney, witness, or juror used is important. In addition, feel free to use quotations to emphasize favorable facts, rules, and cases.

The following example illustrates an effective use of quotations from the record. Because Ms. Elder wants to emphasize that Ms. Whitefish was not bothered by the fact that she was subjected to additional scrutiny at the border but that Mr. Williams was bothered by the fact that police officers seemed to target him, Ms. Elder quotes from the record and places most of those quotations at the end of a paragraph in a position of emphasis.

EXAMPLE 1   **EXCERPT FROM THE APPELLANT'S BRIEF SHOWING USE OF QUOTATIONS FROM THE RECORD TO EMPHASIZE FAVORABLE FACTS**

Later, the prosecutor asked if anyone had ever had negative experiences with law enforcement personnel. (ER 119). Ms. Whitefish, a Native American who was a junior majoring in history at Western Washington University, responded that each time she crossed the border she had been, "pulled aside for additional questions." (ER 119). However, when the prosecutor asked Ms. Whitefish whether she was bothered by the fact that she had been pulled over for additional questions, she stated, "Not particularly. I am a college student, and all of us have had similar experiences. They seem to stop young people more. . . ." (ER 119-20).

Similarly, Mr. Martin, a white man with long hair, told the prosecutor that he had had a number of negative experiences with police officers. (ER 120). For example, Mr. Martin told the prosecutor that on one occasion a police officer had stopped him because one of his taillights was out but that the police had not stopped other individuals who had one of their taillights out. (ER 120). In addition, Mr. Martin told the prosecutor that on two occasions he had been given tickets for jaywalking when other individuals on the same street who had short hair jaywalked but did not get tickets. (ER 120). When the prosecutor asked whether he was bothered by the police officers' actions, Mr. Martin said, "You bet I am." (ER 121).

When you are using quotations for emphasis, you will usually want to begin by making the point using your own language. You can then use the quotation to give that point more airtime or to give that point additional emphasis through the use of detail. The following example illustrates this use of a quotation. Ms. Elder makes her points using her own language, and then she emphasizes those points by quoting from the court's opinion.

Although the quotation is longer than Ms. Elder would have liked, she uses the quotation because it was not possible to edit it without losing coherence and key content, and the point that she uses the quotation to illustrate is an important one.

EXAMPLE 2   SAMPLE SHOWING USE OF A QUOTATION TO EMPHASIZE THE FACTS AND REASONING IN A CASE SUPPORTING AN ARGUMENT

Even though the tip contained a number of details, the United States Supreme Court held that the tip was not, by itself, sufficient to justify a *Terry* stop. *White*, 496 U.S. at 329. According to the Court, it became reasonable to think that the information was reliable only after the police verified not only easily obtained facts but also future actions that are not easily predicted. *Id.* at 332.

> We think it also important that, as in *Gates*, "the anonymous [tip] contained a range of details relating not just to easily obtained facts and conditions existing at the time of the tip, but to future actions of third parties ordinarily not easily predicted." [462 U.S. at 245.] The fact that the officers found a car precisely matching the caller's description in front of the 235 building is an example of the former. Anyone could have "predicted" that fact because it was a condition presumably existing at the time of the call. What was important was the caller's ability to predict respondent's *future behavior*, because it demonstrated inside information—a special familiarity with respondent's affairs.

Id. (emphasis in original).

Although ultimately the Court concluded that the anonymous tip, as corroborated, was sufficient to justify the *Terry* stop, the Court labeled the case as a "close case." *Id.*

PRACTICE

Remember to include a citation to authority for every quotation. If the quotation is from the record, the citation to authority should be to the record; if the quotation is from a statute, the citation to authority should be the statute; and if the quotation is from a case, the citation should be to the case, including the specific page on which the quotation appears.

---

e. Responding to the Other Side's Arguments

In addition to setting out your own arguments, you need to respond to the other side's arguments. If you are the appellee, you do not have a choice about where to set out these responses: you need to set them out in your opening brief. However, when you are the appellant, you do have a choice: you can either anticipate what the appellee is going to argue and try to pre-empt its arguments by setting out your responses in your opening brief, or you can wait to see if the appellee makes the argument and then, if so, set out your response in your reply brief. Although there are pros and cons to both of these approaches, the conventional wisdom is that if you are rela-tively certain that the appellee will make an argument, you should anticipate and respond to that argument in your opening brief. In contrast, if there is a good possibility that the appellee will not make a particular point, you should wait and, if necessary, raise it in your reply brief.

The same considerations apply to deciding when to address cases on which the appellee relies. Although both parties have an ethical obligation to bring to the court's attention a case that is controlling, an appellant can choose to preempt a key, but not controlling, case the other side will likely rely on for support by distinguishing it in the opening brief. If the appellant is not sure the appellee will rely on the case, or the appellant believes the case is not critical to the analysis, the appellant might choose to wait until the reply brief to distinguish cases in the appellee's brief.

In responding to the other side's arguments, avoid repeating the other side's argument. Instead, respond to the argument. Example 1 sets out the appellant's argument that there was purposeful discrimination because the prosecutor excused Native Americans who had a particular experience or commitment but did not excuse white jurors who had similar experiences or commitments. Example 2 is from a weak appellee's brief; it illustrates a poor way of responding to the appellant's argument: by repeating the appellant's argument, thereby giving the appellant's argument additional airtime in the mind of the reader. In addition, instead of attacking the argu-ment, the prosecutor attacks defense counsel when he states that opposing counsel has misstated the law. Example 3 is a rewrite of Example 2, in which the prosecutor does a more effective job of responding to the appellant's argument without repeating the appellant's argument and without attacking defense counsel.

EXAMPLE 1   EXCERPT FROM THE APPELLANT'S BRIEF THAT SETS UP ARGUMENT TO WHICH APPELLEE MUST RESPOND

Moreover, the government cannot lawfully exercise peremptory challenges "against potential jurors of one race unless potential jurors of another race with comparable characteristics are also challenged." *United States v. You*, 382 F.3d 958, 969 (2004) (quoting *Turner*, 121 F.3d 1248, 1252 (9th Cir. 1997)). Accordingly, a "comparative analysis of jurors struck and those remaining is a well-established tool for exploring the possibility that facially race-neutral reasons are a pretext for discrimination." *McClain v. Prunty*, 217 F.3d 1209, 1220-21 (9th Cir. 2000).

Under this comparative analysis, a defendant meets his burden of proving the reason the prosecutor gave for striking a juror was a pretext for discrimination when the reason given applies equally to a juror of another race, but the prosecutor strikes only one of the jurors. *McClain v. Prunty*, 217 F.3d 1209, 1221 (9th Cir. 2000). For instance, in *McClain*, this Court concluded that the reason the prosecutor gave for striking a black juror was a pretext for discrimination when the reason given applied equally to a white juror, but the prosecutor did not strike the white juror. Although the prosecutor stated that he had struck a black juror because the juror lacked experience making decisions, the prosecutor did not strike a white juror who also lacked decision-making experience. *Id.* at 1221-22. As the Court stated, the fact that the prosecutor did not treat jurors of different races in the same way "fatally undermine[d] the credibility of the prosecutor's stated justification." *Id.* at 1222; *see also United States v. Chinchilla*, 874 F.2d 695 (9th Cir. 1989) (reversing a conviction because the prosecutor's stated reason for striking a Hispanic juror — that the juror lived in La Mesa — applied equally to a juror who was not Hispanic and who was not struck).

In *United States v. Josephy*, the reason the prosecutor gave for striking Mr. Williams, a Native American, was a pretext for discrimination because the reason applied equally to Mr. Woods, who is white. In explaining why he struck Mr. Williams, the prosecutor said that Mr. Williams would have difficulty focusing on the facts of the case because he had a meeting scheduled for the following week. (ER 125). However, the prosecutor did not strike Mr. Woods, who told the court that his mother was seriously ill, that the doctors were giving her a 20 percent chance to live, and that he might have to go out of town. (ER 117-18).

In addition, the reason that the prosecutor gave for striking Ms. Whitefish, a Native American, was a pretext for discrimination because the prosecutor did not strike a white juror who had had similar experiences with law enforcement personnel. When the judge asked the prosecutor why he had struck Ms. Whitefish, the prosecutor responded that he did not think Ms. Whitefish would be able "to judge this case fairly and impartially" based on her experiences crossing the border. (ER 125). However, although Ms. Whitefish stated that she had been "pulled aside for additional questions" (ER 19), when asked whether this bothered her, Ms. Whitefish replied, "Not particularly. I am a college student, and all of us have had similar experiences. They seem to stop young people more . . . ." (ER 119).

In contrast, Mr. Martin believed he had been targeted by police officers because he had long hair. (ER 120). He was stopped for having a taillight that was out; others were not. He was ticketed for jaywalking; others, who had short hair, were not. (ER 119-20). When asked whether he was bothered by his experiences with police officers, he said "You bet I am." (ER 121).

Although in some cases the courts have concluded that the subjective reasons prosecutors gave for excusing minority jurors were not pretextual even though prospective jurors of different races provided similar responses and one was excused but the other was not, the Court noted, "While subjective factors may play a legitimate role in the exercise of challenges, reliance on such factors alone cannot overcome strong objective indicia of discrimination such as a clear and sustained pattern of strikes against minority jurors." *Burks v. Borg*, 27 F.3d 1424, 1429 (9th Cir. 1994).

In our case, there are objective indicia of discrimination stemming from a clear and sustained pattern of strikes against minority jurors. The prosecutor used two of his peremptory challenges to strike the only two Native American potential jurors. He struck Mr. Williams, who said he had a meeting scheduled after the trial was expected to end, despite his expressed willingness to serve, even if it meant missing the meeting. He struck Ms. Whitefish based on her experiences at the border, even though Ms. Whitefish assured the Court that her experiences at the border did not bother her.

Because the prosecutor did not excuse white jurors who had similar experiences to the Native Americans whom he did strike, the district court erred in denying Mr. Josephy's *Batson* challenge. Such an erroneous denial is presumed to be prejudicial. *See Gray v. Mississippi*, 481 U.S. 648, 668 (1987). Therefore, this Court should reverse and remand the case for a new trial.

EXAMPLE 2   POOR RESPONSE BY THE APPELLEE

In her brief, defense counsel argues that a "comparative analysis of jurors struck and those remaining is a well-established tool for exploring the possibility that facially race-neutral reasons are a pretext for discrimination." *McClain v. Prunty*, 217 F.3d 1209, 1220-21 (9th Cir. 2000). In addition, defense counsel argues that a defendant meets his burden of proving the reason the prosecutor gave for striking a juror was a pretext for discrimination when the reason given applies equally to a juror of another race, but the prosecutor strikes only one of the jurors. *Id.* at 1221. Based on these rules, defense counsel argues that the appellant has met his burden of proving purposeful discrimination because the prosecutor excused Ms. Whitefish, a Native American, because she had problems crossing the border, but the prosecutor did not excuse Mr. Woods, who is white, even though Mr. Woods said that he believed that the police targeted him because he had long hair. In addition, defense counsel argues that the appellant has met his burden of proving purposeful discrimination because the prosecutor excused a Native American who had a tribal council meeting scheduled for the following week but did not excuse a white juror who said that he might have to go out of town to care for his mother, whom the doctors had given only a 20 percent chance of living.

Defense counsel misstates the law when she states that *Batson* is violated whenever prospective jurors of different races provide similar responses and one is excused but the other is not. *See Burks v. Borg*, 27 F.3d 1424, 1429 (9th Cir. 1994). For example, in *Burks*, this Court held that there was not purposeful discrimination in spite of the fact that a minority juror who was struck shared characteristics with a nonminority juror who was not struck. *Id.* The prosecutor told the Court that he had stricken the minority jurors "because they were 'squishy' on the death penalty, expressed a reluctance to serve, and/or lacked certain life experiences." *Id.* In concluding that there was no purposeful discrimination, the Court reaffirmed that "[t]rial counsel is entitled to exercise his full professional judgment in pursuing his client's 'legitimate interest in using [peremptory] challenges . . . to secure a fair and impartial jury.'" *Id.* (quoting *J.E.B. v. Alabama*, 511 U.S. 127 (1994)). Thus, in using his or her peremptory challenges, trial counsel is entitled to take into account "tone, demeanor, facial expression, emphasis—all those factors that make the words uttered by the prospective juror convincing or not." *Burks*, 27 F.3d at 1429.

EXAMPLE 3   BETTER RESPONSE BY APPELLEE

Furthermore, case law does not support the notion that *Batson* is violated whenever prospective jurors of different races provide similar responses and one is excused but the other is not. *Burks v. Borg*, 27 F.3d 1424, 1429 (9th Cir.1994). For example, in *Burks*, this Court held that there was not purposeful discrimination in spite of the fact that a minority juror who was struck shared characteristics with a nonminority juror who was not struck. *Id.* The prosecutor told the court that he had stricken the minority jurors "because they were 'squishy' on the death penalty, expressed a reluctance to serve, and/or lacked certain life experiences." *Id.* In concluding that there was no purposeful discrimination, this Court reaffirmed that "[t]rial counsel is entitled to exercise his full professional judgment in pursuing his client's 'legitimate interest in using [peremptory] challenges . . . to secure a fair and impartial jury.'" *Id.* (quoting *J.E.B. v. Alabama*, 511 U.S. 127 (1994)). Thus, in using his or her peremptory challenges, trial counsel is entitled to take into account "tone, demeanor, facial expression, emphasis—all those factors that make the words uttered by the prospective juror convincing or not." *Burks*, 27 F.3d at 1429.

---

f. Avoiding the Common Problem of Neglecting to Make Explicit Connections

One of the most common mistakes that attorneys make in writing a brief is that they do not explicitly "connect" the parts of their argument. They set out an assertion but do not connect that assertion to a rule; they set out the rule but do not connect it to the descriptions of analogous cases; or they set out descriptions of analogous cases but do not connect the facts and holdings in those analogous cases to their case. For instance, in the following example, the attorney describes a case, *McClain*, but she does not make it clear that she is using the case to illustrate how the courts have applied the rule that she set out in the first sentence of the paragraph. In addition, although the attorney states that the facts in *McClain* are similar to the facts in her case, she does not explain how they are similar.

EXAMPLE 1   POOR EXAMPLE BECAUSE OF LACK OF EXPLICIT CONNECTIONS

A court may conclude that the prosecutor's reasons are pretextual when the reason that the prosecutor gives for striking a juror applies equally to a juror of a different race who was not stricken. *McClain*, 217 F.3d at 1220. In *McClain*, the reason that the prosecutor gave for excusing a black juror was that she lacked decision-making experience. *Id.* at 1216. However, the prosecutor did not excuse a similar white juror. *Id.* at 1221. Thus, the court concluded that the prosecution's explanations were pretextual. *Id.* Similarly, in our case, the prosecutor excused Mr. Williams, a Native American, but she did not excuse Mr. Woods.

The following example is better because it uses a variety of ways to create connections and coherence. First, the author has gone into more detail in setting out the rules, the cases, and her arguments: the extra detail gives the author the raw material she needs to make the connections. Second, the author has used topic sentences to set up each paragraph. Third, the author has used transitions such as "for example" and "in addition" to make it clear how the information in one sentence is related to the information in the preceding or following sentence. Finally, to create coherence, the author has repeated key terms. For example, she has used the word "reason" and a version of the phrase "not supported by the record" in the statement of the rule, in the description of the analogous case, and in the argument. In the following example, the topic sentences are in all capital letters, the transitions are in large and small caps, the word "reason" is in bold, and the versions of the phrase "not supported by the record" are underlined.

| EXAMPLE 2 | **BETTER EXAMPLE BECAUSE OF CONNECTIONS AND COHERENCE** |

WHEN THE **REASONS** THAT A PROSECUTOR GIVES FOR STRIKING A JUROR ARE <u>NOT SUPPORTED BY THE RECORD</u>, "SERIOUS QUESTIONS ABOUT THE LEGITIMACY OF A PROSECUTOR'S **REASONS** FOR EXERCISING PEREMPTORY CHALLENGES ARE RAISED." *McClain v. Prunty*, 217 F.3d 1209, 1221 (9th Cir. 2000). FOR EXAMPLE, in *McClain*, this Court determined that the first **reason** that the prosecutor gave for striking a black juror, that the juror mistrusted the system and had been treated unfairly, <u>was not supported by the record</u>. *Id.* at 1222. Instead of saying that she mistrusted the system and had been treated badly, the juror stated that she did not trust the public defender and, although she initially believed that her son had been treated unfairly, she had changed her mind. *Id.* at 1221. IN ADDITION, this Court determined that there was <u>nothing in the record to support</u> the prosecutor's second **reason,** that the juror must have lied about being a stewardess because she was heavyset. *Id.* The juror did not state that she was a stewardess; what she said was that she worked in airline maintenance. *Id.* Because the <u>record did not support</u> the **reasons** that the prosecutor gave, this Court held that the **reasons** that the prosecutor gave were a pretext for discrimination. *Id.*

AS IN *MCCLAIN*, IN THIS CASE <u>THE RECORD DOES NOT SUPPORT</u> THE **REASONS** THAT THE PROSECUTOR GAVE FOR EXCUSING MR. WILLIAMS AND MS. WHITEFISH. Although the prosecutor stated that he excused Mr. Williams because Mr. Williams would not be able to focus on the case because he had "other obligations next week" (ER 125), Mr. Williams told the court that he was willing to miss his tribal council meeting should the trial be extended. (ER 117). SIMILARLY, although the prosecutor stated that he excused Ms. Whitefish because her experiences at the border would make it difficult for her "to judge this case fairly and impartially" (ER 125), Ms. Whitefish's response to the prosecutor's question about whether she was bothered by the fact that she had been "pulled aside for additional questions" was the following: "Not particularly. I am a college student, and all of us have had similar experiences. They seem to stop young people more . . . ." (ER 119).

THUS, JUST AS THE *MCCLAIN* COURT HELD THAT THE TRIAL COURT ERRED WHEN IT CONCLUDED THAT THE **REASONS** THAT THE PROSECUTOR GAVE WERE NOT A PRETEXT FOR DISCRIMINATION, THIS COURT SHOULD DECIDE THAT THE DISTRICT COURT ERRED WHEN IT CONCLUDED THAT THE PROSECUTOR'S **REASONS** WERE NOT A PRETEXT FOR DISCRIMINATION. "When there is **reason** to believe that there is a racial motivation for the challenge, [this Court is not] bound to accept at face value a list of neutral **reasons** that are either <u>unsupported in the record</u> or refuted by it. Any other approach leaves *Batson* a dead letter." *Johnson v. Vasquez*, 3 F.3d 1327, 1331 (9th Cir. 1993).

g. Avoiding the Common Problem of Not Dealing with Weaknesses

Another error that attorneys commonly make is that they do not deal with the "weaknesses" in their argument. Although this strategy might work occasionally, more often it does not. Even if the opposing party does not notice the problems, the court will.

Look again at the last example. The writer does not deal with an important weakness: the courts do not always find it a pretext for discrimination when a prosecutor gives a reason for excusing a juror, prospective jurors of different races provide similar responses, and one is excused but the other is not. By not confronting contrary authority, the attorney allows the other side to make an argument like the following one.

EXAMPLE 1   **EXCERPT FROM APPELLEE'S BRIEF TAKING ADVANTAGE OF AN UNADDRESSED WEAKNESS**

Furthermore, case law does not support the notion that *Batson* is violated whenever prospective jurors of different races provide similar responses and one is excused but the other is not. *Burks v. Borg*, 27 F.3d 1424, 1429 (9th Cir. 1994). For example, in *Burks*, this Court held that there was not purposeful discrimination in spite of the fact that a minority juror who was struck shared characteristics with a nonminority juror who was not struck. *Id.* The prosecutor told the court that he had stricken the minority jurors "because they were 'squishy' on the death penalty, expressed a reluctance to serve, and/or lacked certain life experiences." *Id.* In concluding that there was no purposeful discrimination, this Court reaffirmed that "[t]rial counsel is entitled to exercise his full professional judgment in pursuing his client's 'legitimate interest in using [peremptory] challenges . . . to secure a fair and impartial jury.'" *Id.* (quoting

J.E.B. v. Alabama, 511 U.S. 127 (1994)). Thus, in using his or her peremptory challenges, trial counsel is entitled to take into account "tone, demeanor, facial expression, emphasis—all those factors that make the words uttered by the prospective juror convincing or not." *Burks*, 27 F.3d at 1429.

Instead of ignoring problems, the better strategy is to anticipate and respond to arguments that you know the other side will make. In Example 2, Ms. Elder anticipated the government's argument and included the following paragraph.

EXAMPLE 2 **EXCERPT FROM THE APPELLANT'S BRIEF ANTICIPATING OPPONENT'S ARGUMENT**

Although in some cases the courts have concluded that the subjective reasons prosecutors gave for excusing minority jurors were not pretextual even though prospective jurors of different races provided similar responses and one was excused but the other was not, this Court noted, "While subjective factors may play a legitimate role in the exercise of challenges, reliance on such factors alone cannot overcome strong objective indicia of discrimination such as a clear and sustained pattern of strikes against minority jurors." *United States v. Burks*, 27 F.3d 1424, 1429 (9th Cir. 1994).

---

h. Avoiding the Mistake of Overlooking Good Arguments

Finally, sometimes attorneys become so enthusiastic about one argument that they overlook other persuasive arguments. For example, in *United States v. Josephy*, Ms. Elder's strongest arguments are that the prosecutor's reasons are not supported by the record and that a comparative analysis of the Native American jurors who were struck and white jurors who were not reveals that the prosecutor's reasons were a pretext for discrimination. However, Ms. Elder can also argue that a *Batson* violation occurred because the district court failed to do the required sensitive inquiry before ruling on the *Batson* objection. See Appellant's Brief at pages 20-21.

Although adding the additional argument makes the brief a bit longer, in this instance doing so was a good choice. Because both of her arguments are legally sound, Ms. Elder increases her chances of getting a reversal.

See section 1.9.6 for a checklist for critiquing the argument section.

§ 2.16 Drafting the Conclusion or Prayer for Relief

The final section of the brief is the conclusion, or the prayer for relief. In most jurisdictions, this section is short. Unlike the conclusion in an objective memorandum, you do not summarize the arguments. Instead, simply set out the relief you are requesting. *See, e.g.,* Fed. R. App. P. 28(a)(10). For example, as the appellant you usually ask the court to reverse or reverse and remand, and if you are the respondent you usually ask the court to affirm or remand. Sometimes you will ask for a single type of relief; at other times you will ask for different types of relief for different errors or for alternative forms of relief. To determine what type of relief you can request, read cases that have decided the same or similar issues and look to see what type of relief the parties requested and what type of relief the court granted.

In *United States v. Josephy*, Ms. Elder asks the court to reverse or, in the alternative, to remand the case for a new trial. It is possible that the court would reverse and dismiss, holding that the ATF agents did not have probable cause to arrest Mr. Josephy and thus the evidence should have been suppressed and without that evidence there was insufficient evidence to convict. However, the court could also remand the case and leave the decision to the prosecutor as to whether the case is to be retried without the suppressed evidence. Also, if the court reverses on the *Batson* issue, it would remand for a new trial. In contrast, the prosecution asks the appellate court to affirm the district court's decision.

EXAMPLE 1   THE APPELLANT'S CONCLUSION

The district court erred in denying Mr. Josephy's motion to suppress evidence obtained during an investigatory stop unsupported by a reasonable suspicion of criminal activity. Therefore, this Court should reverse his conviction.

In the alternative, the district court erred in denying Mr. Josephy's *Batson* challenge because the prosecution's reasons for striking the only two Native American jurors on the panel were a pretext for purposeful discrimination. Therefore, this Court should reverse his conviction and remand the case for a new trial.

---

§ 2.17 Preparing the Signature Block

Before submitting your brief to the court, you must sign it, listing your name and, in most jurisdictions, your bar number. The format typically used is as follows:

Dated: _____

Respectfully submitted,

_____
Name of attorney
Attorney for [Appellant or Respondent]
Address

§ 2.18 Preparing the Appendix

Most jurisdictions allow the parties to attach one or more appendices to their briefs. Such appendices should not be used to avoid the page limits. Instead, use appendices to set out information that a judge would find useful but that might not be readily available. For example, if you are arguing there was an instructional error, include a copy of the court's instructions to the jury. Likewise, if one of your issues requires the court to interpret the language of a particular statute or set of statutes, set out the text of the statute or statutes in an appendix, and if an issue requires the court to look carefully at the language of a case, particularly an out-of-state case or a recent case, set out a copy of the case in an appendix.

Under Fed. R. App. P. 30(a)(1), an appendix containing specifically listed content is required. In contrast, under the Ninth Circuit local rules, an appendix need not be included, but excerpts of the record must be filed. Ninth Cir. R. 30-1.1(a).

§ 2.19 Revising, Editing, and Proofreading

It is impossible to state strongly enough the importance of revising, editing, and proofreading your brief. You do not want to waste a judge's time by making the judge read and reread a confusing sentence or by taking two pages to make a point that you could make in one page. In addition, you want the judges to focus on your arguments and not on grammar, punctuation, citation, or proofreading errors.

Because she wants to do the best that she can for her clients, Ms. Elder spends as much time revising, editing, and proofreading her brief as she does researching the issues and preparing the first draft. After completing the first draft, she sets it aside for a day or two while she works on other projects. When she comes back to the brief, she looks first at the arguments she has made, asking herself the following questions. Has she identified all of the issues? For each issue, has she made clear her position and what relief she is requesting? Has she provided the best support for each of her assertions? Has she included issues, arguments, or support that is unnecessary?

When she is happy with the content, Ms. Elder then rereads her brief, trying to read it as a judge would read it. Is the material presented in a logical order? Has she made clear the connections between arguments and parts of arguments? Is each argument, paragraph block, paragraph, and sentence easy to read and understand? At this stage, Ms. Elder also works more on writing persuasively. She checks to make sure that she has presented the rules, cases, and facts in a light favorable to her client and that she has used persuasive devices effectively.

Ms. Elder then tries to put the brief down for at least a short period of time so that she can, once again, come back to it with "fresh eyes." This time, she works primarily on two things. She begins by looking at her writing style. Are there places where she could make her writing more eloquent? See Chapter 7 in *Just Writing, Second Edition*. She then goes back through the brief, revising for conciseness and precision, and making sure that her writing is correct. See Chapters 7, 9, and 10 in *Just Writing, Second Edition*. In particular, she looks for the types of mistakes that she knows she has a tendency to make. Finally, she goes back through her brief, checking her citations and adding the page numbers to her table of contents and table of authorities.

Although this process is time-consuming, and thus expensive, Ms. Elder finds that the process pays off in a number of ways. First, and most important, she does a good job of representing her client. Because her briefs are well written, her clients get a fair hearing from the court. Second, because she has worked at it, through the years she has become both a better and a faster writer. Finally, she has protected and enhanced one of her most important assets: her reputation. Because her briefs are well written, judges tend to take them, and her, more seriously.

APPELLANT'S BRIEF

No. 07-12345

UNITED STATES COURT OF APPEALS

FOR THE NINTH CIRCUIT

UNITED STATES OF AMERICA,

Plaintiff-Appellee,

v.

PETER JASON JOSEPHY,

Defendant-Appellant.

On Appeal from the United States District Court
for the Western District of Washington

APPELLANT'S OPENING BRIEF

Susan Elder
Federal Public Defender
Westlake Center Office Tower
1601 Fifth Avenue, Suite 700
Seattle, WA 98101
Tel: (206) 555-4321
Counsel for Appellant

TABLE OF CONTENTS

TABLE OF AUTHORITIES

A. Table of Cases

B. Constitutional Provisions

C. Statutes

D. Rules

I. STATEMENT OF JURISDICTION

The appellant, Peter Jason Josephy, appeals his conviction and sentence on one count of unlawful possession of a controlled substance with the intent to deliver in violation of 21 U.S.C. § 841(a)(1) (2006). The district court asserted jurisdiction pursuant to 8 U.S.C. § 3231 (2006) and entered judgment and commitment on January 17, 2008. (CR 34; ER 205).[1] Mr. Josephy filed his notice of appeal on January 24, 2008, within the ten-day period set out in Fed. R. App. P. 4(b). (CR 35). Therefore, this Court has jurisdiction to review Mr. Josephy's final judgment pursuant to 28 U.S.C. § 1291 (2006).

II. BAIL STATUS

Mr. Josephy is currently serving his seventy-seven-month sentence at the Bureau of Prisons' Washington Correctional Institution.

III. STATEMENT OF THE ISSUES

A. Did the district court err in concluding that a telephone tip created an objective particularized suspicion when the informant declined to give more than his name; the informant called from a public pay phone and gave only a general physical description of Mr. Josephy, Mr. Josephy's vehicle, and Mr. Josephy's location; and the police merely corroborated that Mr. Josephy left a motel shortly before checkout time and got into his vehicle?

B.   Did the district court err in denying Mr. Josephy's *Batson*[2] challenge when the prosecutor used his peremptory challenges to excuse both Mr. Williams and Ms. Whitefish, the only two Native Americans in the jury pool and, in denying the

---

[1] "CR" refers to the Clerk's Record and will be followed by the entry number of the cited document as it appears in the district court docket sheet. "ER" refers to the Excerpts of Record.
[2] *Batson v. Kentucky*, 476 U.S. 79 (1986).

challenge, the trial judge's only statement was "Your objection is noted, Counsel, but the Court finds no purposeful discrimination here"?

IV. STATEMENT OF THE CASE

On June 26, 2007, Peter Jason Josephy was charged with one count of Unlawful Possession of a Controlled Substance with the Intent to Deliver under 21 U.S.C. § 841(a)(1) (2006). (CR 7). After an evidentiary hearing, the district court denied Mr. Josephy's motion to suppress evidence obtained during a warrantless search. (CR 26; ER 30).

The case proceeded to jury trial, the Honorable Alesha J. Moore presiding. (CR 28). During voir dire, Mr. Josephy challenged the government's use of two of its peremptory challenges to excuse the only two Native Americans on the jury panel. (ER 123-24). The district court concluded that although Mr. Josephy had established a prima facie case of discrimination, the reasons given by the Government were race neutral and that Mr. Josephy had not established purposeful discrimination. (ER 124). Thus, the court denied Mr. Josephy's *Batson* challenge.

V. STATEMENT OF THE FACTS

Motion to Suppress

At 10:45 a.m. on June 25, 2007, Peter Josephy left his room at the Travel House Inn in Bellingham, Washington; checked out; and, after talking to a friend for three or four minutes, walked to his car and got in. (ER 22, 43). As Mr. Josephy started his car, Agent Bhasin, an Alcohol, Tobacco, and Firearms (ATF) agent, pulled behind Mr. Josephy's car, and another ATF agent, Agent O'Brien, pulled in front. As a result, Mr. Josephy could not move his car. (ER 44).

Agent Bhasin had gone to the Travel House Inn after receiving a phone call from a 911 operator who reported that she had received a call from a public pay telephone located in the Bellis Fair Mall, which is about a five-minute drive from the Travel House Inn. (ER 30, 34). The informant claimed that a Mr. Josephy was at the Travel House Inn to sell drugs to a man named Oliver. (ER 30). In addition, the informant told the 911 operator that, if the police wanted to catch Mr. Josephy, they should go the Travel House Inn soon because Mr. Josephy would be there for only another hour or two. (ER 32-33).

When asked to describe Mr. Josephy, the informant told the 911 operator that Mr. Josephy was a Native American with black hair in his mid to late twenties and that he was driving a blue Chevy Blazer. (ER 32). When asked about Oliver's last name, the informant said that he did not know Oliver's last name. When pushed for a description, the informant told the 911 operator that Oliver was about six feet tall, that he had brown hair and a beard, and that he was in his thirties. (ER 32).

The 911 operator then asked the informant for his name, address, and a phone number so that the police or ATF agents could recontact him. Although the informant told the 911 operator that his name was Zachary Dillon, he then became uncooperative and refused to give the 911 operator his address, his home telephone number, or a cell phone number. (ER 32, 35).

Despite the fact that he was not able to find anyone by the name of Zachary Dillon in his databases, Agent Bhasin went to the Travel House Inn. (ER 42). When he arrived at the motel, Agent Bhasin searched the parking lot and located a blue Chevy Blazer registered to Peter Jason Josephy. (ER 42). After being told by the motel desk clerk that Mr. Josephy was a registered guest and that Josephy had given his vehicle's make, model, and license plate number when he registered, Agent Bhasin returned to his car and requested a backup unit with a dog from the K-9 unit.

At about 10:45 a.m. Agent O'Brien arrived with his dog. However, before Agent O'Brien could walk the dog around Mr. Josephy's vehicle, Mr. Josephy left his motel room with another man, went into the office and paid his bill, and walked to his car. (ER 43). As soon as Mr. Josephy got in his car and started it, Agent Bhasin pulled in front of Mr. Josephy's car and Agent O'Brien pulled in behind. Blocked, Mr. Josephy could not move his car. (ER 44).

After blocking Mr. Josephy's car, Agent Bhasin got out of his vehicle and approached the driver's side of Mr. Josephy's Blazer. When Agent Bhasin asked Mr. Josephy to step out of his vehicle, Mr. Josephy readily complied. (ER 46). Mr. Josephy did, however, decline Agent Bhasin's request to search the vehicle. (ER 46-47). In response, Agent O'Brien took his dog out of his car and walked the dog around the Blazer. (ER 47). When the dog alerted to the smell of marijuana, Agent Bhasin arrested Mr. Josephy. During a search incident to the arrest, Agent Bhasin found marijuana in the wheel well. (ER 49).

At the suppression hearing, the district court agreed with Mr. Josephy that a seizure occurred when the agents blocked Mr. Josephy's vehicle with their own vehicles. (CR 26; ER 52). However, the district court denied the motion to suppress on the grounds that, at the time they blocked Mr. Josephy's car, the agents had a reasonable suspicion that Mr. Josephy was engaged in criminal activity. (CR 26-27; ER 52).

Voir Dire

Mr. Josephy is a Native American. (ER 124). The government used two of its peremptory challenges to remove the only two Native Americans in the jury pool. (ER 123-24).

At the beginning of voir dire, a Monday, the trial judge told the jurors that the trial was scheduled to last for two or three days and asked the members of the venire whether this schedule would create a hardship. Two jurors responded. (ER 116). Juror No. 12, Mr. Williams, a Native American, told the judge that he had a tribal council meeting scheduled for the following week but that he could

4

miss the meeting if necessary. (ER 117). Juror No. 18, Mr. Woods, who is white, told the judge that he might have to leave town the following week because his mother had suffered a massive heart attack and the doctors had given her a 20 percent chance of surviving. (ER 117-18).

Later, the prosecutor asked if anyone had ever had negative experiences with law enforcement personnel. (ER 119). Ms. Whitefish, a Native American who was a junior majoring in history at Western Washington University, responded that each time she crossed the border she had been "pulled aside for additional questions." (ER 119). However, when the prosecutor asked Ms. Whitefish whether she was bothered by the fact that she had been pulled over for additional questions, she stated, "Not particularly. I am a college student, and all of us have had similar experiences. They seem to stop young people more . . . ." (ER 119-20).

Similarly, Mr. Martin, a white man with long hair, told the prosecutor that he had had a number of negative experiences with police officers. (ER 120). For example, Mr. Martin told the prosecutor that on one occasion a police officer had stopped him because one of his taillights was out but that the police had not stopped other individuals who had one of their taillights out. (ER 120). In addition, Mr. Martin told the prosecutor that on two occasions he had been given tickets for jaywalking when other individuals on the same street who had short hair jaywalked but did not get tickets. (ER 120). When the prosecutor asked whether he was bothered by the police officers' actions, Mr. Martin said, "You bet I am." (ER 121).

At the end of voir dire, the government used two of its peremptory challenges to remove Mr. Williams and Ms. Whitefish. (ER 122). Because the prosecutor used his peremptory challenges to remove both Native Americans in the jury pool, Mr. Josephy made a *Batson* challenge to the exclusion of the two jurors based on race. (ER 123). Concluding that Mr. Josephy had established a prima facie case of discrimination, the judge asked the prosecutor to provide reasons for his strikes. The prosecutor stated that he struck Juror No. 5, Ms. Whitefish, because he believed that Ms. Whitefish would have difficulty being impartial given her personal experiences at the border, which could lead her to have negative feelings about law enforcement personnel in general. He said that he struck Mr. Williams because Mr. Williams would have difficulty focusing on the facts of the case given his meeting scheduled for the following week. (ER 125).

Mr. Josephy responded, stating that the reasons provided were not neutral and "are only a mask for unconstitutional race . . . discrimination." (ER 125). The trial judge's only statement was, "Your objection is noted, Counsel, but the Court finds no purposeful discrimination here." (ER 126).

VI. SUMMARY OF THE ARGUMENT

Mr. Josephy's conviction should be reversed for two reasons: (1) his Fourth Amendment rights were violated when the district court failed to suppress evidence obtained by police from an investigative detention unsupported by a reasonable suspicion of criminal activity, and (2) his constitutional right to equal protection was violated because the reasons that the prosecutor gave for using his peremptory challenges to excuse the only two Native Americans in the jury pool were a pretext for discrimination.

First, the district court erred in failing to suppress evidence obtained by police following an illegal seizure. At the time that the ATF agents seized Mr. Josephy by pulling their vehicles in front and behind his vehicle, the only information that the agents had came from a telephone tip made from a public pay telephone at a mall. Although the informant gave his name, the tip should be treated as being from an anonymous source: the informant gave no other identifying information, he ensured he could not be located by calling 911 from a public pay telephone at a shopping mall, and the police were unable to locate anyone by the name that he gave in the greater Bellingham area. Because there was no way to assess the caller's reputation or hold him responsible if the tip turned out to be a fabrication, the tip was less reliable than a tip from a known informant.

The tip also lacked sufficient indicia of reliability because it contained only a general description of Mr. Josephy, his location, and his vehicle. Although such information helped the police locate the person the caller accused, it did not show that the caller had information about hidden criminal activity. Moreover, police observations did no more than corroborate innocuous details, such as the time Mr. Josephy would check out of a motel. Because the agents did not have a reasonable suspicion of criminal activity, the investigatory detention was unconstitutional, and all evidence obtained should have been suppressed.

Second, Mr. Josephy's constitutional right to equal protection was violated when the prosecutor used his peremptory challenges to remove the only Native Americans from the jury pool. In denying Mr. Josephy's *Batson* challenge, the district court erred for two reasons: First, the reasons that the prosecutor gave for striking the only two Native Americans in the jury pool were a pretext for discrimination both because the reasons are not supported by the record and because a comparative analysis shows that the prosecutor did not excuse white jurors who had similar obligations and experiences. Second, the district court erred by not doing the "sensitive analysis required" under *Batson* and by not setting out its reasoning on the record. In fact, the trial judge's ruling on this crucial third step of the analysis consisted of only one statement: "Your objection is noted, Counsel, but the Court finds no purposeful discrimination here."

7

VII. ARGUMENT

A. THE ATF AGENTS VIOLATED MR. JOSEPHY'S FOURTH AMENDMENT RIGHTS BECAUSE THEY DID NOT HAVE A PARTICULARIZED OBJECTIVE SUSPICION THAT MR. JOSEPHY WAS ENGAGED IN CRIMINAL ACTIVITY.

The district court erred in denying Mr. Josephy's motion to suppress because, at the time that the ATF agents seized Mr. Josephy, they did not have a particularized objective suspicion that Mr. Josephy was engaged in criminal activity. This Court reviews a district court's determination of reasonable suspicion *de novo*. *Ornelos v. United States*, 517 U.S. 690, 699 (1996); *United States v. Fernandez-Castillo*, 324 F.3d 1114, 1117 (9th Cir. 2003).

"The Fourth Amendment allows government officials to conduct an investigatory stop of a vehicle only upon a showing of reasonable suspicion: 'a particularized and objective basis for suspecting the particular person stopped of criminal activity.' " *United States v. Thomas*, 211 F.3d 1186, 1189 (9th Cir. 1999) (quoting *United States v. Jimenez-Medina*, 173 F.3d 752, 754 (9th Cir. 1999)); see U.S. Const. amend. IV. In determining whether the government officials had a reasonable suspicion, the courts look at the totality of the circumstances, including whether the informant was a known or unknown informant; whether the tip included sufficient indicia of reliability; and whether the law enforcement officer verified, through an independent investigation, details other than innocuous details. *See, e.g., Alabama v. White*, 496 U.S. 325, 330 (1990); *Illinois v. Gates*, 462 U.S. 213, 238-40 (1983).

1. The ATF agents did not have a particularized objective suspicion that Mr. Josephy was engaged in criminal activity because the tip came from an unknown informant; although the informant gave the 911 operator his name, he refused to give his address or phone number.

Where an informant declines to be identified, there is a risk the tip has been fabricated, undercutting its reliability. *Florida v. J.L.*, 529 U.S. 266, 269-70, 272 (2000). The unknown informant's reputation cannot be accessed, nor can the informant be held responsible for a false accusation. *Id.* This possibility that the informant might be lying outweighs the value of the information provided unless there are other factors that establish that the informant is reliable, for example, the informant provides law enforcement officers with information about the suspect's future actions, which law enforcement officers then independently verify. *United States v. Morales*, 253 F.3d 1070, 1075 (9th Cir. 2001).

In *United States v. Josephy*, the Court should treat the tip as a tip from an unknown informant. Although the informant gave the 911 operator a name, "Zachary Dillon," he called from a public pay phone in a large mall, and he refused to give the 911 operator his address or phone number. (ER 32, 35). In addition, when Agent Bhasin tried to locate an individual by the name of Zachary Dillon in his databases, he was not able to find anyone by that name in the greater Bellingham area. (ER 42). Consequently, neither Agent Bhasin nor any other law enforcement officer was able to contact Zachary Dillon to determine how he obtained the information that he gave to the 911 operator or to hold him accountable if the statements that he made turned out to be false.

Thus, the facts in this case can be distinguished from the facts in *United States v. Terry-Crespo*, 356 F.3d 1170, 1172 (9th Cir. 2004), a case in which the court held that information provided by an individual who had called 911 to report that the defendant had threatened him with a firearm was sufficient to support a *Terry* stop even though the police were not able to locate anyone by the caller's name in their databases. Unlike the caller in *Terry-Crespo*, who was the victim of a crime, *id.* at 1177, in this case the informant, "Dillon," was not the victim of a crime. In addition, unlike the caller in *Terry-Crespo*, who made the call from the scene of the crime, in this case, *id.* at 1176, "Dillon" made the call from a mall five minutes from the motel where the drug buy was allegedly occurring. Finally, in *Terry-Crespo* the caller did not give the 911 operator his phone number because he did not know the number of the cell phone that he had borrowed to make the emergency call, *id.*, but in this case "Dillon" refused to give the operator his address, home phone number, or a cell phone number. Consequently, in *Terry-Crespo* the facts supported the court's conclusion that the caller was not trying to hide his identity, but in this case the facts suggest just the opposite.

Thus, because "Dillon" appears to have taken steps to hide his identity, this Court should treat his tip as a tip from an unknown informant. However, even if this Court does not treat the tip as coming from an unknown informant, the tip is not reliable because it lacks sufficient indicia of reliability.

> 2. <u>The ATF agents did not have a particularized objective suspicion that Mr. Josephy was engaged in criminal activity because the tip included only general physical descriptions, it omitted any description of clothing, and the only action it predicted was that Mr. Josephy would be leaving a motel shortly before checkout time.</u>

A tip from an unknown informant that does no more than describe an individual's readily observable location and appearance does not have sufficient indicia of reliability to support a stop. *Florida v. J.L.*, 529 U.S. 266, 272 (2000). Although such a tip might help the police identify the person whom the informant means to accuse, such a tip does not establish that the informant has knowledge of concealed criminal activity. *Id.* at 272.

In the cases in which the courts have held that the tip lacked sufficient indicia of reliability, the tip lacked predictive information and included only a general description of the defendant and his location, and the informant did not explain how he had acquired the information. *See, e.g., Florida v. J.L.*, 529 U.S. at 272. For instance, in *J.L.*, an anonymous caller reported to police that "a young black male standing at a particular bus stop and wearing a plaid shirt was carrying a gun." *Id.* at 269. In concluding that this tip was not sufficient to establish a reasonable suspicion of criminal activity, the Court said that "[t]he anonymous call concerning J.L. provided no predictive information and therefore left the police without means to test the informant's knowledge or credibility." *Id.* at 270. The court went on to say that the fact that the allegation about the gun turned out to be true did not establish a reasonable basis for suspecting J.L. of engaging in unlawful conduct:

> The reasonableness of official suspicion must be measured by what the officers knew before they conducted their search. All the police had to go on in this case was the bare report of an unknown, unaccountable informant who neither explained how he knew about the gun nor supplied any basis for believing he had inside information about J.L.

Id. at 271.

In contrast, in most of the cases in which the courts have held that the tips had sufficient indicia of reliability to support a *Terry* stop, the callers were reporting what they had recently seen or experienced, *see, e.g., United States v. Terry-Crespo,* 356 F.3d 1170, 1172 (9th Cir. 2004), or the callers provided the police with not only details about the defendant and his or her current location but also information about what the defendant was about to do, *see, e.g., United States v. Fernandez-Castillo,* 324 F.3d 1114, 1119 (9th Cir. 2003). For example, in *Terry-Crespo,* the court held that a 911 call contained sufficient indicia of reliability for four reasons: (1) the call was not anonymous because the caller provided the 911 operator with his name and the call was recorded; (2) the caller was the victim of a crime, and the police must be able to take seriously, and respond promptly to, emergency 911 calls; (3) the caller jeopardized any anonymity he might have had by calling 911 and providing his name to an operator during a recorded call; and (4) the caller was giving first-hand information about an event that had just occurred. *Terry-Crespo,* 356 F.3d at 1172-77. Similarly, in *Fernandez-Castillo,* the court held that a tip had sufficient reliability because it came from a Montana Department of Transportation (MDOT) employee and there are relatively few MDOT employees; the MDOT employee who reported the erratic driving not only provided the dispatcher with the make and model of the car but also told the dispatcher that the car had North Dakota license plates; the MDOT employee made the report almost immediately after he observed the defendant driving erratically; and the report contained predictive information: that the car was driving eastbound near milepost 116. *Fernandez-Castillo*, 324 F.3d at 1119.

In the case before this Court, the tip lacked the required indicia of reliability. Like the informant in *J.L.*, who called from a borrowed cell phone and did not give the 911 operator either his own phone number or his own address, Mr. Dillon called from a public pay telephone and refused to give the operator his phone number or his address. (ER 30). As a consequence, in both cases law enforcement officers were not able to contact the informants to determine the basis for their allegations or to hold them accountable if the information that they provided turned out to be false.

More important, though, Dillon's tip lacked sufficient indicia of reliability because he failed to give a description of Josephy's clothing, he failed to provide information based on first-hand observation, and he failed to give specific predictive information. First, in *J.L.*, the caller told the operator that the defendant was wearing a plaid jacket; in this case, Dillon did not describe either Mr. Josephy's or Oliver's clothing (ER 32), which suggests that Dillon had not seen Mr. Josephy or Oliver on the day of the call. Second, unlike *Terry-Crespo* and *Fernandez-Castillo*, in which it was clear that the callers were providing first-hand information, in this case, there is nothing to suggest that Dillon's statements were based on his own observations. At no time during the call did Dillon tell the operator how he knew that Mr. Josephy was at the motel or why he believed that Mr. Josephy was involved in illegal activity. (ER 30-35). Third, unlike *Fernandez-Castillo*, in which the caller provided the operator with specific predictive information about the defendant's location and direction of travel, in this case Dillon provided the operator with only general information: that Mr. Josephy was going to leave the motel shortly before checkout time. (ER 32-33). While predicting where a car will be at a given time provides evidence that the tip is reliable, predicting that a guest will check out of motel at checkout time does not.

Thus, under the totality of the circumstances, the tip did not have the required indicia of reliability and was not, therefore, sufficient to support a *Terry* stop unless the police independently verified more than innocuous details.

3. The ATF agents did not have a particularized objective suspicion that Mr. Josephy was engaged in criminal activity because the police corroborated only innocuous details, for example, Mr. Josephy's physical appearance, his vehicle, and his departure from a motel shortly before checkout time.

When a tip lacks the required indicia of reliability, the tip is not sufficient to support a Terry stop unless law enforcement officers independently corroborate more than innocuous details. *See Alabama v. White*, 496 U.S. 325, 330 (1990). As the Court noted in *White*, when a tip has a relatively low degree of reliability, more information will be required to establish the requisite quantum of suspicion than would be required if the tip were more reliable. *Id.*

In *White*, the police received an anonymous tip in which the caller stated that "Vanessa White would be leaving 235-C Lynnwood Terrace Apartments at a particular time in a brown Plymouth station wagon with the right taillight lens broken, that she would be going to Dobey's Motel, and that she would be in possession of about an ounce of cocaine inside a brown attaché case. *Id.* at 327. After receiving this tip, two police officers went to the Lynnwood Terrace Apartments, where they located a brown Plymouth station wagon with a broken right taillight in the parking lot in front of the 235 building. *Id.* As the police officers sat in their vehicle, they observed the defendant leave the 235 building, carrying nothing in her hands, and enter the station wagon. *Id.* The officers followed the vehicle as it drove the most direct route to Dobey's Motel. When the vehicle reached the Mobile Highway, on which Dobey's Motel is located, the officers had a patrol unit stop the vehicle. *Id.*

Even though the tip contained a number of details, the United States Supreme Court held that the tip was not, by itself, sufficient to justify a *Terry* stop. *White*, 496 U.S. at 329. According to the Court, it became reasonable to think that the information was reliable only after the police verified not only easily obtained facts but also future actions that are not easily predicted. *Id.* at 332.

> We think it also important that, as in *Gates,* "the anonymous [tip] contained a range of details relating not just to easily obtained facts and conditions existing at the time of the tip, but to future actions of third parties ordinarily not easily predicted." [462 U.S. at 245.] The fact that the officers found a car precisely matching the caller's description in front of the 235 building is an example of the former. Anyone could have "predicted" that fact because it was a condition presumably existing at the time of the call. What was important was the caller's ability to predict respondent's *future behavior,* because it demonstrated inside information—a special familiarity with respondent's affairs.

Id. (emphasis in original).

Although ultimately the Court concluded that the anonymous tip, as corroborated, was sufficient to justify the *Terry* stop, the Court labeled the case as a "close case." *Id.*

If *White* was a close case, this case is an easy case. First, in *White*, the informant provided the police with far more details than Dillon gave the 911 operator. For example, in *White*, the informant provided the police with the defendant's apartment number and the fact that the car had a broken taillight, but in this case Dillon did not provide anything more than the name of the motel and the make and model of the vehicle. (ER 32). Second, in *White*, the informant provided the police with information about the defendant's future actions that only someone who had a special familiarity with the defendant could know, but in this case, Dillon only predicted that Mr. Josephy would leave the motel shortly before checkout

14

time. (ER 32-33). Finally, in *White*, the police independently verified most of the information that the informant had provided, including the fact that the defendant would leave the apartment at a particular time and drive to a particular motel; in this case, the police did not verify anything more than Mr. Josephy owned a vehicle and that he left the motel at checkout time. (ER 42-43).

Although in this case the *Terry* stop might have been justified if Dillon had told the 911 operator that Mr. Josephy would leave the motel and drive to a particular house or restaurant at a particular time, and the ATF agents had verified these facts through their own surveillance, those facts are not the facts of this case. Under the facts of this case, the stop was not justified for three reasons: (1) the tip was, for all practical purposes, an anonymous tip; (2) the tip did not contain sufficient indicia of reliability; and (3) the ATF agents were not able to verify, through their own independent investigation, facts that established a "particularized and objective basis" for suspecting Mr. Josephy of criminal wrongdoing. *See United States v. Velazco-Durazo*, 372 F. Supp. 2d 520, 528 (D. Ariz. 2005).

    B.   THE DISTRICT COURT ERRED IN DENYING MR. JOSEPHY'S *BATSON* CHALLENGE BECAUSE THE PROSECUTOR STRUCK THE ONLY TWO NATIVE AMERICANS IN THE JURY POOL, AND THE COURT'S ENTIRE RULING CONSISTED OF A SINGLE SENTENCE.

For more than a century, the United States Supreme Court has "consistently and repeatedly . . . reaffirmed that racial discrimination by the State in jury selection offends the Equal Protection Clause." *Miller-El v. Dretke*, 125 U.S. 2317, 2324 (2005) (quoting *Georgia v. McCollum*, 505 U.S. 42 (1992)); *see also* U.S. Const. amend. XIV. Racial discrimination in jury selection denies defendants their right to a jury trial, denies jurors the right to participate in public life, and undermines public confidence in the fairness of our justice system. *Batson v. Kentucky*, 476 U.S. 79, 86-87 (1986); *Williams v. Runnels*, 432 F.3d 1102, 1108 (9th Cir. 2006). Therefore, the "Constitution forbids striking even a single prospective juror for a discriminatory purpose." *United States v. Vasquez-Lopez*, 22 F.3d 900, 902 (9th Cir. 1992).

In *Batson*, the Court developed a three-step test to uncover discrimination masked by peremptory challenges. 476 U.S. at 96-97. Under the first step of the test, the defendant need only establish a prima facie case of purposeful discrimination by showing that the prosecutor has struck a member of a cognizable class and that the circumstances raise an inference of discrimination. *Id.* at 96. Once the defendant establishes a prima facie case, the burden shifts to the government: the government must provide a race-neutral explanation for striking a member of a cognizable class. *Id.* at 97. If the government does meet its burden, the court must do a sensitive analysis to determine whether the government has engaged in purposeful discrimination. *See Johnson v. California*, 545 U.S. 162, 169 (2005).

In this case, the district court erred when it denied Mr. Josephy's *Batson* challenge for two reasons: First, the district court erred when it concluded that the reasons that the prosecutor gave were not a pretext for discrimination. (ER 126). Second, the district court erred by not doing the "sensitive analysis required" under *Batson* and by not setting out its reasoning on the record. (ER 126).

    1.   <u>The reasons the prosecutor gave for striking the only two Native Americans in the jury pool were a pretext for discrimination because they were not supported by the record and the prosecutor did not excuse white jurors who had similar obligations and experiences.</u>

When the reasons that a prosecutor gives for striking a juror are not supported by the record, "serious questions about the legitimacy of a prosecutor's reasons for exercising peremptory challenges are raised." *McClain v. Prunty*, 217 F.3d 1209, 1221 (9th Cir. 2000). For example, in *McClain*, this Court determined that the first reason that the prosecutor gave for striking a black juror, that the juror mistrusted the system and had been treated unfairly, was not supported by the record. *Id.* at 1222. Instead of saying that she mistrusted the system and had been treated badly, the juror stated that she did not trust the public defender and, although she initially believed that her son had been treated unfairly, she had changed her mind. *Id.* at 1221. In addition, this Court determined that there was nothing in the record to support the prosecutor's second reason, that the juror must have lied about being a stewardess because she was heavyset. *Id.* The juror did not state that she was a stewardess; what she said was that she worked in airline maintenance. *Id.* Because the record did not support the reasons that the prosecutor gave, this Court held that the reasons that the prosecutor gave were a pretext for discrimination. *Id.*

As in *McClain*, in this case the record does not support the reasons that the prosecutor gave for excusing Mr. Williams and Ms. Whitefish. Although the prosecutor stated that he excused Mr. Williams because Mr. Williams would not be able to focus on the case because he had "other obligations next week," (ER 125), Mr. Williams told the court that he was willing to miss his tribal council meeting should the trial be extended. (ER 117). Similarly, although the prosecutor stated that he excused Ms. Whitefish because her experiences at the border would make it difficult for her "to judge this case fairly and impartially," (ER 125), Ms. Whitefish's response to the prosecutor's question about whether she was bothered by the fact that she had been "pulled aside for additional questions" was the following: "Not particularly. I am a college student, and all of us have had similar experiences. They seem to stop young people more . . . ." (ER 119).

Thus, just as the *McClain* court held that the trial court erred when it concluded that the reasons that the prosecutor gave were not a pretext for discrimination, this Court should decide that the district court erred when it concluded that the prosecutor's reasons were not a pretext for discrimination. "When there is reason to believe that there is a racial motivation for the challenge, [this Court is not] bound to accept at face value a list of neutral reasons that are either unsupported

in the record or refuted by it. Any other approach leaves *Batson* a dead letter."
Johnson v. Vasquez, 3 F.3d 1327, 1331 (9th Cir. 1993).

Moreover, the government cannot lawfully exercise peremptory challenges
"against potential jurors of one race unless potential jurors of another race with
comparable characteristics are also challenged." *United States v. You*, 382 F.3d
958, 969 (2004) (quoting *Turner v. Marshall*, 121 F.3d 1248, 1252 (9th Cir. 1997)).
Accordingly, a "comparative analysis of jurors struck and those remaining is a
well-established tool for exploring the possibility that facially race-neutral reasons
are a pretext for discrimination." *McClain v. Prunty*, 217 F.3d 1209, 1220-21 (9th
Cir. 2000).

Under this comparative analysis, a defendant meets his burden of proving
the reason the prosecutor gave for striking a juror was a pretext for discrimination when the reason given applies equally to a juror of another race, but the
prosecutor strikes only one of the jurors. *McClain v. Prunty*, 217 F.3d 1209, 1221
(9th Cir. 2000). For instance, in *McClain*, this Court concluded that the reason the
prosecutor gave for striking a black juror was a pretext for discrimination when
the reason given applied equally to a white juror, but the prosecutor did not strike
the white juror. Although the prosecutor stated that he had struck a black juror
because the juror lacked experience making decisions, the prosecutor did not
strike a white juror who also lacked decision-making experience. *Id.* at 1221-22.
As the court stated, the fact that the prosecutor did not treat jurors of different
races in the same way "fatally undermine[d] the credibility of the prosecutor's
stated justification." *Id.* at 1222; *see also United States v. Chinchilla*, 874 F.2d 695
(9th Cir. 1989) (reversing a conviction because the prosecutor's stated reason for
striking a Hispanic juror—that the juror lived in La Mesa—applied equally to a
juror who was not Hispanic and who was not struck).

In *United States v. Josephy*, the reason the prosecutor gave for striking Mr. Williams, a Native American, was a pretext for discrimination because the reason applied equally to Mr. Woods, who is white. In explaining why he struck Mr. Williams, the prosecutor said that Mr. Williams would have difficulty focusing on the facts of the case because he had a meeting scheduled for the following week. (ER 125). However, the prosecutor did not strike Mr. Woods, who told the court that his mother was seriously ill, that the doctors were giving her a 20 percent chance to live, and that he might have to go out of town. (ER 117-18).

In addition, the reason that the prosecutor gave for striking Ms. Whitefish, a Native American, was a pretext for discrimination because the prosecutor did not strike a white juror who had had similar experiences with law enforcement personnel. When the judge asked the prosecutor why he had struck Ms. Whitefish, the prosecutor responded that he did not think Ms. Whitefish would be able "to judge this case fairly and impartially" based on her experiences crossing the border. (ER 125). However, although Ms. Whitefish stated that she had been "pulled aside for additional questions," (ER 19), when asked whether this bothered her, Ms. Whitefish replied, "Not particularly. I am a college student, and all of us have had similar experiences. They seem to stop young people more . . . ." (ER 119).

In contrast, Mr. Martin believed he had been targeted by police officers because he had long hair. (ER 120). He was stopped for having a taillight that was out; others were not. He was ticketed for jaywalking; others, who had short hair, were not. (ER 119-20). When asked whether he was bothered by his experiences with police officers, he said, "You bet I am." (ER 121).

Although in some cases the courts have concluded that the subjective reasons prosecutors gave for excusing minority jurors were not pretextual even though prospective jurors of different races provided similar responses and one was excused but the other was not, the Court noted, "While subjective factors may play a legitimate role in the exercise of challenges, reliance on such factors alone cannot overcome strong objective indicia of discrimination such as a clear and sustained pattern of strikes against minority jurors." *Burks v. Borg*, 27 F.3d 1424, 1429 (9th Cir. 1994).

In our case, there are objective indicia of discrimination stemming from a clear and sustained pattern of strikes against minority jurors. The prosecutor used two of his peremptory challenges to strike the only two Native American potential jurors. He struck Mr. Williams, who said he had a meeting scheduled after the trial was expected to end, despite his expressed willingness to serve, even if it meant missing the meeting. He struck Ms. Whitefish based on her experiences at the border, even though Ms. Whitefish assured the Court that her experiences at the border did not bother her.

Because the prosecutor did not excuse white jurors who had similar experiences to the Native Americans whom he did strike, the district court erred in denying Mr. Josephy's *Batson* challenge. Such an erroneous denial is presumed to be prejudicial. *See Gray v. Mississippi*, 481 U.S. 648, 668 (1987). Therefore, this Court should reverse and remand the case for a new trial.

2. <u>In addition, the district court erred by not conducting the required sensitive inquiry and by not stating its reasoning on the record.</u>

A trial court commits an error if it fails to conduct "a sensitive inquiry into such circumstantial and direct evidence of intent as may be available," *Batson*, 476 U.S. at 93, or if it fails to show on the record that its decision was deliberate. *United States v. Alanis*, 335 F.3d 965, n.2 (9th Cir. 2003).

A trial court commits reversible error if it fails to do the required "sensitive inquiry" or if the trial court's decision is made in haste or is imprecise. *Jordan v. Lefevre*, 206 F.3d 196, 198 (2d Cir. 2006). In *Jordan*, the trial judge attempted to save "an awful lot of time" by ruling on the defendant's *Batson* challenge without considering all of the facts and arguments and without setting out its analysis in the record. *Id.* at 199. As a result, the reviewing court concluded that the trial court had violated the defendant's right to equal protection by making a hasty decision and not stating on the record its analysis of why the reasons that prosecutor gave for striking jurors were not a pretext for discrimination. *Id.*

As in *Jordan*, in this case the court made a hasty decision and did not state on the record its analysis of why the reasons that the prosecutor gave were not a pretext for discrimination. In fact, the record consists of a single sentence: "Your objection is noted, Counsel, but the Court finds no purposeful discrimination here." (ER 126).

The "duty of assessing the credibility of the prosecutor's race-neutral reasons [embodies] the 'decisive question' in the *Batson* analysis." *Jordan*, 206 F.3d at 200 (citing *Hernandez v. New York*, 500 U.S. 352, 365 (1991)). Although the lack of a reasoned analysis does not seem to stem from a blatant impatience with the proceedings as it did in *Jordan*, the result and the violation are the same: this Court is left with a record devoid of the reasoned credibility analysis regarding each challenged juror that due process requires.

Because the district court's erroneous denial of Mr. Josephy's *Batson* challenge is presumed to be prejudicial, *see Gray*, 481 U.S. at 668, this Court should reverse and remand the case for a new trial.

VIII. CONCLUSION

The district court erred in denying Mr. Josephy's motion to suppress evidence obtained during an investigatory stop unsupported by a reasonable suspicion of criminal activity. Therefore, this Court should reverse his conviction.

In the alternative, the district court erred in denying Mr. Josephy's *Batson* challenge because the prosecutor's reasons for striking the only two Native

American jurors on the panel were a pretext for purposeful discrimination and because the district court failed to conduct the required sensitive inquiry or state its reasoning. Therefore, this Court should reverse his conviction and remand the case for a new trial.

Dated: _____

Respectfully submitted,

_____

Susan Elder
Federal Public Defender
Westlake Center Office Tower
1601 Fifth Avenue, Suite 700
Seattle, WA 98101

STATEMENT OF RELATED CASES

The appellant knows of no other related cases pending in this Court.

23

APPELLEE'S BRIEF

No. 07-12345

UNITED STATES COURT OF APPEALS

FOR THE NINTH CIRCUIT

UNITED STATES OF AMERICA,

Plaintiff-Appellee,

v.

PETER JASON JOSEPHY,

Defendant-Appellant.

On Appeal from the United States District Court
for the Western District of Washington

BRIEF OF APPELLEE

Andrew Froh
United States Attorney
Western District of Washington
James Jorgenson
Assistant United States
Attorney
700 Stewart Street
Seattle, WA 98101
Tel: (206) 555-1234
Counsel for Appellee

TABLE OF CONTENTS

TABLE OF AUTHORITIES

A. Table of Cases

B. Statutes

I. STATEMENT OF JURISDICTION

The appellee agrees with the appellant's statement of jurisdiction.

II. STATEMENT OF THE ISSUES

A. Whether police had a reasonable articulable suspicion that Mr. Josephy was engaged in criminal activity when (1) Zachary Dillon called 911 to report that Mr. Josephy was in possession of drugs he planned to sell; (2) Mr. Dillon provided the 911 operator with descriptions of Mr. Josephy, Mr. Josephy's car, and Mr. Josephy's companion; (3) Mr. Dillon told the 911 operator that Mr. Josephy and his companion were at the Travel House Inn and that Mr. Josephy would soon leave the motel in a blue Chevy Blazer; and (4) ATF agents verified that the blue Blazer in the motel parking lot was registered to Mr. Josephy and observed men matching the descriptions that Mr. Dillon had given leave the motel in the predicted time frame.

B. Whether Mr. Josephy failed to prove that the government engaged in purposeful discrimination when (1) the prosecutor excused a 21-year-old Native American juror who volunteered that she had experienced problems each time she had crossed from the United States into Canada and (2) the Government excused both a Native American juror who told the judge that he had a tribal council meeting the following week and a white juror who was worried about missing work.

III. STATEMENT OF THE FACTS

Motion to Suppress

At about 9:30 a.m. on June 25, 2007, Zachary Dillon called 911 and reported that Peter Josephy was involved in selling drugs that had been brought into the United States from Canada. (ER 30). Two hours later, Alcohol, Tobacco, and Firearms (ATF) agents searched Mr. Josephy's vehicle and found four kilos of marijuana in the wheel well. (ER 49).

During the 911 call, which was recorded, Mr. Dillon told the operator that Mr. Josephy was at the Travel House Inn to meet with, and deliver marijuana to, a man named Oliver. (ER 30-31). Although Mr. Dillon declined to give the 911 operator his address or phone number, Mr. Dillon did tell the 911 operator that Mr. Josephy was a Native American, that Josephy had black hair, and that Josephy was in his mid to late twenties. (ER 32). Mr. Dillon also told the operator that Mr. Josephy owned, and was driving, a blue Chevy Blazer. (ER 32). Although Mr. Dillon did not know Oliver's last name, he described Oliver as in being his thirties, about six feet tall, and with brown hair and a beard. (ER 32). Finally, Mr. Dillon told the police not to wait too long because Mr. Josephy would be leaving the motel in the next hour or two. (ER 33).

The 911 operator relayed the information from Mr. Dillon to Agent Bhasin, an ATF agent with more than ten years of service. (ER 4). Not finding anyone by the name of Zachary Dillon in the ATF databases, Agent Bhasin drove to the Travel House Inn in an unmarked car to determine whether there was a blue Chevy Blazer in the parking lot. (ER 35, 40). When he arrived at the motel at approximately 10:15 a.m., Agent Bhasin located a blue Chevy Blazer in the parking lot; when he ran the license plates, he was told that the Blazer was registered to Peter Jason Josephy. (ER 42).

After confirming with the desk clerk not only that the blue Chevy Blazer in the parking lot was registered to Josephy but also that Josephy was a registered guest, Agent Bhasin called for backup and a K-9 unit. (ER 43).

Agent O'Brien arrived with his dog in an unmarked car at about 10:45 a.m. (ER 43). However, before Agent O'Brien could walk his dog around the Blazer, Agents Bhasin and O'Brien saw two men matching the descriptions of Josephy and Oliver come out of a motel room. (ER 43). The man matching Oliver's description walked out of the parking lot. (ER 44). The other man, who was later confirmed to be Peter Josephy, walked to the blue Blazer. (ER 43).

Based on Dillon's tip and his own observations, Agent Bhasin believed Mr. Josephy had possession of a controlled substance with intent to deliver. (ER 44). Therefore, when Mr. Josephy got into the Blazer and started the engine, Agent Bhasin pulled in front of Josephy's car, and Agent O'Brien pulled behind. (ER 44). Although Josephy complied with Agent Bhasin's request to get out of the Blazer, Josephy refused the request for permission to search the Blazer. As a consequence, Agent O'Brien walked his dog around the Blazer. (ER 46-7). After the dog alerted, Agent Bhasin arrested Mr. Josephy for possession of a controlled substance. (ER 49). During a search incident to the arrest, Agent Bhasin found the four kilos of marijuana. (ER 49).

After a pretrial hearing, the district court denied Mr. Josephy's motion to suppress, concluding that the *Terry* stop was justified because Agent Bhasin had a reasonable suspicion that Mr. Josephy was engaged in criminal conduct. (CR 26-27; ER 52).

<u>Voir Dire</u>

Out of a venire of twenty-four potential jurors, twelve jurors and one alternate were chosen by use of the Struck Jury Method. (ER 130). After Judge Moore explained the selection process to the jurors (ER 113-15), she asked whether serving on the jury would create a hardship. (ER 116). Juror No. 12, Mr. Williams, indicated that, although he could forego attending a tribal council meeting scheduled for Thursday and Friday, he would prefer not to. (ER 117). In addition, Juror No. 2, Mr. Feldman, told the judge that he was scheduled to go to Africa on the following Saturday and that his "boss would be unhappy if he did not finish some projects before he left." (ER 117). However, Mr. Feldman also told the judge that his boss would have to accept it if he was selected for the jury. (ER 117). Finally,

Juror No. 18, Mr. Woods, revealed that his mother had recently had a heart attack, that the doctors had given her a 20 percent chance of surviving, and that he was unsure whether he would have to go out of town the next week to attend to her. (ER 117-18). None of these jurors were excused for cause. (ER 118).

During voir dire, the prosecutor asked the members of the jury panel whether anyone had had a negative experience with a law enforcement officer. (ER 119). Juror No. 5, a young Native American, responded that she had negative experiences each time she crossed the border between the United States and Canada. (ER 119). Although Juror No. 5 stated that she was not bothered by her experiences at the border, she also stated that she had been pulled aside for additional questioning every time that she had crossed the border. (ER 119).

In contrast, Juror No. 11, Mr. Martin, a white man in his forties with long hair, told the prosecutor that he had been stopped by the police on one occasion because he had a taillight out and on two other occasions because he was jaywalking. (ER 120). Although Mr. Martin said that he was bothered by the fact that he had been stopped by the police, he also said he felt that police officers tended to stop people with long hair more often than people with short hair. (ER 120).

After defense counsel questioned the jury, both the prosecutor and defense counsel were permitted to exercise their peremptory challenges. (ER 122). The prosecutor excused Mr. Feldman, Ms. Whitefish, and Mr. Williams. (ER 122).

At sidebar, defense counsel objected to the prosecutor's use of his peremptory challenges on the grounds that they were based on race, arguing that the prosecutor had excused Mr. Williams and Ms. Whitefish because they were Native Americans. (ER 123). After a hearing outside the presence of the jury, Judge Moore concluded that Mr. Josephy had established a prima facie case for racial discrimination and asked the prosecutor to explain why he had used his peremptory challenges to excuse Mr. Williams and Ms. Whitefish. (ER 124). The

4

prosecutor explained that he excused both Mr. Feldman and Mr. Williams because he thought they would be unable to keep their minds on the case because of their other obligations—namely, Feldman's trip to Africa and Williams's tribal council meeting. (ER 125). The prosecutor then explained that he had excused Ms. Whitefish because her experiences at the border would make it difficult for her to remain impartial. (ER 125).

The judge ruled that these explanations were race neutral and that Josephy had not met his burden of proving that the reasons that the prosecutor had given were a pretext for discrimination. (ER 125). Thus, based on these facts and explanations, Judge Moore overruled the *Batson* objection. (ER 126).

IV. SUMMARY OF THE ARGUMENT

Mr. Josephy's conviction should be affirmed: the district court correctly concluded that the evidence obtained during an investigatory stop was admissible because Agent Bhasin had a reasonable suspicion that Mr. Josephy was involved in criminal activity, and the district court properly exercised its discretion in finding that Mr. Josephy did not meet his burden of establishing that the reasons that the prosecutor gave for using two of his peremptory challenges to excuse Mr. Williams and Ms. Whitefish were a pretext for discrimination.

First, the district court correctly concluded that, under the totality circumstances, the *Terry* stop was permissible because Agent Bhasin had a reasonable suspicion that Mr. Josephy was engaged in criminal activity. The informant, Zachary Dillon, gave the 911 operator his name; Mr. Dillon's 911 call was recorded and transcribed; Mr. Dillon provided the 911 operator not only with a description of Mr. Josephy, Mr. Josephy's car, and Mr. Josephy's companion but also with the name of the motel where Mr. Josephy was staying; Mr. Dillon predicted when Mr. Josephy would leave the motel; and Agent Bhasin verified that Mr. Josephy was staying at the motel, that the vehicle found in the parking lot was registered to Mr. Josephy, and that men matching the descriptions given by Mr. Dillon left the motel during the time frame that Mr. Dillon had predicted.

Second, the district court properly exercised its discretion in denying Mr. Josephy's *Batson* objection based on a finding that Mr. Josephy failed to meet his burden of showing discrimination in the prosecutor's use of peremptory challenges. Peremptory challenges are an important trial tool that permits both parties' counsel to use their professional judgment and educated hunches about individual jurors to ensure a fair and impartial jury. As a result, a *Batson* violation is not established whenever prospective jurors of different races provide similar responses and one is excused but the other is not. Thus, in this case, the district court correctly found that the prosecutor's reasons for exercising peremptory challenges were not a pretext for discrimination. The prosecutor excused one juror because he was concerned that the juror would be distracted by his outside obligations, and the prosecutor excused the second juror because he was concerned that the juror's negative experiences when crossing the border would affect her ability to judge the Government's case fairly. In addition, the district court did the required analysis, and the record supports its conclusion that no *Batson* violation occurred. The court allowed Mr. Josephy to present his prima facie case and then asked the prosecutor to explain his reasons for excusing the jurors before stating that Mr. Josephy had not met his burden of proof.

V. ARGUMENT

A. THE *TERRY* STOP WAS PERMISSIBLE BECAUSE THE ATF AGENTS HAD A REASONABLE SUSPICION THAT MR. JOSEPHY WAS INVOLVED IN CRIMINAL ACTIVITY.

Both the United States Supreme Court and this Court have repeatedly held that law enforcement officers have the authority to conduct an investigatory stop anytime they have a reasonable suspicion that a suspect is engaged in criminal activity. *See, e.g., Florida v. J.L.*, 529 U.S. 266, 272 (2000); *United States v. Fernandez-Castillo*, 324 F.3d 1114, 1119 (9th Cir. 2003). In addition, both the United States Supreme Court and this Court have repeatedly held that evidence obtained during a permissible *Terry* stop is admissible. *J.L.*, 529 U.S. at 272; *Fernandez-Castillo*, 324 F.3d at 119.

In determining whether a *Terry* stop was permissible, the courts do a de novo review, looking at the totality of the circumstances and considering all relevant factors, including those factors that "in a different context, might be entirely innocuous." *Florida v. J.L.*, 529 U.S. at 277-78; *accord United States v. Terry-Crespo*, 356 F.3d 1170, 1172 (9th Cir. 2004). For example, in *Terry-Crespo*, this Court held that the informant's preliminary phone call was, by itself, sufficient to establish a reasonable suspicion that the defendant, Terry-Crespo, was engaged in criminal activity. *Id.* at 1172. In doing so, this Court rejected Terry-Crespo's argument that the informant, Mr. Domingis, should be treated as an anonymous informant because he was not able to provide the 911 operator with the number of the phone from which he placed the call; he changed the subject when the operator asked him to provide another number; and, when asked for his location, he gave the operator a nonexistent intersection. *Id.* at 1174-75. As the court stated in its opinion,

> [d]uring the course of the 911 call, the operator asked Mr. Domingis for his telephone number. Mr. Domingis explained that he did not know the return number because he was calling from someone else's cellular telephone. When the operator asked if there was another number where she could reach him, he did not answer her question but returned to discussing the subject of the suspect's location. The operator asked Mr. Domingis for his location. Initially, he responded by providing a nonexistent intersection on Portland's grid system and then stammeringly told the operator that "I don't want . . . . I don't want . . . . I don't want . . . ." While not certain, it appears that Mr. Domingis did not want police contact.

Id. at 1172.

The Court then went on to note that, although the police tried to locate Mr. Domingis in a number of different databases, including the Yahoo! databases, they were not able to locate anyone by that name. *Id.* However, the Court concluded that the tip had sufficient indicia of reliability because Mr. Domingis was reporting that he had just been the victim of a crime and because Mr. Domingis risked any anonymity that he might have enjoyed by giving the 911 operator his name during a recorded call. *Id.* at 1174-76. As the Court stated, "Merely calling 911 and having a recorded telephone conversation risks the possibility that the police could trace the call or identify Mr. Domingis by his voice." *Id.* at 1176. Thus, even though the police did not independently verify any of the information contained in the tip, the court held that, under the totality of the circumstances, the tip was sufficient to support a finding that Terry-Crespo was engaged in criminal activity. *Id.* at 1177.

Similarly, in *Alabama v. White*, 496 U.S. 325, 330 (1990), the United States Supreme Court held that the police had a reasonable suspicion that the defendant, White, was engaged in criminal activity. In *White*, an anonymous caller phoned 911 and told the operator that Vanessa White would be leaving the Lynnwood Terrace Apartments at a particular time in a brown Plymouth station wagon with a broken taillight to go to Dobey's Motel. *Id.* at 327. In addition, the caller told the 911 operator that White would have about "an ounce of cocaine inside a brown attaché case." *Id.* Although the two police officers who went to the apartment complex saw White get into a brown Plymouth station wagon with a broken taillight, they did not see anything in White's hands. *Id.* Moreover, although White appeared to be driving to Dobey's Motel, the officers had a patrol unit stop the vehicle before it reached the motel. *Id.* The Court held that the officers had a reasonable suspicion despite failing to verify White's predicted destination. *Id.* at 330.

In considering the totality of the circumstances, the Court noted that "the anonymous [tip] contained a range of details relating not just to easily obtained facts and conditions existing at the time of the tip, but to future actions of third

parties ordinarily not easily predicted." As the Court stated,

> The general public would have had no way of knowing that respondent
> would shortly leave the building, get in the described car, and drive the
> most direct route to Dobey's Motel. Because only a small number of people
> are generally privy to an individual's itinerary, it is reasonable for police
> to believe that a person with access to such information is likely to also
> have access to reliable information about that individual's illegal activities.
> See *ibid.* When significant aspects of the caller's predictions were verified,
> there was reason to believe not only that the caller was honest but also
> that he was well informed, at least well enough to justify the stop.

Id. at 332.

In contrast, in *Florida v. J.L.*, the court held that the officers did not have a

reasonable suspicion that the defendant, a minor, was engaged in criminal activity.

Id. at 271. In *J.L.*, the only information the officers had at the time they stopped J.L.

was a tip from an anonymous caller reporting that a "young black male standing

at a particular bus stop and wearing a plaid shirt was carrying a gun." *Id.* at 269.

Two officers were dispatched to the bus stop and, when they arrived, they saw

three black males, one of whom was wearing a plaid shirt. *Id.* The officers did

not, however, see a firearm, and J.L. made no threatening or otherwise unusual

movements. *Id.* In concluding that, under the totality of the circumstances, the

officers did not have a reasonable suspicion that J.L. was involved in criminal

conduct, the Court considered three factors: (1) that the tip came from an indi-

vidual who did not give his name; (2) that the call was not recorded; and (3) that

the call did not contain any predictive information that would have allowed the

police "to test the informant's knowledge or credibility." *Id.* at 270-72.

In contrast, in this case, under the totality of the circumstances, Agent Bhasin

had a reasonable suspicion that Mr. Josephy was engaged in criminal activity.

First, like the caller in *Terry-Crespo*, in this case, the caller gave the 911 opera-

tor his name: Zachary Dillon. (ER 30). Although the ATF agents were not able

to locate anyone by that name in their databases (ER 42), the same was true in

Terry-Crespo, and in *Terry-Crespo*, the court concluded that a tip was not turned into an anonymous tip simply because the police officers were unable to find anyone by the informant's name in their databases.

Second, like the 911 call in *Terry-Crespo*, in this case the 911 call was recorded and transcribed. (ER 30). As a result, there is no risk that the tip was manufactured after the fact. *See id.* at 1175. In addition, the fact that Mr. Dillon gave his name in a recorded call subjected Mr. Dillon to the risk that the police could locate him and that, if he had provided false information, he would be subjected to criminal sanctions. Wash. Rev. Code § 9A.76.175 (2006).

Third, like the caller in *White*, in this case, Mr. Dillon provided the 911 operator with a number of details. For example, Mr. Dillon provided the operator not only with a physical description of Josephy, but also with a physical description of the man Josephy was meeting. (ER 32). Moreover, Mr. Dillon gave the operator the make, model, and color of Josephy's car and the name of the motel where Mr. Josephy was staying. (ER 30, 32). Although there may be a number of individuals who could provide the police with a description of a particular individual and his car, only a small number of people are generally privy to an individual's itinerary.

Fourth, as in *White*, in which the caller predicted that White would be leaving the apartment complex at a particular time, in this case, Mr. Dillon predicted that Josephy would be leaving the motel within an hour or two. (ER 33). That the time frame that Mr. Dillon provided coincides with the standard checkout time is not dispositive. Many motel guests check out long before the established checkout time, and many guests stay more than one night.

Finally, in this case the ATF agents verified all of the information that Mr. Dillon provided. As a consequence, the facts in this case are stronger than the facts in *Terry-Crespo*, in which the officers did not independently verify any of the information in the tip, and they are stronger than the facts in *White*, in which the officers did not see White carrying a brown attaché case and did not verify that she was in fact going to the motel.

Taken together, these factors establish that, under the totality of the circumstances, the tip was far more reliable than the tip in *J.L.*, in which the caller did not give his name, provided the police with only a general description of J.L., and did not provide the police with any predictive information. In fact, these factors establish that, under the totality of the circumstances, the tip is even more reliable than the tip in *Terry-Crespo*. In *Terry-Crespo*, Mr. Domingis reported that Terry-Crespo assaulted him, but the police did not independently verify this fact or any of the other information contained in the tip, and Mr. Domingis appears to have tried to hide from the police by changing the topic when asked for his phone number, by giving a nonexistent intersection as his location, and by making statements that suggested that he did not want the police to contact him. *Id.* 1172.

Because the totality of the circumstances establish that Agent Bhasin had a reasonable suspicion to believe that Mr. Josephy was engaged in criminal activity, the stop was permissible and the Court should affirm the district court's denial of Mr. Josephy's motion to suppress.

B.   THE DISTRICT COURT PROPERLY EXERCISED ITS DISCRETION IN OVER-
       RULING MR. JOSEPHY'S *BATSON* OBJECTION.

Peremptory challenges are an important trial tool that permits both parties' counsel to use their professional judgment and educated hunches about individual jurors to select a fair and impartial jury. *United States v. Bauer*, 84 F.3d 1549, 1555 (9th Cir. 1996). While the Supreme Court has acknowledged difficulties in balancing the need to protect constitutional rights with the proper use of peremptory challenges, the Court has not indicated a willingness to deprive the parties of their right to use peremptory challenges. *See Miller-El v. Dretke*, 545 U.S. 231, 239-40

(2005). Indeed, Justice Breyer's concurrence, in which he posited that the Court should reconsider the *Batson* test and the peremptory system as a whole, failed to garner a single co-signer. *Id.* at 266-67 (Breyer, J. concurring).

Thus, the courts continue to apply the three-step test set out in *Batson. Batson*, 476 U.S. at 89, 96-98. Under the test, a defendant's rights are not violated unless (1) the defendant establishes a prima facie case of purposeful discrimination in the government's use of peremptory challenges by showing that the challenged juror is a member of a cognizable class and that the circumstances raise an inference of discrimination; and (2) the government fails to meet its burden to provide a race-neutral explanation for its strike; or (3) the government offers a race-neutral reason, but the defendant meets his burden of showing that a review of all relevant circumstances shows purposeful discrimination. *See Johnson v. California*, 545 U.S. 162, 169 (2005); *Batson v. Kentucky*, 476 U.S. 79, 89, 96-98 (1986).

In the case before the court, Mr. Josephy has not argued that the district court erred in deciding that the reasons the prosecutor gave for exercising the peremptory challenges were not facially neutral. Thus, the only issues before this Court are whether the district court properly concluded that Mr. Josephy had not met his burden of proving that the reasons the prosecutor gave for exercising the peremptory challenges were a pretext for discrimination and whether the record is adequate.

1. Mr. Josephy has not met his burden of proving that the reasons that the prosecutor gave for the peremptory challenges were a pretext for purposeful discrimination.

In reviewing the third step in the *Batson* analysis, appellate courts give great deference to the trial court's determination and reverse a trial court only when the appellate court has a "definite and firm conviction" that a mistake has been made. *United States v. U.S. Gypsum Co.*, 333 U.S. 364, 395 (1948); *Bauer*, 84 F.3d 1555. While such a mistake occurs when the record contradicts the prosecutor's stated reasoning, *see, e.g., McClain v. Prunty*, 217 F.3d 1209, 1220-21 (9th Cir. 2000), in this case there is no such contradiction.

United States v. Josephy stands in stark contrast to *McClain*, where a review of the record revealed a clear contradiction in objectively verifiable facts. *Id.* In *McClain*, the first reason the prosecutor gave for excusing a black juror was that the juror had stated that she mistrusted the system and had been treated unfairly. *Id.* at 1221. In fact, what the juror said was that *her son* did not trust the public defender and that, although she initially believed that her son had been treated unfairly, this was no longer true. *Id.* In addition, the record contradicted the second reason the prosecutor gave for striking the juror. *Id.* Although the prosecutor stated that he was excusing the juror because she had lied about being a stewardess because she was heavyset, the juror had actually said she worked in airline maintenance. *Id.*

In contrast, in *United States v. Josephy*, the record supports the reasons that the prosecutor gave for excusing Mr. Williams and Ms. Whitefish. When asked why he had excused Mr. Williams, the prosecutor stated that he was concerned that, because Mr. Williams had a tribal council meeting scheduled for the following week, Mr. Williams might be distracted. (ER 125). The record supports this explanation: Mr. Williams told that court that although he could forego attending a tribal council meeting scheduled for the following week, he would prefer not to. (ER 117). Similarly, the prosecutor excused Ms. Whitefish because the prosecutor believed she would be unable "to judge this case fairly and impartially" based on her prior experiences crossing the border. (ER 125). The record supports the prosecutor's reason: Ms. Whitefish acknowledged that she had been subjected to additional questioning at the border. (ER 119).

Furthermore, case law does not support the notion that *Batson* is violated whenever prospective jurors of different races provide similar responses and one is excused but the other is not. *Burks v. Borg*, 27 F.3d 1424, 1429 (9th Cir. 1994). For example, in *Burks*, this Court held that there was not purposeful discrimination in spite of the fact that a minority juror who was struck shared characteristics with a nonminority juror who was not struck. *Id.* The prosecutor told the court that he had stricken the minority jurors "because they were 'squishy' on the death penalty, expressed a reluctance to serve, and/or lacked certain life experiences." *Id.* In concluding that there was no purposeful discrimination, this Court reaffirmed that "[t]rial counsel is entitled to exercise his full professional judgment in pursuing his client's 'legitimate interest in using [peremptory] challenges . . . to secure a fair and impartial jury.'" *Id.* (quoting *J.E.B. v. Alabama*, 511 U.S. 127 (1994)). Thus, in using his or her peremptory challenges, trial counsel is entitled to take into account "tone, demeanor, facial expression, emphasis—all those factors that make the words uttered by the prospective juror convincing or not." *Burks*, 27 F.3d at 1429.

In this case, such a comparison supports the district court's decision that there was no purposeful discrimination. For example, in response to the trial judge's question regarding other obligations, three jurors answered that they had conflicts the following week, and all stated a willingness to still serve on the jury. (ER 117-18). The prosecutor used two of his peremptory challenges against the two jurors who already had definite plans—one had a tribal council meeting and the other was going to Africa. (ER 117). In addition, the prosecutor provided the same neutral reason for both strikes—that the jurors would be too distracted to tend to the business of the jury. (ER 125). Therefore, the prosecutor acted consistently: he struck the two jurors who had definite plans for the following week, and he did not strike the one whose plans were not definite. Finally, in making his decision, the prosecutor was allowed to consider factors that are difficult to discern from a paper record, for example, the demeanor of each of the potential jurors.

Likewise, the district court did not err in concluding that the prosecutor had not engaged in purposeful discrimination when he excused Ms. Whitefish but not Mr. Martin. Although both Ms. Whitefish and Mr. Martin volunteered that they had negative experiences with law enforcement personnel, there may have been other factors that influenced the prosecutor in his decision about how to use his peremptory challenges. For example, the prosecutor may have taken into consideration Ms. Whitefish's young age or limited set of experiences. Because this type of judgment call is not based on race, it falls well within the purpose behind peremptory challenges of providing a "useful instrument for molding a more impartial jury." *See Burks*, 27 F.3d at 1429.

   2. <u>The record establishes that the district court conducted the required sensitive inquiry because the court ensured that both parties had the opportunity to respond at each of the three steps of the *Batson* analysis.</u>

Mr. Josephy's reliance on *Jordan v. Lefevre*, 206 F.3d 196, 198 (2d Cir. 2000), is misplaced: in this case, the district court did the required analysis, and the record is sufficient.

In *Jordan*, the defendant objected to the prosecutor's use of his peremptory challenges to strike several black jurors. *Id.* at 199. However, before the defendant could even make his prima facie case, the court cut him short "in order to save us an awful lot of time." *Id.* Instead, the trial court immediately asked the prosecutor for a "non-racial reason for exercising the challenges," prefacing the request with a statement that "I don't think it's necessary or required." *Id.*

The prosecutor gave neutral reasons, and the trial court summarily overruled the defendant's objection, stating only, "to the extent there is any application [on] the *Batson*, I'm denying it. It seems to me there is some rational basis for the exercise of the challenge." *Id.* When defense counsel later tried to create a record, the trial judge told him, "You've already made your record." *Id.* When defense counsel made a second objection, arguing that "the record is not complete," the judge replied "do it very succinctly, because I'm not going to be spending more time in here listening to you." *Id.* Given this specific set of facts, the Court of Appeals agreed with the defendant that "the district court's conclusory statement that the prosecutor's explanations were race neutral did not satisfy *Batson*'s third step." *Id.* at 200.

In contrast, in this case, the district court allowed Mr. Josephy to present his prima facie case and then asked the prosecutor to explain why he had excused Mr. Williams and why he had excused Ms. Whitefish. (ER 123-24). It was not until after the prosecutor had set out his reason that the district court judge stated that Mr. Josephy had not met his burden of proof. (ER 125-26). Therefore, in this case, the district court did the required analysis, and the record supports its conclusion.

VI. CONCLUSION

For the reasons set out above, the Government respectfully requests that the Court of Appeals affirm the district court. The district court properly denied the motion to suppress because the investigatory stop was supported by a reasonable suspicion that Mr. Josephy was involved in drug trafficking. In addition, the district court properly overruled the *Batson* objection because it properly found that Mr. Josephy failed to meet his burden of proving purposeful discrimination.

Dated: _____   Respectfully submitted,

_____
Andrew Froh
United States Attorney
Western District of Washington
James Jorgenson
Assistant United States Attorney
700 Stewart Street
Seattle, WA 98101
Tel: (206) 555-1234
Counsel for Appellee

EXCERPTS FROM APPELLANT'S AND RESPONDENT'S BRIEFS IN *STATE V. MORRISON*, A CASE BEING HEARD BY THE WASHINGTON COURT OF APPEALS SHOWING HARMLESS ERROR ANALYSIS

The following examples of harmless error arguments are taken from *State v. Morrison*, a case heard by the Washington Court of Appeals. Because the briefs were filed in a Washington court, the authors used Washington's citation rules. The facts are as follows:

The defendant, Mr. Morrison, was convicted of the murder of Mr. Louis Wall, a drug runner who was shot to death in his car in the parking lot of the Southcenter Shopping Mall. The State's case was circumstantial: there were no witnesses to the murder; the murder weapon was never found; the cell phone Mr. Wall used that day was never recovered; and, despite the fact that Mr. Morrison and Mr. Wall had planned to meet for a drug transaction, there was no cocaine and only a small amount of change in the car. Although Mr. Morrison was the last person known to have met with Mr. Wall that day, he met with Mr. Wall at a fast food restaurant and not in the Southcenter parking lot.

On appeal, Mr. Morrison raised three issues, including that the trial court erred when it granted the State's motion to exclude other suspect testimony: a defense witness would have testified that Kevin Phillips, another person involved in the local drug culture, was seen after the murder, within a few miles of the murder scene, with a gun, cocaine, and a phone similar to Wall's cell phone.

In the following examples, we have excerpted just the harmless error arguments from the briefs from both sides.

Appellant's Harmless Error Argument

B. <u>The erroneous exclusion of other suspect evidence requires reversal because the State's circumstantial case, which did not place Mr. Morrison at the scene of the crime or establish that he had a weapon with him that day, was not overwhelming.</u>

The trial court's erroneous exclusion of other suspect evidence violated Mr. Morrison's constitutional right to present a defense. Therefore, the error is presumed to be prejudicial. *State v. Stephens*, 93 Wn.2d 186, 190-91, 607 P.2d 304 (1980).

A constitutional error requires reversal when the appellate court is not convinced beyond a reasonable doubt that any reasonable jury would have reached the same result in the absence of the error. *State v. Maupin*, 128 Wn.2d

918, 929, 913 P.2d 808 (1996). When the evidence is not so overwhelming that it necessarily leads to a finding of guilt, the error is not harmless. *State v. Guloy*, 104 Wn.2d 412, 425, 705 P.2d 1182 (1985). The burden of proving an error was harmless rests on the State. *State v. Stephens*, 93 Wn.2d at 190-91.

In the present case, the State has not met its burden of proof because the circumstantial case against Mr. Morrison was not overwhelming: it does not place him at the scene of the murder, nor does the timeline support his involvement in the crime. Moreover, the evidence neither places a gun on him on the day of the crime nor establishes that the gun later recovered was involved in the crime.

First, no evidence places Mr. Morrison at the scene of the crime. RP 44. Mr. Wall's body was found in his car one-quarter mile away and across a very busy road, RP 42, from the Jack in the Box parking lot where Mr. Morrison met with Mr. Wall. RP 45. Mr. Wall was found with his seatbelt on and a cigarette in his hand, resting on his leg. RP 44. The evidence was uncontroverted that he was killed as he sat in his car in that parking lot, not at another location. Further, although Mr. Billings testified that he saw what he thought was Mr. Morrison's truck leaving the Jack in the Box after the transaction was over, he could not positively identify the vehicle or who was in it. RP 44, 88.

Moreover, the timeline does not support Mr. Morrison's involvement in the murder. The manager of the hotel where Mr. Morrison was staying with his former girlfriend testified that Mr. Morrison's security deposit was returned when Mr. Morrison checked out of the hotel the day of the murder. RP 94. The manager stated that the deposit would not have been returned if Mr. Morrison had checked out any later than 11:30 a.m. RP 95. Another witness testified that Mr. Wall's car was not parked in the Southcenter parking lot at 11:40 a.m. when he arrived, but was there at 1:00 p.m. RP 172. Therefore, when Mr. Wall was murdered, Mr. Morrison was not in the parking lot.

Second, there was no evidence that Mr. Morrison had a gun that day. RP 110. Moreover, there were no readable fingerprints, RP 87, or blood on the gun that was recovered weeks later. RP 84. Nor could the ballistics examiner say for certain that was the gun that killed the victim. Indeed, the muzzle stamp on the victim's head was consistent with two different types of guns. RP 76.

In contrast, the excluded evidence would have shown that another possible suspect, Kevin Phillips, had a gun shortly after the time of the murder: Mr. Wall was found dead in his car at around 12:30 p.m. RP 44. A witness, Jeanne Smith, would have testified that, when she saw Phillips in the late morning or early afternoon of that day, he had a gun. CP 10.

Given that the State's case relied on merely circumstantial evidence against Mr. Morrison that was not overwhelming, the error in excluding the other suspect evidence violated Mr. Morrison's constitutional right to present a defense. Therefore, this error requires a reversal.

Respondent's Harmless Error Argument

C. <u>Any error in excluding the evidence was harmless because the evidence against the defendant was overwhelming: he was the last known person to see Mr. Wall alive and to speak on Mr. Wall's cell phone, he needed money, and he owned a gun of the same caliber as the gun used to murder Mr. Wall.</u>

An error can be so insignificant that it is harmless. *Maupin*, 128 Wn.2d 918, 928, 913 P.2d 808 (1996). Although an error infringing on the defendant's constitutional rights is presumed to be prejudicial, *State v. Fowler*, 114 Wn.2d 59, 63, 785 P.2d 808 (1990), *rev'd on other grounds by State v. Blair*, 117 Wn.2d 479, 816 P.2d 718 (1991), once the State proves that the error was harmless beyond a reasonable doubt, the court should affirm the conviction despite the error. *State v. Maupin*, 128 Wn.2d at 929.

This Court should affirm the conviction because the evidence against the defendant was overwhelming; therefore, any error was harmless beyond a reasonable doubt. *See State v. Dixon*, 159 Wn.2d 65, 147 P.3d 991 (2006).

The evidence against the defendant was overwhelming for three reasons: (1) the defendant was the last known person to see Mr. Wall alive and the last known person to speak on Mr. Wall's cell phone. RP 79, 101; (2) the defendant had an expensive cocaine habit and needed money; and (3) the defendant owned the same caliber gun as the one used to murder Mr. Wall. RP 45, 96.

First, the defendant was the last known person to see Mr. Wall alive. The defendant met with Mr. Wall at the Jack in the Box on the day of the murder to buy cocaine. RP 44. When an associate of Mr. Wall, Mr. Billings, called to check in with Mr. Wall, the defendant answered Mr. Wall's cell phone. RP 88. Mr. Billings testified that when he drove to the location he saw what he thought was the defendant's truck leaving the Jack in the Box thirty minutes after the drug deal should have been over. RP 88.

Second, the defendant needed money to support his $75–$100 per day cocaine habit. RP 78. Although he was receiving unemployment benefits, the defendant asked to borrow money from others and rented his house in exchange for money and cocaine. RP 44, 79, 90. Moreover, the defendant told his girlfriend he was going out the morning of the murder to get more money, there was no cocaine found in Mr. Wall's car, and a money bag found in Mr. Wall's car contained only fifty-five cents. RP 73, 111.

Finally, although the ballistics expert could not definitively tie the gun to the murder because the barrel was missing, RP 75, the defendant owned a gun of the same caliber as one of only two types of gun that could have been used to commit the murder, RP 76. In addition, although the defendant claimed to have lost the barrel of the gun, he never explained how or when he lost the barrel. RP 97.

Given the overwhelming evidence against the defendant, any error in excluding the evidence was harmless beyond a reasonable doubt.

Oral Advocacy

Oral argument. For some, it is the part of practice they most enjoy; for others, it is the part they most dread.

Whichever group you fall into, oral argument is probably not what you expect. It is not a speech, a debate, or a performance. Instead, when done right, it is a dialogue between the attorneys and the judges. The attorneys explain the issues, facts, and law, and the judges ask questions, not because they want to badger the attorney or because they want to see how much he or she knows, but because they want to make the right decision.

§ 3.1 Audience

In making an oral argument, who is your audience? At the trial court level, the audience is the trial judge who is hearing the motion; at the appellate level, it is the panel of judges hearing the appeal. In both instances, the audience is extremely sophisticated. Although an eloquent oral argument is more persuasive than an oral argument that is not eloquent, form seldom wins out over substance. If you do not have anything to say, it does not matter how well you say it.

At oral argument, the court can be either "hot" or "cold." The court is hot when the judges come prepared to the oral argument. The judges have studied the briefs and, at least in some appellate courts, have met in a pre-oral argument conference to discuss the case. In contrast, a cold court is not as prepared. The judge or judges are not familiar with the case, and if they have not yet read the briefs, they have done so only quickly.

As a general rule, hot courts are more active than cold courts. Because they have studied the briefs, they often have their own agenda. They want to know more about point A, or they are concerned about how the rule being advocated might be applied in other cases. As a consequence, they often take more control over the argument, directing counsel to discuss certain issues and asking a number of questions. A cold court is usually comparatively passive. Because the judges are not as familiar with the case, most of their questions are informational. They want counsel to clarify the issue, supply a fact, or explain in more detail how the law should be applied.

§ 3.2 Purpose

In making your oral argument, you have two goals: to educate and to persuade. You want to explain the law and the facts in such a way that the court rules in your client's favor.

§ 3.3 Preparing for Oral Argument

The key to a good oral argument is preparation. You must know what you must argue to win, you must know your case, and you must have practiced both the text of your argument and your responses to the questions the court can reasonably be expected to ask.

§ 3.3.1 Deciding What to Argue

In making your argument, you will have only a limited amount of time. Depending on the case and the court, you will be granted ten, fifteen, or thirty minutes to make your points; answer the judge or judges' questions; and, if you are the appellant, to make your rebuttal. Because time is so limited, you will not be able to make every argument that you made in your brief. You must be selective.

PRACTICE POINTER In selecting the issues and arguments that you will make, choose those that are essential. Do not spend your time on the easy argument if, to get the relief you want, you must win on the hard one. Make the arguments that you must make to win.

Also anticipate the arguments that the other side is likely to make. Although you do not want to make the other side's arguments, try to integrate your responses into your argument. Similarly, anticipate the court's concerns and decide how they can best be handled.

§ 3.3.2 Preparing an Outline

Do not write out your argument. If you do, you will either read it, or perhaps worse yet, memorize and recite it. Neither is appropriate. A dialogue does not have a predetermined text. Instead, prepare either a list of the points you want to cover or an outline.

Because it is difficult to predict how much of the time will be spent answering the court's questions, many advocates prepare two lists or outlines: a short version, in which they list only those points that they must make, and a long version, in which they list the points they would like to make if they have time. If the court is hot and asks a number of questions, they argue from the short list or outline; if the court is cold, they use the long one.

§ 3.3.3 Practicing the Argument

The next step is to practice, both by yourself and with colleagues. Working alone, practice your opening, your closing, your statements of the law, and the arguments themselves. Think carefully about the language you will use and about how you will move from one issue to the next and, within an issue, from argument to argument. Also list every question that a judge could be reasonably expected to ask, and decide (1) how you will respond and (2) how you can move from the answer to another point in your argument.

Then, with colleagues, practice delivering the argument. Ask your colleagues to play the role of the judge(s), sometimes asking almost no questions and at other times asking many. As you deliver the argument, concentrate on "reading" the court, adjusting your argument to meet its concerns; on responding to questions; and on the transitions between issues and arguments. Before a major argument, you will want to go through your argument five to ten times, practicing in front of as many different people as you can.

§ 3.3.4 Reviewing the Facts and the Law

You will also want to review the facts of the case, the law, and both your brief and your opponent's brief. When you walk into the courtroom, you should know everything there is to know about your case.

PRACTICE POINTER   In practice, months or years might pass between the writing of the brief and the oral argument. When this is the case, it is essential that you update your research, and, when appropriate, file a supplemental brief with the court or statement of additional authorities.

§ 3.3.5 Organizing Your Materials

Part of the preparation is getting your materials organized. You do not want to be flipping through your notes or searching the record during oral argument.

a. Notes or Outline

To avoid the "flipping pages syndrome," limit yourself to two pages of notes: a one-page short list or outline and a one-page long list or outline, which you can staple to the inside of a manila folder. Use colored markers to highlight the key portions of the argument.

b. The Briefs

You will want to take a copy of your brief and your opponent's brief with you to the podium, placing them on the inside shelf. Make sure that you know both what is in the briefs and where that information is located.

c. The Record

In arguing an appeal, you will usually want to have the relevant portions of the record in the courtroom, either on the podium shelf or on counsel table. You should also be fully familiar with the record, as with the briefs, knowing both what is in the record and where particular information can be found. So that they can locate information quickly, many attorneys tab the record or prepare an index.

d. The Law

Although you do not need to have copies of all of the statutes and cases with you, you should be familiar with both the statutes and cases you cited in your brief and those on which your opponent's case is based. If you do bring cases with you, have them indexed and highlighted for quick reference.

§ 3.4 Courtroom Procedures and Etiquette

Like much of law, oral argument has its own set of conventions and procedures.

§ 3.4.1 Seating

In many jurisdictions, the moving party sits on the left (when facing the court) and the responding party sits on the right.

§ 3.4.2 Before the Case Is Called

If court is not in session, sit at counsel table, reviewing your notes or quietly conversing with co-counsel. If court is in session, sit in the audience until the prior case is completed. When your case is called, rise and move to counsel table.

§ 3.4.3 Courtroom Etiquette

Stand each time you are instructed to do so by the bailiff. For example, stand when the bailiff calls court into session and announces the judge or judges, and stand when court is recessed or adjourned. In the first instance, remain standing until the judges are seated, and in the latter instance, remain standing until the judges have left the courtroom.

Also stand each time you address the court, whether it be to tell the court that you are ready to proceed, to make your argument, or to respond to a question.

In addressing the court, you will want to use the phrases "Your Honor," "Your Honors," "this Court," "the Court," or, occasionally, the judge's name: "Judge Yu" or "Justice Smith." Never use a judge's or justice's first name.

PRACTICE

The title judge or justice can vary depending on your jurisdiction and on whether you are in an intermediate court or the jurisdiction's highest court. Make sure that you are using the correct title to address the members of the bench.

Finally, during the argument, do not speak directly to opposing counsel. Instead, address all of your statements to the court. Also remember that you are always "on." While opposing counsel is arguing, sit attentively at counsel table, listening and, if appropriate, taking notes.

§ 3.4.4 Appropriate Dress

As a sign of respect, both for the court and the client, most attorneys wear suits. Men wear conservative suits and ties, and women wear a suit coat and matching pants or skirts. The key is to look professional but not severe. During oral argument, the judge's attention should be focused on your argument, not on your attire.

§ 3.5 Making the Argument

Like the brief, the oral argument has a prescribed format. The following example sets out the typical outline for an oral argument.

EXAMPLE 1   OUTLINE OF ORAL ARGUMENT

A. *Moving party* (party bringing the motion or, on appeal, the appellant)
   1. Introductions
   2. Opening
   3. Statement of the issue(s)
   4. Brief summary of the significant facts (when appropriate)
   5. Argument
   6. Conclusion and request for relief
B. *Responding party* (party opposing the motion or, on appeal, the respondent or appellee)
   1. Introductions
   2. Opening
   3. Statement of position
   4. Brief summary of significant facts (when appropriate)
   5. Argument
   6. Conclusion and request for relief
C. *Moving party's rebuttal*
D. *Sur-rebuttal* (when allowed)

§ 3.5.1 Introductions

Begin your oral argument by introducing yourself and your client. At the trial court level, the language is relatively informal. Most attorneys say "Good morning, Your Honor," and then introduce themselves and the client. At the appellate level, the language is more formal. By convention, most attorneys begin by saying, "May it please the Court, my name is _____, and I represent the [appellant] [respondent], _____."

PRACTICE POINTER

In many courts, the introduction is also used to reserve rebuttal time. The attorney for the moving party reserves rebuttal either before introducing himself or herself or immediately afterwards: "Your Honor, at this time, I would like to reserve _____ minutes for rebuttal." If you do not reserve rebuttal time, the court might not allow you to present a rebuttal.

§ 3.5.2 Opening

The first minute of your argument should be memorable. The opening sentences should catch the judge's attention, making the case's importance clear, establishing the theme, and creating the appropriate context for the argument that follows.

§ 3.5.3 Statement of the Issues

a. The Moving Party

If you are the moving party, you need to set out the issues. Sometimes this is best done as part of the opening. From the issue statement alone, the case's importance is clear: "In this case, the appellant asks the Court to overrule *Roe v. Wade*." At other times, such a strategy is not effective. For example, few trial judges would find the following opening memorable: "In this case, the defendant asks the court to suppress identification testimony." In such cases, the opening and the statement of the issues should not be combined.

As a general rule, the statement of the issues should precede the summary of the facts. Before hearing the facts, the court needs a context. There are times, however, when it is more effective to set out the issues after the summary of the facts.

Wherever they are presented, the issue statements must be tailored to oral argument. What is effective in writing might not be effective when spoken. For example, although the under-does-when format works well in a brief, it does not work well orally. In oral argument, the issue needs to be presented more simply: "In this case, the court is asked to decide whether . . ." or "This case presents two issues: first, whether . . . and second, whether . . . ." An issue statement can be even stronger if it is stated as a positive assertion, much like an argumentative heading: "This court should reverse because Mr. Josephy's constitutional rights were violated by the admission of evidence obtained from an unlawful search and by the prosecutor's purposeful discrimination in the use of its peremptory challenges to remove Native Americans from the jury. The search was unlawful because . . . ."

Even though they are streamlined, the issues should be presented in the light most favorable to the client. The questions should be framed as they were in the brief, and the significant and emotionally favorable facts should be included. See sections 1.6 and 2.12.

b. The Responding Party

As a general rule, the responding party does not restate the issue or issues. Instead, it states its position, either as part of its opening or as a lead-in to its arguments: "The trial court did not err in denying Mr. Josephy's motion to suppress because the officers had a reasonable suspicion that the defendant was engaged in criminal activity."

§ 3.5.4 Summary of Facts

a. The Moving Party

When arguing to a cold court, you will want to include a summary of the facts, in one to three minutes telling the court what the case is about. You might also want to include a summary of the facts when arguing to a hot court. If the facts are particularly important, you will want to summarize them, refresh the court's memory, and present the facts in the light most favorable to the client. There will, however, be times when a separate summary of the facts is not the best use of limited time. In these cases, instead of presenting the facts in a separate summary at the beginning, integrate them into the argument.

b. The Responding Party

As the responding party, you do not want to use your time repeating what opposing counsel just said. Consequently, for you a summary of the facts is optional even if the court is cold. If opposing counsel has set out the facts accurately, the summary can be omitted. Just integrate the significant facts into the argument. You will, however, want to include a summary if opposing counsel has misstated key facts or has omitted facts that are important to your argument or if you need to present the facts from your client's point of view.

PRACTICE 	In presenting the facts, you will not, as a matter of course, include references to the record. You must, however, be able to provide such references if asked to do so by the court or if you are correcting a misstatement made by opposing counsel.

§ 3.5.5 The Argument

Unless the issues and arguments build on each other, start with your strongest issue and, in discussing that issue, your strongest argument. This allows you to take advantage of the positions of emphasis and ensures that you will have the opportunity to make your best, or most crucial, arguments. In addition, it usually results in better continuity. Because the moving party's strongest issue is usually the responding party's weakest, the moving party's final issue will be the responding party's first, providing the responding party with an easy opening for his or her argument.

Moving Party	*Responding Party*
Issue 1 → Issue 2	Issue 2 → Issue 1

In presenting the arguments, do what you did in your brief but in abbreviated form. When the law is not in dispute, begin by presenting the rule of law, presenting that law in the light most favorable to your client (see sections 1.9.3 and 2.15.3). Then argue that law, explaining why the court should reach the result that you advocate. When it is the law itself that is in dispute, argue your interpretation.

In both instances, you must support your position and present arguments based on the plain language of the statute or rule, legislative intent, policy, facts of the case, or analogous cases. When appropriate, cite to the relevant portions of a statute or to a common law rule and, in using analogous cases, be specific: explain the rule that the court applied, the significant facts, and the court's reasoning. Although you should have the full case citations available, you do not need to include them in your argument.

Although you want to cite to the relevant authorities, you do not, as a general rule, want to quote them or your own brief. Reading more than a line is seldom effective. If it is important that the court have specific language before it, refer the judge or judges to the appropriate page in the brief or, better yet, prepare a visual aid.

There are several other things that you need to keep in mind in making your argument. First, it is usually more difficult to follow an oral argument than a written one. As a result, it is important to include sufficient roadmaps, signposts, and transitions. Make both the structure of your argument and the connections between ideas explicit.

Second, you need to manage your time. Do not spend so much time on one issue or argument that you do not have time for the other issues or arguments. Because it is difficult to predict how many questions the court will ask, practice both a short version and a long version of each argument.

§ 3.5.6 Answering Questions

You should welcome the court's questions. They tell you what the court is thinking about your case, what the judges understand, and what they still question. If you are not getting questions, it is usually a bad sign. The judges have either already made up their minds or are not listening.

Questions from the bench fall into several categories. Some are mere requests for information. The judge wants to clarify a fact or your position on an issue or wants to know more about the rule or how you think it should be applied.

Other questions are designed to elicit a particular response from you: Judge A agrees with your position and wants you to pursue a particular line of argument for the benefit of Judge B, who is not yet persuaded. Still other questions are designed to test the merits of your argument. These questions may have as their focus your case or, at the appellate level, future cases. If the court applies rule A, what does that mean for cases X, Y, and Z?

Whatever the type of question, when the judge begins to speak, you must stop. Although judges can interrupt you, you should not interrupt them. As the judge speaks, listen—not only to the question that is being asked, but also for clues about how the judge is perceiving the case.

The hardest part comes next. Before answering the judge, think through your answer. Although the second or two of silence might make you uncomfortable, the penalty for answering too quickly can be severe. Although few cases are won at oral argument, some are lost, usually because in answering a question an attorney conceded or asserted too much. The second or two of silence is by far better than an unfavorable ruling.

When you know what you want to say, answer. In most instances, you will want to begin by giving the judge a one-, two-, or three-word answer. "Yes," "No," "Yes, but . . . ," "No, but . . . ," or "In some cases, ..." Then explain or support your answer, integrating the points that you want to make into your answer when possible. Instead of thinking of questions as interruptions, think of them as another vehicle for making your argument.

There are a number of things that you should not do in responding to a question. First, do not tell the judge that you will answer the question later. It is you, not the judge, who must be flexible.

Second, do not argue with the judge. Answer all questions calmly and thoughtfully. Do not raise your voice, and even if you are frustrated, do not let it show. If one line of argument is not working and the point is essential to your case, try another, and if that line does not work, try still another. When the point is not important or you have given all the answers you have, answer, and then, without pausing, move as smoothly as you can into the next part of your argument.

Third, after answering the question, do not stop and wait for the judge's approval or permission to continue. Answer the question, and then, unless asked another question, move to the next part of your argument. Finally, do not answer by asking the judge a question. In oral argument, it is inappropriate to question a judge.

§ 3.5.7 The Closing

The closing is as important as the opening. Because it is a position of emphasis, you want to end on a favorable point.

One way of doing this is to end with a summary of your arguments, reminding the court of your strongest points and requesting the appropriate relief. Although this is often effective, it can also be ineffective. Many judges stop listening when they hear the phrase "In conclusion" or "In summary." Consequently, when using a summary, avoid stock openers. Catch the court's attention by repeating a key phrase, weaving the pieces together, or returning to the points made in your opening.

Another way is to end on a strong point. If you are running out of time, it might be better to stop at the end of an argument or after answering a question than to rush through a prepared closing. Like a good comedian, a good advocate knows when to sit down.

§ 3.5.8 Rebuttal

Perhaps the hardest part of the oral argument is rebuttal. In one or two minutes you must identify the crucial issues and make your strongest argument or response.

If you try to make too many points in rebuttal, you dilute the power of each. Therefore, as a general rule, do not try to make more than one or two points. The points should be selected because of their importance to your case: do not merely repeat what you said in the main portion of your argument or respond to trivial points made by opposing counsel. Instead, make your rebuttal a true rebuttal by responding to significant points made by opposing counsel or questions or concerns raised by the court during opposing counsel's argument.

Because time is so limited, most advocates begin their rebuttal by telling the court how many points they plan to make: "I would like to make two points." This introduction tells the court what to expect. The advocate then makes his or her first point and supports it and, unless interrupted by a question, moves to the second point. Most advocates close by quickly repeating their request for relief.

§ 3.6 Delivering the Argument

Every advocate has his or her own style. Some are soft-spoken and others are dynamic; some are plain-speaking and others strive for eloquence. As an advocate, you will need to develop your own style, building on your strengths and minimizing your weaknesses. Whatever your style, there are, however, certain "rules" that you should follow.

§ 3.6.1 Do Not Read Your Argument

The first, and perhaps most important, rule is not to read your argument. Similarly, do not try to deliver a memorized speech. Know what you want to say and then talk to the court. You are a teacher, sharing information and answering the court's questions.

§ 3.6.2 Maintain Eye Contact

If you do not read, you will be able to maintain eye contact with the judge or judges. Eye contact is important for several reasons. First, it helps you keep the judge's attention. It is very difficult not to listen to a person who is looking you in the eye. Second, it helps you "read" the court. By studying the judges, you can often determine (1) whether they already agree with you on a point and you can move to the next part of your argument, (2) whether they are confused, or (3) whether you have not yet persuaded them. Finally, eye contact is important because of what it says about you and your argument. An advocate who looks the judge in the eye is perceived as being more confident and more competent than one who does not.

PRACTICE POINTER   When you are arguing to an appellate court, maintain eye contact with all of the judges, even when you are answering a specific judge's question.

---

§ 3.6.3 Do Not Slouch, Rock, or Put Your Hands in Your Pockets

In delivering an oral argument to the court, stand erect, but not stiffly, behind the podium. Do not rock from foot to foot, and do not put your hands in your pockets.

Although it might be appropriate to move around the courtroom when arguing to a jury, you should not do so when arguing to the court.

§ 3.6.4 Limit Your Gestures and Avoid Distracting Mannerisms

Gestures are appropriate in an oral argument. They should, however, be natural and relatively constrained. If you talk with your hands, mentally put yourself inside a small telephone booth.

You also want to avoid distracting mannerisms. Do not play with a pen, the edge of your notes, or the keys in your pocket. In addition, do not repeatedly push hair out of your eyes or your glasses back up on your nose.

§ 3.6.5 Speak So that You Can Be Easily Understood

In delivering your oral argument, speak loudly and clearly enough that you can be easily heard by the judges.

Also try to modulate your voice, varying both the pace and volume of your speech. If you want to emphasize a point, speak more slowly and either more softly or more loudly.

§ 3.7 Making Your Argument Persuasive

In delivering your oral argument, you will want to use many of the same techniques that you used in writing your brief. In stating the issue, frame the question so that it suggests the answer favorable to your client and, in presenting the facts, emphasize the favorable facts by placing them in positions of emphasis and by using detail and sentence structure to your advantage. See sections 1.5.3 and 2.12.5. Also present the law in the light most favorable to your client. State favorable rules broadly, use cases to your advantage, and emphasize the policies that support your client's position. See sections 1.9.3 and 2.15.3.

You should also pick your words carefully. Select words both for their denotation and their connotation and avoid words and phrases that undermine the persuasiveness of your argument. If you represent the defendant, do not say, "It is the defendant's position that the officers violated the defendant's Fourth Amendment rights when they searched his car." Instead, say, "The officers violated the defendant's Fourth Amendment rights when they searched his car." Similarly, do not say, "We feel that the State engaged in purposeful discrimination when it used its peremptory challenges to excuse the only two Native Americans in the jury pool." Instead, say, "The State engaged in purposeful discrimination when it used its peremptory challenges to excuse the only two Native Americans in the jury pool."

§ 3.8 Handling the Problems

Because an oral argument is not scripted, you need to prepare for the unexpected and decide in advance how you will handle the problems that might arise.

§ 3.8.1 Counsel Has Misstated Facts or Law

If opposing counsel misstates an important fact or the governing law, you will usually want to bring the error to the attention of the court. You should, however, use care in correcting opposing counsel.

First, make sure you are right. If there is time, double-check the record, the statute, or the case. Second, make sure you are correcting a misstatement of fact or law, not the opposing party's interpretation of a fact, statute, or case. Third, correct the mistake, not opposing counsel. Instead of criticizing or attacking opposing counsel, simply provide the court with the correct information and, if possible, the citation to the record or the language of the statute or case.

EXAMPLE 1 **CORRECTING A STATEMENT MADE BY OPPOSING COUNSEL**

"Ms. Martinez did not see the assailant three times. She testified that she saw him twice: once when he drove by slowly and then when he pulled in front of her."

Finally, correct only those errors that are significant.

§ 3.8.2 You Make a Mistake

If you make a significant mistake, correct it as soon as you can.

§ 3.8.3 You Do Not Have Enough Time

Despite the best planning, you will sometimes run out of time. You might have gotten more questions than you expected, leaving you little or no remaining time for your last issue or your final points. When this happens, you have two options. You can either quickly summarize the points that you would have made, or you can tell the court that, because you are out of time, you will rely on your brief for the issues and arguments that you did not cover.

What you do not want to do is exceed the time that you have been allotted. Unless the court gives you permission to continue, you must stop when your time is up.

§ 3.8.4 You Have Too Much Time

Having too much time is not a problem. You do not need to use all of your allotted time. When you have said what you need to say, thank the court and sit down.

§ 3.8.5 You Do Not Know the Answer to a Question

Occasionally you will be asked a question that you cannot answer. If it is a question about the facts of your case or about the law, do not try to bluff. Instead, do one of the following: (1) if you can do so in a few seconds, look up the answer; (2) tell the judge that at this point you cannot answer the question but that you will be glad to provide the information after oral argument; or (3) give the best answer you can.

EXAMPLE 1 **STATEMENTS THAT YOU CAN MAKE WHEN YOU DO NOT KNOW THE ANSWER**

"So that I can answer correctly, let me quickly check the record."
"I'm not sure what the actual words were. I will check and provide you with that information after oral argument."
"As I recall, the police officer testified that he asked the question twice."

If the question raises an issue you have not considered, the options are slightly different. You can either trust yourself and, on the spot, give your best answer, or you can tell the court that you need to give the question some thought.

§ 3.8.6 You Do Not Understand the Question

If you do not understand a question, tell the judge and either ask him or her to repeat the question or repeat the question in your own words, asking the judge whether you understood correctly: "I'm sorry, I'm not sure that I understand your question. Could you please rephrase it?" "If I am correct, you are asking whether . . . ."

§ 3.8.7 You Become Flustered or Draw a Blank

It happens, at some time or another, to almost everyone. You become flustered or draw a blank. When this happens, "buy" a few seconds by either taking a drink of water or taking a deep breath and looking down at your notes. If you still cannot continue with the point you were making, move to another one.

§ 3.8.8 You Are Asked to Concede a Point

Concessions can work both to your advantage and to your disadvantage. You will win points by conceding points that you cannot win or that are not important to your argument. You can, however, lose your case if you concede too much. Therefore, before you walk into court, decide what you can and cannot concede, concede when appropriate, and otherwise politely but firmly stand your ground. If the court presses for a concession, you can try to move the court past the issue: "Assuming, *arguendo,* that this Court decides that the trial court erred, the error was harmless because . . . ."

§ 3.9 A Final Note

No matter how much they dread it initially, most individuals end up enjoying oral argument for what it is, a stimulating dialogue among intelligent people.

§ 3.9.1 Checklist for Critiquing the Oral Argument

I. Preparation

- The advocate has anticipated and prepared rebuttals for the arguments the other side is likely to make.
- The advocate has anticipated and prepared responses to the questions the court is likely to ask.
- The advocate knows the law and the facts of the case.
- The advocate has determined what arguments he or she needs to make to win.
- The advocate has determined what points he or she can, or cannot, concede.
- The advocate has prepared two outlines: a long outline, which can be used if the court asks only a few questions, and a short outline, which can be used in case the court asks more questions.

II. Content and Organization

A. Introduction

- The advocate identifies himself or herself and the client.
- When appropriate, the advocate requests rebuttal time.

B. Opening and Statement of Issues or Position

- The advocate begins the argument with a sentence or phrase that catches the attention of the court and establishes the client's theory of the case.
- The advocate then presents the question or states his or her position.
- The question or statement of position is framed so that it supports the advocate's theory of the case and suggests an answer favorable to the client.
- The question or statement of position is presented using language that is easily understood.

C. Summary of Facts

- When appropriate, the advocate includes a short summary of the facts in which he or she explains the case and establishes an appropriate context. When a separate summary of the facts is not appropriate, the advocate weaves the facts into the argument.
- The facts are presented accurately but in the light most favorable to the client. The positions of emphasis and detail are used effectively, and words have been selected for both their denotation and their connotation.

D. Argument

- The advocate discusses the issues and makes the arguments needed to win.
- The argument is structured in such a way that it is easy to follow: (1) issues and arguments are discussed in a logical order and (2) sufficient roadmaps, signposts, and transitions are used.
- The arguments are supported. The advocate uses the law, analogous cases, policy, and the facts to support each of his or her assertions.
- The law, analogous cases, policies, and facts are presented accurately.
- The law, analogous cases, policies, and facts are presented in the light most favorable to the client.

E. Questions from the Bench

- When a judge asks a question, the advocate immediately stops talking and listens to the question.

- The advocate thinks before answering.
- As a general rule, the advocate begins his or her answer with a short response ("Yes," "No," "In this case") and then supports that answer.
- After answering the question, the advocate moves back into his or her argument without pausing or waiting for the judge to give permission to continue.
- The advocate sees questions, not as an interruption, but as another opportunity to get his or her argument before the court.
- As he or she listens to the questions, the advocate adjusts the argument to match the concerns and interests of the court.

F. Closing

- The advocate ends the argument with a summary of the main points or on a strong point.
- When appropriate, the advocate includes a request for relief.

G. Rebuttal

- The advocate uses rebuttal to respond to the one or two most important points raised by opposing counsel or the court.

III. Delivery

- The advocate treats the argument as a dialogue; he or she does not read or recite the argument.
- The advocate maintains eye contact with all of the judges.
- The advocate has good posture, uses gestures effectively, and speaks so that he or she can be easily understood.
- The advocate does not use phrases like "I think," "We maintain," or "It is our position that."
- The advocate is composed and treats the court and opposing counsel with respect.

Glossary of Terms

Active voice. Active voice is the quality of a transitive verb in which the action of the verb is performed by the subject: "Judges decide cases." (Compare with **Passive voice**.)

Analogous case. An analogous case is a case that is factually similar to the client's case. An argument based on an analogous case is an argument in which the attorney compares or contrasts the facts in a factually similar case with the facts in the client's case.

Analysis. When you analyze something, you examine it closely, identifying each part and determining how the parts are related. In law, there are two types of analysis: statutory analysis, which involves the close examination of a statute, and case analysis, which involves the close examination of a case. (Compare with **Synthesis**.)

Background fact. A background fact, while not necessary to decide the legal issue, is a fact that helps put the legally significant facts in context to tell a clear story. (Compare with **Emotionally significant fact** and **Legally significant fact**.)

Case briefing. Case briefing is a technique used to analyze a court's written opinion. A case brief usually contains a summary of the facts, a statement of the issue(s), the court's holding, and the court's rationale.

Case law. Although the term "case law" is often used to refer to common law, in fact its meaning is broader. It refers to all court decisions including those interpreting or applying enacted law.

Chronological organization. A writer using chronological organization for the facts in a brief sets the facts out in the order in which the related events occurred. (Compare with **Topical organization**.)

Citation (also Cite). A citation is a reference to a legal authority. Because different courts use different citation systems, always check the court rules to see which citation system is used by the court to which you are submitting your brief.

Cite checking. Cite checking is the process used to determine the current status of an authority and to locate sources that have cited that authority. The two most common systems for cite checking an authority are *Shepard's,* which is available both in print and on LEXIS, and KeyCite, an on-line service available on Westlaw.

Common law. The common law is a system of law created by the judicial branch. For example, much of tort law is common law: The causes of action and rules were created by the courts rather than by the legislature.

Concluding sentence. A concluding sentence in a paragraph is the sentence that sums up the main point of the paragraph. Although not every paragraph will have a concluding sentence, in those that do the concluding sentence is invariably the last sentence in the paragraph.

Connotation. The connotation of a word is all the associations the word carries with it. For example, the word "lawyer" may have positive connotations for individuals who respect lawyers or who aspire to be lawyers, but it may have negative connotations for people who have had bad experiences with lawyers. (Compare with **Denotation.**)

Denotation. The denotation of a word is its dictionary definition. (Compare with **Connotation.**)

Dicta. Comments made by a court that are not directly related to the issue before it or that are not necessary to its holding are dicta. Such comments are often preceded by the word "if": "If the evidence had established. . . ." Although in some cases dicta are easily identifiable, in other cases they may not be. If the issue is broadly defined, the statement may be part of the court's holding; if the issue is narrowly defined, the statement is dicta. (Compare with **Holding.**)

Dovetailing. Dovetailing is the overlap of language between two sentences that creates a bridge between those two sentences. Dovetails are often created by moving the connecting idea to the end of the first sentence and the beginning of the second sentence, repeating key words, using pronouns to refer back to nouns in an earlier sentence, and using "hook words" (this, that, these, such) and a summarizing noun. (Compare with **Substantive transitions**.)

Elements analysis. When you do an elements analysis, you systematically analyze a set of requirements set out either in a statute or as part of a common law doctrine by determining whether, given a particular set of facts, each requirement is met.

Emotionally significant fact. An emotionally significant fact is a fact that, while not necessary to decide the legal issue, may have an emotional impact. For example, emotionally significant facts may lead a jury to feel more favorably towards a plaintiff or a defendant. (Compare with **Background fact** and **Legally significant fact**.)

Finding. A finding is a decision on a question of fact. For example, a trial court judge may find a defendant incompetent to stand trial, or a jury may find that a police officer acted in good faith. (Compare with **Holding.**)

Gender-neutral language. Gender-neutral language is language that treats males and females as having equal value. It does not assume being male is the norm or that certain jobs or positions are primarily filled by males or females.

Generic transition. Generic transitions are those transitions that are commonly used in writing to describe standard mental moves, such as "consequently" to show cause/effect or "however" to show contrast. (Compare with **Dovetailing** and **Substantive transitions**.)

Harmless error. An error is harmless when an appellate court determines that an error occurred at trial but the error does not require reversal because the outcome would likely have been the same absent the error. The test the court applies in deciding if reversal is required turns on whether the error was a constitutional or a non-constitutional error. (Compare with **Reversible error**.)

Headnote. A headnote is a one-sentence summary of a rule of law found at the beginning of a court's opinion. Because headnotes are written by an attorney employed by the company publishing the reporter in which the opinion appears and not the court, they cannot be cited as authority.

Holding. A holding is the court's decision in a particular case. "When the court applied the rule to the facts of the case, it held that. . . ." Thus a holding has two components: a reference to the applicable rule of law and a reference to the specific facts to which that rule was applied. Because the holding is the answer to the legal question, it can be formulated by turning the issue (a question) into a statement. (Compare with **Dicta**.)

Legalese. Legalese is a broad term used to describe several common features of legal writing such as the use of archaic language, Latin terms, boilerplate language, and long and convoluted sentences. "Legalese" is usually a pejorative term.

Legally significant fact. A legally significant fact is a fact that a court would consider significant, either in deciding that a statute or rule is applicable, or in applying that statute or rule. (Compare with **Background fact** and **Emotionally significant fact**.)

Legislative intent. Legislative intent is what a legislative body intended when it enacted a particular statute. Attorneys and courts use legislative histories to determine what a state legislature or Congress intended in enacting a statute. In addition, some statutes include a purpose section setting out the underlying intent of the statute.

Main clause. A clause is a group of related words that has both a subject and a verb. A main clause is a clause that can stand alone as a sentence. (Compare with **Subordinate clause**.)

Mandatory authority. Mandatory authority is law that a court must apply in deciding the case before it.

Metaphor. Metaphor is a direct comparison. For example, a journey is often a metaphor for life.

Nominalization. Nominalization is the process of converting verbs into nouns (determine → determination).

Orienting transitions. Orienting transitions are transitions that provide a context for the information that follows. They locate the reader physically, logically, or chronologically. (Compare with **Generic transition** and **Substantive transitions**.)

Paragraph block. A paragraph block is a group of two or more paragraphs that together develop a point within a larger document.

Paragraph coherence. A paragraph has coherence when the various points raised in the paragraph are connected to each other. Common connecting devices include repetition of key words, transitional phrases, parallelism, and pronouns.

Paragraph unity. A paragraph has unity when all the points raised in the paragraph are related to one larger point, the paragraph's topic.

Parallel citation. A parallel citation is a citation to another source that contains a copy of a case. Many state decisions are published in a state reporter as well as a regional reporter. The two citations for the same case are considered "parallel." Some decisions (such as those of the United States Supreme Court) have more than one parallel citation. Other decisions have no parallel citation.

Parallel construction. Parallel construction is the use of the same part of speech or similar grammatical structures in a pair or series of related words, phrases, or clauses. In other words, a noun is matched to a noun, a verb is matched to a verb, a phrase to a phrase, etc. Parallel construction is also required with correlative conjunctions such as *either/or, neither/nor,* and *not only/but also.*

Parenthetical case description. A parenthetical case description can be used when a full description of the case is not required, for example when the case is being used to illustrate a specific point, or when one or two cases have already been described in full in the text and the writer wants to alert the reader to additional case law.

Passive voice. Passive voice is the quality of a transitive verb in which the subject receives rather than performs the action of the verb: "Cases are decided by judges." (Compare with **Active voice**.)

Persuasive authority. Persuasive authority is law or commentary that a court may consider in deciding the case before it.

Plain language. Plain language is the term used to describe a movement to encourage the use of simple, straightforward language (in professions such as law) that is readily understandable by lay people.

Policy argument. A policy argument is one in which the attorney argues that a particular interpretation of a statute, regulation, or common law rule is (or is not) consistent with current public policy, that is, the objective underlying a particular law. For example, child custody laws usually seek to provide stability for children; environmental laws seek to balance the interest of developers and preservationists.

Primary authority. A primary authority is a source that sets out the law. Sources of primary authority include codes and reporters. (Compare with **Secondary authority**.)

Published case. A published case is a case that the court determines is part of the legal precedent in a jurisdiction. While the highest court in each jurisdiction publishes all of its opinions, intermediate courts of appeal (and district courts in the federal system) look to specified criteria to determine whether a case should be published based on whether it adds to the body of law. Generally, the decision to publish a case is made when the case is filed and is not related to whether the case has yet been included in a reporter's advance sheet or bound volume.

Purple prose. Purple prose is the overuse of flowery language that draws attention to itself.

Raise and dismiss. You can raise and dismiss issues, elements, and arguments. Because both sides will agree on the point, extensive analysis is not necessary.

Record. An appeal is based on the record created in the trial court. The record generally consists of documents filed, exhibits admitted, and transcripts of testimony.

Reversible error. Reversible error occurs when an appellate court determines that an error occurred at trial and the error affected the outcome of the trial. The test the court applies in deciding if reversal is required turns on whether the error was a constitutional error or a non-constitutional error. (Compare with **Harmless error**.)

Roadmap. Roadmaps are introductory paragraphs that give readers an overview of an entire document or a section of a document.

Rule. The rule is the legal standard that the court applies in deciding the issue before it. In some cases, the rule will be enacted law (a constitutional provision, statute, or regulation); in other cases, it will be a court rule (one of the Federal Rules of Civil Procedure); and in still other cases, it will be a common law rule or doctrine. Although in the latter case the rule may be announced in the context of a particular case, rules are not case-specific. They are the general standards that are applied in all cases. (Compare with **Test**.)

Secondary authority. A secondary authority is a source that describes or comments on the law. Sources of secondary authority include treatises, law review articles, legal encyclopedias, and restatements. Secondary authority never has binding effect, but it can be used as persuasive authority based on its reasoning or the eminence of its author. (Compare with **Primary authority**.)

Shepardizing. Shepardizing is the process used to determine the current status of an authority and to locate sources that have cited that authority. For example, an attorney would shepardize a court's opinion to determine whether it had been reversed, overruled, questioned, or followed and to locate other, more recent authorities that have cited the case as authority.

Signposts. Signposts are words and phrases that keep readers oriented as they move through a document. Transitional phrases, particularly ones like "first," "second," and "third," are the most common signposts. Topic sentences can also be considered a type of signpost.

Standard of review. "Standard of review" refers to the level of scrutiny an appellate court will use to review a trial court's decision. For example, in *de novo* review the appellate court does not give any deference to the decision of the trial court; it decides the issue independently. In contrast, when the standard of review is abuse of discretion, the appellate court defers to the trial court, reversing its decision only when there is no evidence to support it.

Subordinate clause. A clause is a group of related words that has both a subject and a verb. A subordinate clause cannot stand alone as a sentence because it is introduced by a subordinating conjunction (for example, "although") or relative pronoun (for example, "which"). (Compare with **Main clause**.)

Substantive transitions. Substantive transitions are connecting words and phrases that also add content. Unlike generic transitions, which signal standard mental moves, substantive transitions tend to be document-specific. (Compare with **Dovetailing** and **Generic transition**.)

Synthesis. When you synthesize, you bring the pieces together into a coherent whole. For example, when you synthesize a series of cases, you identify the unifying principle or principles. (Compare with **Analysis**.)

Term of art. Although sometimes used to describe any word or phrase that has a "legal ring" to it, "term of art" means a technical word or phrase with a specific meaning. "Certiorari" is a true term of art; "reasonable person" is not.

Test. Although the words "rule" and "test" are sometimes used interchangeably, they are not the same. A test is used to determine whether a rule is met. (Compare with **Rule**.)

Theory of the case. The theory of the case is the "theme" created for the case. A good theory of the case appeals both to the head and to the heart; it combines the law and the facts in a way that is legally sound and that produces a result the court sees as just.

Topic sentence. A topic sentence is the sentence in a paragraph that introduces the key point in the paragraph or that states the topic of the paragraph. Topic sentences are often the first sentence in a paragraph.

Topical organization. A writer using topical organization groups facts by topics. Topical organization generally works best when there are a number of facts not related by dates (for example, the description of several pieces of property), or a number of related events that occurred during the same time period (for example, four unrelated crimes committed by the same defendant over the same time period). (Compare with **Chronological organization**.)

Unpublished case. An unpublished case is a case filed for public record that the issuing court has determined has no precedential value. An unpublished case decides the issue for the parties involved, but does not become part of the body of law in a jurisdiction. While unpublished opinions are not included in reporters, they are often available on electronic databases (with a notation if the jurisdiction prohibits citation to unpublished decisions). Some jurisdictions prohibit citations to unpublished cases.

Voice. Voice is the active or passive quality of a transitive verb.

Index